All the Juicy Pastures

All the Juicy Pastures

Greville Texidor and New Zealand

Margot Schwass

VICTORIA UNIVERSITY PRESS

TE WHARE WĀNANGA O TE ŪPOKO O TE IKA A MĀUI

VICTORIA UNIVERSITY PRESS
Victoria University of Wellington
PO Box 600 Wellington
vup.victoria.ac.nz

Cataloguing-in-Publication Data is available from the
National Library of New Zealand

ISBN 9781776562251

Published with the assistance of

ARTS COUNCIL OF NEW ZEALAND *TOI AOTEAROA*

Printed by 1010 Printing, China

Contents

Foreword

In 1941, New Zealand's pre-eminent writer of short fiction, Frank Sargeson, met an elderly English woman recently arrived in Auckland. Silver-haired and gracious, Mrs Editha Foster (née Prideaux) immediately captivated Sargeson with what he called her 'English gentry' ways. He later wrote to a friend:

> Apparently the Prideaus [sic] are so old their ancestors lie on the top of their tombs in Cornwall with their feet crossed. Anyhow this one is 76 & looks not more than 56 . . . She has 2 daughters by the way who apparently reacted away from the stone ancestors with their feet crossed. The girls couldn't keep theirs crossed – they won beauty contests, became Follies girls, married Spaniards, Arabs etc – not to mention those they didn't marry. One of them . . . told me she & her sister have dragged Mother all over the world chasing after men. The only remark mother has ever been known to make was that she hoped all these affairs were Platonic. The daughter's nice too and can write . . .[1]

And with that offhand observation, the arrival of Greville Texidor – elder daughter of Editha, one-time Bloomsbury insider, globetrotting chorus-line dancer, former heroin addict, anarchist militia-woman and recent inmate of Holloway Prison – was announced to New Zealand.

Although Greville had been many things by the time she stepped off the boat in Auckland, she was not yet a writer, despite

Sargeson's endorsement. But when she left this country less than a decade later, she was a published author whose modernist-inflected short fiction had appeared in New Zealand, Australia and England. She had written a novella that Sargeson considered 'one of the most beautiful prose pieces ever achieved in this country'.[2] Her work had 'impressed and quietly depressed' Janet Frame with its assurance and sophistication.[3] She had been one of the first authors to receive a grant from the fledgling New Zealand Literary Fund. An Australian publisher wanted an option to publish all her work for the next three years, including novels; at least one was already well-advanced.[4]

Sargeson was instrumental in Greville's invention as a writer – encouraging, advising, cajoling, sometimes bullying her into print. So too were some of the younger New Zealand writers who were her neighbours on Auckland's North Shore, notably Maurice Duggan. Their frequent, sometimes daily correspondence documents a shared literary apprenticeship, the concurrent gestation of two writing lives at a time when a national literary culture was also coming into being. Their intense and productive literary relationship – characterised by camaraderie, robust critique and intermittent bitchiness – anticipates that far more recent phenomenon, the creative writing workshop.

But Greville's career as a published writer essentially ended when she left New Zealand for Australia in 1948. The only fiction she published in her lifetime – short stories that mostly appeared in journals, and a novella – was written during her years here. Some has endured. One story earned a place in Sargeson's anthology *Speaking for Ourselves* (1945) and another in Davin's *New Zealand Short Stories* (1953); her work has also appeared in some more recent anthologies, such as the *Penguin Book of New Zealand War Writing* (2015). Long after her death, Victoria University Press published her collected fiction, *In Fifteen Minutes You Can Say A Lot* (1987), which included six previously unseen pieces. Another unpublished story emerged in a local online journal in 2006.[5]

After leaving New Zealand, Greville continued to write in a variety of genres. Among her papers at the State Library of New South Wales are the typescripts of numerous short stories, translations, poems and three novels in varying stages of completeness – including multiple drafts of a copious novel based on her Spanish Civil War experiences. She wrote plays for stage and radio, two of which were broadcast by the Australian Broadcasting Commission in 1953. Some of the fifty Lorca poems she translated were also broadcast by the ABC or appeared in Australian and American journals. Greville turned her hand to non-fiction, too; in 1951, her essay about life in a post-war Australian camp for displaced persons was published in New Zealand. But most of the work she wrote in Australia never made it into print. Over her lifetime she accumulated a pile of publishers' rejection letters that were, she noted drily, 'unsurpassed for variety and originality'.[6] She moved on again, this time to Franco's Spain, where her dwindling literary output ceased completely. Unhappy, regretful, as restless as ever, Greville returned to Australia, where she took her own life in 1964.

Greville Texidor's body of published work is, by any measure, slender. Most accounts of mid-century New Zealand literature pay it scant attention, except to challenge her credentials as a bona fide local. The woman herself can be glimpsed in the occasional literary biography or cultural history as an exotic footnote – the promising newcomer who failed to kick on, the woman who drew a knife on Denis Glover at a party, the glamorous adornment to Sargeson's circle of enslaved male disciples. But she remains largely unknown and her work unread. When I received funding from Creative New Zealand to help with this book, journalist Steve Braunias reported it was a grant to write 'about the life of someone called Greville Texidor'.[7]

Well, exactly. Greville lived and wrote in New Zealand for less than a decade. She started late, left much unfinished, published little and destroyed a great deal. Most of the unpublished material is apprentice work – experiments with form, style and voice that do not warrant publication. There are no undiscovered masterpieces, although much of interest. Outside her fiction, Greville engaged only minimally with the country and people among whom she found refuge in the 1940s. She mixed with some of the period's leading cultural figures but remained essentially outside the mission of creating a national culture that preoccupied many of them. She was bored by New Zealand – its meagre cultural life, its enervating respectability, its puritanism. She once said that 'being brought up in N.Z. is the worst preparation for the struggle to live'.[8] Why, indeed, should we be interested in the life of someone whose engagement with this country was so brief and contingent? Why should we care about 'someone called Greville Texidor' when it was not even her real name but one of many identities constructed in a determined lifelong flight from conformity?

The sheer glamour of the Texidor back-story and its fictional treatment is a partial answer, admittedly a rather shallow one. Glamour was certainly what originally entranced me when I first came across her collected stories in 1987 – the irresistible allure of her pre-war European life, made even more dazzling by its utter erasure in 1940s New Zealand. The gulf between the two seemed almost too much for a single lifetime to accommodate. How did someone who had been painted by Augustus John and Mark Gertler, who had danced the Charleston in theatres from Paris to Buenos Aires and fought for the doomed Left in Spain, end up washing her clothes in a Kaipara farm creek? But, as I read on, the fiction itself began to work on me. Until then, local writing of the 1940s and 50s had seemed a zone of unmitigated dreariness (an unfair judgement, I know now) – tight-lipped, monochrome, insular, resolutely male. Here was something else: fiction redolent with exotic elsewheres, animated by strong political and personal passions and an unapologetically cosmopolitan sensibility. The stories – whether located in the bohemian enclaves of pre-war Europe, in Civil War Spain, or in a rural New Zealand rendered oddly unfamiliar – were restless and unsettled, full of tonal ambiguities, switches and the occasional razor blade. It was as if the early Jean Rhys had washed up here with her brew of bitter comedy and psychological pain, her cast of doomed and desperate women on the verge of abandonment, hysteria or suicide. Some of Greville's stories deployed, if not always successfully, the heavy weaponry of high European modernism (symbolism, surrealism, dream writing and more) alongside biting social satire and spare realism. They slipped between registers as easily as they straddled hemispheres. They revealed a set of artistic and intellectual responses that I had never met in New Zealand writing – responses to a lifetime of strandings, reinventions and displacement, all compelled by a combination of personality, circumstance and what James K. Baxter called the 'winds of a terrible century'.[9]

How those winds brought Greville Texidor to New Zealand, and what happened when she got here, is central to this book. It tells the story of a cosmopolitan, adventurous and politically-engaged woman who briefly flourished as a writer in the apparently uncongenial environment of wartime New Zealand. But *All the Juicy Pastures* also acknowledges the frustrations of telling that story. Chronicling Greville's 'life and times' required constant vigilance; it was all too easy for the 'life' to be swamped by the 'times', for the personal and particular to become representative, generic and thus indistinct. Like Woody Allen's Leonard Zelig, Greville's life was entangled with and shaped by some of the century's most defining moments, both profound and prosaic. She experienced first-hand the Roaring Twenties, the birth of movie-making, the destruction of political ideals in the Spanish Civil War, the mutilating effects of exile. She rubbed shoulders with personalities as various as the sixth Earl of Ilchester, D.H. Lawrence, George Gershwin and the revolutionary anarchist Emma Goldman. How to particularise an individual life which, in its sweep and scale, seems a kind of proxy for the twentieth century itself, for all the best and worst which that 'terrible century' could unleash?

And how to write about an individual so comprehensively erased – by herself, and by others – from the official record? Diaries and most correspondence from Greville's early life simply vanished when she abruptly left Britain for New Zealand. But she colluded in her own erasure too, sealing off experiences and events like flooded underground chambers, never to be reopened or discussed; Greville's own daughters learned little directly from her about the most significant periods of her life. She burnt many personal papers and manuscripts when she left New Zealand, and more still when she returned to Europe a decade later. Greville's footprint, in this country and elsewhere, was light to the point of invisibility.

And so I've gone searching for her in the memoirs and letters of contemporaries, in long-forgotten *romans à clef* from the 1920s and 30s, in theatre programmes and shipping lists, in exhibition catalogues and prison records. I've looked for her in accounts of Bloomsbury parties, West End shows, anarchist meetings and battlefield skirmishes on the windswept plains of Aragón. All too often, I've found nothing more than a glimpse, an echo of her voice, a keen sense of having arrived somewhere she has just left. Surveyors, watchmakers and others rely on the revelations of 'witness marks' – physical signs, often faint or cryptic, left on the surface of an object – to guide their precise, exacting work. I soon discovered that the story of Greville's life was singularly lacking in witness marks and obstinately resistant to precision.

By way of compensation, I've turned to proxies – other people whose lives occasionally intersected with Greville's or mirrored it. The stage-struck girls in gym slips and bathing costumes Ethel Mannin describes queuing in the wings to audition for the chorus line.[10] The crop-haired young women dancing the toddle, the jog-trot, the shimmy, the scandalising Charleston in Soho nightclubs, hip to hip with shabby painters and jazz musicians or the scions of old Bloomsbury families.[11] The young poet Iris Tree taking 'spoonfuls of hashish mixed into jam at intervals through the course of an inspiring evening' with Augustus John.[12] The young Britons travelling abroad in the early 1920s, arriving at the Gare du Nord for the very first time 'and smelling that combination of coffee and garlic and French cigarettes and drains which is forever Paris'.[13] Greville's own sister Kate Kurzke, 'high on danger' in the Spanish Civil War, writing ardent propaganda 'for a cause I believed in at a time when I had the illusion that propaganda could make a difference'.[14]

These lives followed similar trajectories to Greville's; some collided with hers at various points. But they are not Greville's. The only really reliable way in to her life is through the handful of letters and manuscripts surviving in the archives, and of course through her published fiction – and there is precious little of that.

The small body of fiction she left behind can certainly be read as forensic evidence of her life story, or for the literary pleasures I've already described. But it has something more to yield. Her work allows us to discover another story – one about this place. Seen from today, New Zealand's mid-century cultural and social landscape can seem drab and uniform, its inhabitants myopically obsessed with kicking around what has been called the 'dried turd' of cultural nationalism[15] – that relentless quest to articulate the local in prose and poetry, to express a (Pākehā) national identity and the history and geography that were said to have shaped it. But in fact, as the 1940s progressed, the cultural landscape was being subtly reconfigured and enriched: by war, the aftermath of economic depression, the influence of European modernism, the emergence of new forms of popular culture and other forces. In many art forms, cultural nationalism was far from the only new show in town, if indeed it ever had been. Internationalism and a distinctly exilic sensibility were taking root too, thanks at least in part to the presence of wartime émigrés, refugees and wanderers like Greville Texidor. To many local writers and artists – some of whom knew all too well what it felt like to be on the outside – these new arrivals offered access to the more expansive aesthetic, intellectual and political horizons they themselves yearned for. They too wanted to experience what Greville called 'all the juicy pastures of civilisation', not by travelling 'Home' as their parents had done, but by reimagining and reinhabiting *this* home. The relationships they forged with the exotic strangers in their midst helped opened doors to new possibilities.

So while *All the Juicy Pastures* is about Greville Texidor, it's also about some of the well-worn historical and literary narratives that have shaped our view of the twentieth century, and the assumptions on which they're based. Literary history has an inherent tendency to tidy up the past as it periodises it; to slice and sort it into settled and orderly categories, schools, cultural movements, political ideologies, success stories and failures, the mainstream and the marginalised. In doing so, it can often overlook evidence of cultural unruliness, the outliers who don't quite fit. Greville's life in New Zealand and the fiction she wrote here – both full of contradictions and incongruities – belong among that rich cultural messiness. She is someone who stands both here and there, an outsider with an insider's intuitive sensitivity to place and people, a cosmopolitan sophisticate who became a writer in the most uncongenial environment imaginable for writing, an exilic writer who learned her craft from the prose writer most closely associated with the nationalist project.

Situating Greville Texidor in the well-documented cultural landscape of 1940s New Zealand makes us see it anew. We're invited to notice its variety and elasticity, to pay more attention to the mavericks and outsiders who were part of it, and to imagine it as a more porous, fluid, internationally-connected and frankly interesting place than we might have believed.

The literary landscape of the 1940s

Had Greville Texidor wanted to enquire into the state of New Zealand literary culture in the 1940s, this image could have told her a lot. Betty Curnow's snap shows four men sitting in a Christchurch street. Crouching beside Betty's poet husband Allen (far left) are Denis Glover, Bob Lowry and Donald McWilliams, an old school-friend of Glover's. Curnow – bespectacled, rumpled, a pipe clapped between his teeth – holds a bottle and glass. The pugilistic Glover, just home from distinguished war service with the British Navy, makes a fist with one hand. Lowry, a printer and typesetter, holds up two ink-stained thumbs to the camera.

McWilliams, another recently-returned soldier and pipe-smoker, grins a little awkwardly at finding himself in the company of these faintly disreputable literary lions. A boisterous drinking binge seems imminent. Behind the group, an enormous movie billboard advertises *Gaslight* (1944); the technicolor décolletage of Ingrid Bergman looms over their shoulders, an extravagantly female encroachment into this otherwise blokey moment.

It's not only the conspicuous masculinity that makes this photo so suggestive of its times. It memorialises one of the twentieth century's most enduring cultural myths; the invention of New Zealand literature by Curnow, Glover, Lowry and a handful of other 'marvellously talented young men' in the 1930s and 40s.[16] The story is well-known. It begins in 1932 with the provocative but short-lived journal *Phoenix*, which founding editor James Bertram declared a platform for the young writers to whom 'this country must look, if it is to look anywhere for a national literature'.[17] Not

Allen Curnow, Denis Glover, Bob Lowry and Donald McWilliams, 1946
Alexander Turnbull Library, PAColl-2146-008

long after, in Christchurch, the student-poet and amateur printer Glover founded the Caxton Press with Lowry's help; it too would be an engine of indigenous literary expression and invention. Publications like the landmark anthology *New Poems* (1934) – featuring work by Curnow, Charles Brasch, A.R.D. Fairburn, R.A.K. Mason and Glover himself – were soon tumbling off the Caxton press, along with work by Frank Sargeson, Monte Holcroft, D'Arcy Cresswell and others. Glover meanwhile helped launch the left-wing paper *Tomorrow* in 1934, which included regular literary contributions from local young writers alongside progressive political and economic commentary. Those contributors included Sargeson, and his gradual mastery of the stripped-down prose style that became his signature can be traced in the pages of *Tomorrow*.

Thus the *Phoenix*–Caxton men became uniquely powerful. Simultaneously, they were creating, publishing and championing what they declared to be a new literature. It would unsettle more than it consoled, they cautioned, but in it New Zealanders would finally find what they called 'a home in thought'.[18] The *Phoenix*–Caxton writers have been described, retrospectively, as nationalists. Their best-known works – for example, Curnow's 'The Unhistoric Story', Fairburn's *Dominion*, John Mulgan's *Man Alone*, nearly every story Sargeson wrote before 1945 – came to be read as a collective manifesto of a programme dedicated above all to the expression of a national identity and voice. Yet the *Phoenix*–Caxton writers never called themselves nationalists and several emphatically rejected the term. If their project can be called 'nationalist', it is nationalism of a very particular complexion; bleak, unromantic, as improving as castor oil. Unlike nationalist writing elsewhere, it was neither celebratory, nostalgic nor intended as an instrument of anti-colonial resistance. Its pervasive tone was a kind of self-lacerating gloom. The *Phoenix*–Caxton writers, like their counterparts in other white settler cultures, wrote out of what has been called a shared 'perception of non-identity', as 'cultural migrants, overburdened with values and attitudes which belonged in an older or other world', acutely conscious of the lack of fit between an imported aesthetic vocabulary and the reality of their location.[19] And even more so than their Australian and Canadian counterparts, New Zealand's nationalists were hell-bent on clearing away this colonial literary heritage with all the purifying vigour of a 'hard frost'.[20]

Although Curnow's demeanour in the photo is admittedly bookish, Lowry's inky thumbs and Glover's physicality speak of the urgency and vigour of their mission. These are not effete aesthetes but men of action literally *making* a national literature from scratch, pushing aside a moribund past. Their project seeks no less than the moral and aesthetic regeneration of the nation and they, this image announces, are the men for the task – courageous, muscular and more than a little bolshy.

Importantly, though, this photograph was taken in 1946. As such, it records a very specific moment in the evolution of the *Phoenix*–Caxton writers' enterprise. In the 1930s, their project had been single-minded and oppositional, its sights trained firmly on specific enemies. Bad writing was one. In some senses, what the *Phoenix*–Caxton writers sought then was, quite simply, quality improvement – an end to a century of 'colonial literaturishness' and 'tui and treacle' sentimentality.[21] Their literary forebears had been transplanted spiritual exiles writing nostalgically of an England they scarcely knew, or fancifully of a local environment to which they had never truly reconciled themselves. Their work was also, sneered Glover, despicably feminine in attitude, subject matter and idiom. Now was the time for an injection of 'new vitality', he announced in 1934: 'no more leisurely-whimsy, feminine-mimsy stuff'.[22]

But the *Phoenix*–Caxton writers were not only repudiating the *literary* practices and culture of the past: they also wanted to cast off the progressivist colonial myth they had inherited. That myth spoke of New Zealand as a prosperous pastoral paradise built by pioneers who had tamed the bush, subdued the natives with a firm yet kind hand, and formed themselves into a modest and decent outpost of Britain. Against this complacent, self-congratulatory myth, the younger writers fought back with what

Curnow called their own 'anti-myth', a much darker story attuned to the Depression era in which they had reached maturity.[23] Where their elders spoke smugly of a society sustained by solid, respectable values, in the 1930s the *Phoenix*–Caxton writers saw a spiritually- and materially-impoverished nation suffocating under repressive puritanism. Where the colonial myth portrayed a smiling and fertile land tamed by the pioneers' toil, the anti-myth told of a country despoiled for profit – a debased, sometimes hostile environment in which the European, even after a century of occupation, remained essentially homeless. Māori, if they were visible at all, were the shadowy remnants of a more admirable past that the colonial project had extinguished. Throughout the 1930s and early 1940s, the *Phoenix*–Caxton writers relentlessly laid bare these uncomfortable truths. And in doing so, they claimed a newly prophetic role for local writers: to articulate the unrealised meaning of this unformed and spiritually arid place, using a voice that sprung from here and nowhere else.

But in the immediate post-war period of this photograph, the *Phoenix*–Caxton writers' project was losing some of these earlier prophetic certainties, along with its self-consciousness. Perhaps this was inevitable as its champions matured: the men in the photo have now reached their fourth decade. For the past few years, even those who had earlier considered themselves pacifists have been fighting the Old World's wars. The moment recorded in Betty Curnow's snapshot signals the new dispensation that is emerging in the post-war world, bringing with it new anxieties and possibilities. 'Nationalism' is now a more problematic term than ever, the war having graphically confirmed its destructive potential. Just three years earlier, essayist and journalist Monte Holcroft had written of the need 'to identify a racial soul with the processes of history, a consecration of soil and mind to the service of the spirit' if New Zealanders were 'to make a spiritual home' through literature.[24] By 1946, such language seemed disturbingly resonant of the hateful rhetoric that had so recently spawned atrocities in Europe. As the German-born art historian Dr Gerda Eichbaum wrote in *Art New*

Zealand: 'Ever since Hitler has made "blood and soil" his one and only creed, all tendencies pointing in this direction . . . appear to have some sinister meaning, even if not intended by the author.'[25] In the post-war era, the *Phoenix*–Caxton writers – including those pictured here – were even less comfortable with the 'nationalist' label than they had been in the 1930s.

And despite the bullish confidence Glover and friends project, some of the *Phoenix*–Caxton writers were puzzled and dismayed by the very different world emerging in 1946. What has been called a 'new cultural tuning' was in the air.[26] The Depression-era material these writers had once mined so successfully, and the audience they had sought to create, had both changed in ways they could not yet fully apprehend. Even in 1942, Sargeson had complained to a friend that the 'out-of-work pattern of society of which I was a part [and] the people I understand best' had disappeared, leaving him adrift 'in a dreary pretentious middle-class suburb with people I don't understand and hence despise'.[27] As the Hollywood imagery in Betty Curnow's snap demonstrates, foreign, international and transnational forces were indeed exerting new pressures on the cultural project these men had set in motion more than a decade earlier. New accommodations and responses would be required.

So, as much as the photograph can be seen to *embody* the well-worn cultural nationalist myth – the invention of New Zealand literature by the *Phoenix*–Caxton writers, the belligerent masculinity of their project – the image also reminds us that it is just one story (albeit one that was received, sanctified and transmitted from decade to decade more or less unquestioned). In twentieth-century anthologies and literary histories, and in some university English departments, the myth of heroic invention was burnished and retold to the point where it seemed that the *Phoenix*–Caxton writers and their acolytes were the sole source of 'authentic' New Zealand writing; out of a void, they had single-handedly brought it into being. Equally, it seemed that the only thing that mattered about their work was what it had to say about the condition of being a New Zealander, or its fidelity to something agreed to be 'the real

New Zealand'. Sargeson's subversive manipulations of narrative and language, Curnow's shift from declamatory public verse to a more austere private poetic voice, the current of sentiment rippling through Glover's lyrics; all were of less importance than the images of ourselves, our history and our geography we could purportedly find in their work. Literary nationalism gained purchase as *the* mid-century national narrative, a force consuming all the oxygen in the era's cultural landscape.

Since at least the 1980s, the *Phoenix*–Caxton writers' claim to have invented New Zealand literature anew has been energetically contested. Other writers whose work was excluded by the period's powerful literary gatekeepers – including the 'lost matrix' of women jettisoned from Curnow's first *Book of New Zealand Verse* (1945)[28] – have been rediscovered and rehabilitated. Greater attention has been given to the concealed strands of cultural variety, cross-fertilisation and unorthodoxy also running through the thirties and forties. Instead of an anxious, uniform and inward-looking era, historians such as James Belich and Felicity Barnes have shown us a period in which new patterns of cultural traffic and transnational connections were becoming established across time and space. The strongly internationalist element that always inhered in the so-called nationalist project has also been acknowledged. Fairburn may have compared the task of 'build[ing] up a national literature' to a committee of scientists trying to create a test-tube baby, but the *Phoenix*–Caxton writers never claimed to be working in isolation.[29] Most continued to regard publication and critical acclaim in England as the highest confirmation of literary value, the only imprimatur that really mattered (and, of course, an economic lifeline at a time when it was virtually impossible to make a living in New Zealand just by writing). The 'founding document' of literary nationalism, *The Phoenix*, was explicitly modelled on contemporary British literary trends in its design, typography and content, which attended as much to the international and ideological as the local and literary.

From the perspective of the twenty-first century, then, the

Phoenix–Caxton writers' project looks neither as original and revolutionary as its champions initially asserted, nor as myopic and uniform as its critics (especially the ardent 'internationalists' of the next generation) liked to claim. The culture of the times was porous and surprisingly plural. It drew on and reflected a range of sources, foreign and indigenous. Importantly for this story, those sources included the exilic sensibilities and the tradition of European modernism brought to New Zealand by refugees and émigrés during the Second World War, including Greville Texidor.

Contrapuntal narratives: exiles and nationalists

Nationalist and exilic sensibilities are often imagined as 'conflicting poles of feeling'.[30] But it's also possible to think of them as interdependent forces, as Edward Said famously proposed. They 'inform and constitute each other,' he writes in 'Reflections on Exile', each arising out of an analogous 'condition of estrangement'.[31] Said's argument makes particular sense in the New Zealand cultural landscape of the 1930s and 40s, where the nationalist and the exilic can be seen working as strangely compatible mentalities – converging, intersecting and projecting themselves onto each other in sometimes unexpected ways.

Here, I use the term 'exile' as a deliberately loose, catch-all description for those who came to New Zealand from other countries in search of safety or respite from the Second World War. They were a far from homogenous group. Some arrived before or during the war, and others immediately after. Some came from continental Europe, some from Britain or elsewhere. Some sought a permanent home, while for others New Zealand was simply a staging post in a lifetime of itinerancy. By 1939, they included more than a thousand refugees from Hitler's Europe, primarily German-speaking Jews (mostly secular) from a range of countries; in a pattern repeated across the world, thousands more had been turned away.[32]

Wartime New Zealand was also a refuge for others whose origins, nationalities, intentions and migrant status could not be readily classified. Greville – a Spanish Civil War veteran recently released from internment in Britain, married to the non-Jewish German Werner Droescher – typifies the eclectic circumstances of the wanderers and travellers who, whether by choice or happenstance, washed up in New Zealand. So too does the Indonesian-born Dutch artist Theo Schoon who arrived from Java after fleeing the advancing Japanese army.[33] Another exile from Java was the Hungarian-born concert pianist Lili Kraus, who had been interned there.[34] Anna Kavan, a writer whose self-invented and vaguely continental name belies her English home-county origins, came here by way of Sweden, California, Bali and New York. In New Zealand, she joined her lover Ian Hamilton, a wealthy conscientious objector who owned land in Hawke's Bay but had spent much of his earlier life in England; he would settle here permanently after the war.[35] Peripatetic, nebulously tied to their countries of origin, often eager to move on, these exotic itinerants nonetheless became absorbed for a time into New Zealand's refugee milieu and were often treated as de facto 'European' refugees. Sargeson for one apparently drew no distinction: after first encountering Greville and Werner in 1941, he simply told a friend of meeting 'more refugees'.[36]

While their origins and circumstances were diverse, New Zealand's wartime exiles had important experiences in common. Many had lived in major European cities where cafés, restaurants, concerts, exhibitions, a sophisticated press and intellectual debate were part of daily life. They tended to be highly educated, and included a disproportionate number of professionals, business people and scholars. Some were full-time artists, musicians and writers, but many more were gifted amateurs or enthusiastic patrons of the arts. In general, they embodied what George Steiner has called the 'moral, intellectual and artistic noon of bourgeois Europe'[37] – although bourgeois Europeans might well have been discomfited by the radical politics of some, like Greville and Werner. Their reactions to their new homeland, even if it was only a staging post, had similarities too. Alongside the gratitude and relief most felt at finding a safe haven from the war in Europe, there was a degree of dismay. To many, New Zealand cities and towns seemed primitive, ugly and mean; there were few places to eat out at night and cultural activities were limited largely to the movies. They were astounded by New Zealanders' attitudes to alcohol, and by displays of public drunkenness. Typical houses, even middle-class ones, struck them as poorly-planned, cold and awash in ugly Victoriana. The abundance of corrugated iron was astonishing. Social behaviours – the separation of men and women at parties and dances, the reluctance to display affection in public – puzzled and sometimes shocked them.

Official New Zealand demanded the exiles become 'new Britishers: by procreation, and by assimilation' and 'vectors of the British way of life that still has so much to give to the world'.[38] Yet even those willing to assimilate found they remained highly conspicuous. According to the (later controversial) immigration official Reuel Lochore, some of the arrivals

> revel in displays of emotionalism and self-pity, and fail to realize how we despise such lack of self-control. [. . .] On social occasions, and other occasions too, they talk loudly and untiringly about their own affairs. Being bad listeners they cannot take a hint, nor sense an attitude from what we prefer to leave unsaid.[39]

The exiles' visible differences were amplified by the community's wartime anxieties, and their alien status was confirmed by official decree. Some were interned and many more harassed.[40] Others – including Greville and Werner – had their movements restricted, their correspondence monitored and their freedoms curbed by official measures ranging from the petty to the intrusive.

The demographic impact of the European wartime exiles was not large. But their social and cultural impact was transformative. It helped reshape New Zealand's post-war economic, social and intellectual landscape to an extent that belies their numbers. Over recent years, the contributions of numerous individuals have received greater attention, including in the arts, where wartime exiles made perhaps their most visible and vitalising contributions. Steeped in non-Anglophone traditions, these exilic artists introduced fresh talent, new artistic practices and professionalism into New Zealand cultural life. Crucially, they also brought to New Zealand a set of cultural sensibilities that were largely unfamiliar: an assured conviction of the value of 'high' culture and intellectual life, a sophisticated view of the relationship between artist and society, and an understanding of the creative and formal possibilities offered by European modernism.

The influence of exilic artists from Europe was perhaps most evident in architecture and the visual arts (even if, as scholar Leonard Bell argues, their contributions were frequently overshadowed by their 'nationalist' local contemporaries or ignored by Anglocentric professional bodies). Bell has shone new light on their achievements, showing that the talent and skills they introduced – as well as the unmistakeable exilic sensibility that permeates their work – opened up new creative and technical possibilities to their local counterparts.[41] The Czech refugee architect Imric Porsolt, for example, helped invigorate and professionalise local criticism of art and architecture; his writing appeared regularly in *Landfall*, and was informed by a deep immersion in European modernism. He championed Toss Woollaston and Colin McCahon but urged New Zealanders to see their work 'through a wider lens, situating it internationally, not nationally'.[42]

However, the literary contributions of wartime exiles have received less attention, even those written in English (of the exiles who did not write in English, the German poet Karl Wolfskehl was perhaps the most celebrated).[43] But the 'talented transient'[44] Anna Kavan, who lived in New Zealand for less than two years, made a conspicuous impact in 1943 with her scathing essay 'New Zealand: An Answer to an Inquiry'. It offers a damning account of the local scene she encountered on arrival in Auckland: 'It's null, it's dull, it's tepid, it's mediocre: the downunder of the spirit,' she wrote. The moribund cities were mired in 'quiet parochial slowness . . . Everything's shut, there's nothing to do except go to the pub or the cinema, or, if it happens to be the right day, to the races. No music, no theatres, no pictures . . .' New Zealanders seemed to exist in a perpetual condition of unease, she observed, acutely conscious of being 'only a few transplanted ordinary people, not specially tough or talented, walking . . . among the appalling impersonal perils and strangeness of the universe, living in temporary shacks, uneasily, as reluctant campers too far from home.'[45]

Kavan's unsympathetic account was not really very different from the national critique the *Phoenix*–Caxton writers had been advancing since 1932. Nonetheless, it raised local hackles when published in the prestigious London literary journal *Horizon*, striking many as the condescending and ill-informed opinions of a short-term visitor; Kavan left New Zealand in 1944. In the post-war period, she and her work received little attention until 2009 when *Anna Kavan's New Zealand* (edited by Jennifer Sturm) appeared. Although some of these newly-discovered pieces are unfinished, they show Kavan could also respond more thoughtfully to her temporary home than her sometimes flippant essay suggests. They are also faintly marked by local literary influences, notes C.K. Stead in his introduction; he argues that Kavan's evident engagement with this country and its literary climate made her, at least for the time she was here, 'a New Zealand writer'.[46] His judgement stands as a reminder of Edward Said's argument that exilic and the nationalist sensibilities are not mutually exclusive poles of feeling, but 'opposites informing and constituting each other'.[47]

Writers at the vanguard of the national literary project – Sargeson, Fairburn, Brasch, Curnow and others – could not help but respond, both personally and creatively, to the exilic European sensibilities they encountered in the 1940s. The two worlds came together at parties, dinners and other gatherings that ranged in tone from the cultivated to the riotous. Such occasions allowed two marginal groups to enjoy common ground and, often, mutual admiration. In Christchurch, for example, the refugee and artistic communities regularly converged at the modernist house designed by Ernst Plischke for the German-Jewish scientist Otto

Frankel and his artist wife Margaret Anderson; at the home of German refugees Paul and Otti Binswanger; or at Betty and Allen Curnow's.[48] Among the regulars were Curnow, Glover (before he went away to the war), Rita Angus, Helen Shaw, Douglas Lilburn, Leo Bensemann and others associated with the Caxton Press – all self-consciously in rebellion against 'the conventional, formulaic, Anglo-oriented parochial and "polite" arts of the city'.[49]

In Auckland, which had become the locus of the cultural nationalist project by the mid-1940s, the exilic community had several centres of gravity, mostly on the North Shore. At Torbay, recent European arrivals might gather at the home of Ian Hamilton and Anna Kavan or the nearby house of lawyer Frank Haigh, a friend and supporter of many wartime exiles. In either place, they could rub shoulders with Fairburn, Mason, Sargeson, the critic Eric McCormick or the architect Vernon Brown. Sargeson's bach in Takapuna was another place where Auckland exiles and the wider artistic community congregated, Sargeson plying them with copious amounts of Lemora, exotic vegetables from his garden and discourses on his favourite authors. As well as the Torbay set, Sargeson's regular visitors included the young Maurice Duggan, Wolfskehl, the Shanghai-born German Odo Strewe,[50] sculptor Molly Macalister and her future husband, the Jewish-Hungarian George Haydn – and Texidor and Droescher. As I describe in chapter 3, Greville and Werner's nearby home (and caravan) soon became another gathering point where North Shore writers and artists could gossip, argue, drink and eat audaciously un-English food. More refined evenings could be enjoyed in the newly-built modernist homes of wealthy émigrés such as the Kulkas, who regularly invited refugee and local friends to share food, wine, conversation and music. For those seeking more excitement, there were the legendary parties of printer Bob Lowry at One Tree Hill which, over time, became 'synonymous with Auckland Bohemian depravity'.[51]

But the encounters between exilic and local artists, writers and intellectuals took place not only in person. As Stead observed of Kavan's fiction, European sensibilities can be seen bumping up against local idioms and critical realism on the page as well. Tonal registers slip and slide, horizons broaden as new voices make themselves heard. Little by little, local literature was becoming animated by what Said has called a 'plurality of vision [that] gives rise to an awareness of simultaneous dimensions, an awareness that – to borrow a phrase from music – is *contrapuntal*'.[52]

That exilic-nationalist counterpoint is present in some emblematic moments. Conversing with visitors in his shabby Auckland lodgings, poet Karl Wolfskehl – the towering incarnation of 'German-Jewish symbiosis' – lovingly reconstructs his lost library of books for anyone who will listen; as he talks, all the riches of a vanished European tradition come to life again, volume by volume.[53] In Wellington, Allen Curnow listens to a recording of Beethoven in the light-filled, sky-blue house that Ernst Plischke designed for his fellow refugees Joachim and Gertrud Kahn. Curnow registers the moment in 'At Joachim Kahn's', a poem that suggests new possibilities – of crossing 'motionless horizons as if not marooned', of finding a more sophisticated, expansive and *international* cultural space within which a New Zealand artist might make a home. In German-Jewish refugee Maria Dronke's seaside cottage – bought with compensation she and her husband received as victims of Nazi persecution – the actress asks composer Douglas Lilburn to set Curnow's poem 'The Changeling' to music. Here, in this palpable reminder of the recent European past, a new addition to the canon of cultural nationalism is brought into being.[54]

And Greville Texidor, disembarking from the RMMV *Rangitata* in Auckland on 9 May 1940; this too is the start of another encounter between the exilic and the local, between the cultural sensibilities of the Old World and the New. But how on earth had she ended up here?

Photograph courtesy Cristina Patterson Texidor

1. And now Greville has turned up . . .

The woman who became Greville Texidor was born plain Margaret Greville Foster in 1902, in the Midlands town of Wolverhampton.[1] Her mother Editha Greville Prideaux was an accomplished painter who had studied at the Slade School of Fine Art; her father William Arthur Foster was a local solicitor. When they married in 1900, they bought The Limes, an impressive Italianate-style house (complete with belvedere tower) on the outskirts of Sedgley, a little south of Wolverhampton proper.[2] Two years after Margaret's birth, she was joined by a sister, Katharine Prideaux Foster, known as Kate (later Kate Kurzke), and the family was complete.

It was a thoroughly comfortable start to life in a thoroughly comfortable town in the heart of England. William's practice was flourishing, with offices in Wolverhampton and nearby Tipton. The Fosters had servants, nannies and a governess for the two girls. William and Editha enjoyed holidays abroad and a busy life full of social and public engagements. A degree of free-thinking was encouraged of the kind encountered in more progressive corners of the prosperous Edwardian upper-middle class. Certain artistic interests were sanctioned. Editha continued to paint, although she did not exhibit; William, who at one time had hankered for a career on the stage, enjoyed the theatre and read avidly. Although William held office in the local Conservative Party and reportedly had political aspirations of his own, Editha's politics leaned towards the liberal. During the industrial unrest that swept the Midlands and north of England between 1910 and 1920, she regularly served lunches for families of striking miners on the lawn at The Limes. William's reaction to this declaration of solidarity is unknown; if there were political tensions, the Fosters did not air them in front of the children.

William brought professional status and social ambition to the marriage; Editha a cosmopolitan outlook, distinguished lineage and modest family wealth. Born in Devon in 1866, she belonged to an ancient family of Norman origin whose progenitors, as Sargeson had so admiringly recorded, were entombed in state in Cornwell. The name Greville had been handed down through many generations of Prideauxs, who included distinguished Anglican churchmen, a member of parliament and other prominent citizens. Editha's father William Prideaux was a Bristol vicar, but his missionary and educational work had taken the family to all corners of the world. They spent some years in China, one of Editha's siblings was born in Canada, and another in the West Indies. Importantly for Greville's future, the Prideauxs also lived in New Zealand on at least one occasion and Editha's brother remained there for many years. It was in Auckland that Editha began painting, exhibiting her oils with the Auckland Society of Arts from 1887 onwards. A guide to nineteenth-century New Zealand artists says Editha was seen as a 'painter of great promise' before she returned to England with her family.[3] Back in London, she entered the Slade School of Art, which – unlike most other art schools of the time – had welcomed women students since its establishment in 1871. By the 1890s, the Slade's respectable reputation was enough to reassure even the most nervous Victorian parent. Significant numbers of female students from 'good' families arrived each morning by carriage or escorted by servants, and they prospered at the Slade under the teaching of instructors like Professor of Art Alphonse Legros (whose devoted following of female students, the 'Slade Girls', were celebrated especially for their medal-casting skills).[4]

Editha was not the only woman in her family to have an independent life, a higher education and a profession. According to family tradition, her sister Ethelwynn was a suffragette who had been imprisoned for her convictions. Editha's first cousin Helen Prideaux was a brilliant young surgeon and one of the first women appointed to a post at a London hospital; she died of diphtheria aged just twenty-seven while Editha was at the Slade.[5] Neither the Prideaux family nor the Fosters may have deviated radically from the conventions of their class and times. But on the Prideaux side especially, they included a sprinkling of women willing to test and transgress boundaries, and who had the talents to create unusually expansive lives.

As a child, though, Greville was closest to her father, whose 'buoyant and manic' personality she shared. Kate recalled that it was William who called her sister by her androgynous middle name, and Greville alone was regularly invited into his study to discuss books and theatre. At home, Greville was unquestionably the 'Queen Bee' – a dominant and domineering presence. By her own admission, Kate herself was dreamy, solitary and somewhat immature; even in her early teens, she liked nothing better than reading fairy stories and tending to her doll family. Greville, meanwhile, was more likely to be found outdoors on top of a pile of other youngsters, engaged in what they called their 'struggling games'. She was the ring-leader among the local children, an 'over-poweringly vital, active and extrovert' child whose relentless energy outlasted all others. But Greville was not entirely wild: like Kate, she learnt dancing, kept diaries and read voraciously (Kate had read Boswell's *Life of Johnson*, complete with Latin notes, by the time she was a teenager). Fragments of Kate's diaries from the First World War years recall long, unsupervised summer days playing in their neighbour Colonel Law's hay paddock, once burying the teapot so deeply in the hay to keep it hot that it was lost forever.

As they grew older, the sisters' friendships with the sons of neighbouring families turned to crushes, and Kate remembered competing with Greville for the affections of uniformed young

William Foster – buoyant, manic and politically ambitious

State Library of New South Wales, ref. PXA 1210

Well away – Greville as a schoolgirl

Photograph courtesy Cristina Patterson Texidor

*Greville and her mother Editha
on the Costa Brava*

Photograph courtesy Cristina
Patterson Texidor

*Kate Foster (Kurzke) – artist, model, war
correspondent, teacher*

Photograph courtesy Cristina Patterson Texidor

men home on leave during the First World War, even Colonel Law himself. By twelve, Greville was already physically mature and 'well away', hiding love letters from boys in which they enclosed rather greasy locks of hair; her obsession with boys lasted until she was 'about 30', commented Kate drily. While 'Miss Kitty' played with her dolls, Greville was out with local boys, racing round the village on the backs of motorbikes. She was indeed 'well away', running headlong towards whatever juicier pastures might lie beyond the confines of The Limes.

Perhaps for that very reason, Editha and William sent Greville to board at the prestigious Cheltenham Ladies' College in September 1917. Since the 1850s, Cheltenham had built a reputation for the quality of its teaching and learning, and its commitment to moulding independent-minded – rather than conventionally 'accomplished' – young women. But Greville did not allow it to mould her. She did join the Dramatic Society and learned elocution from an elderly actress; back at The Limes, her dramatic recitation of Tennyson's 'The Splendour Falls on the Castle Walls' was especially memorable. She played lacrosse. But Greville otherwise left little mark on Cheltenham, and vice versa – there are no records of her having passed any examinations whatsoever.[6] Her poor spelling remained legendary throughout her life. Friends later marvelled at Greville's apparent resistance to her elite education; her brother-in-law Sherry Mangan speculated that what he called her 'illiteracy' was in fact an act of protest against the Cheltenham regime. Greville told Frank Sargeson that she hated school and is variously said to have been expelled or run away. In any event, she was sure she learned nothing.[7]

Her schooling did indeed come to an abrupt end in 1919, when she was seventeen. In that year, her father committed suicide after being named a defendant in a highly-publicised libel trial. Following the 1918 'khaki' election, the unsuccessful Labour candidate for the Wolverhampton seat of Bilston claimed to have been slandered by his Conservative rival, the sitting MP Colonel Hickman, and two of Hickman's supporters.[8] One of those supporters was William Foster who, as well as being Hickman's legal adviser, chaired his constituency association.[9] At the end of 1918, William learned Kynaston intended to sue him for slander. This in itself was ruinous for a man of his social and political ambitions. But even worse – according to unverified family stories – was the likelihood that a trial would expose some decidedly rackety business transactions William had been part of, possibly involving illegal arms sales. On a snowy night in January 1919, while his wife and daughters were in London, William made his way from Sedgley to nearby Coseley, purportedly to meet a client. Instead he stepped into the path of the London express train, meeting with what the local newspaper called 'a terrible death'. His umbrella 'was smashed to atoms'; pieces were found some distance away from the scene, reported the *Express and Star* with unnecessary relish.[10]

Perhaps out of kindness to the family, the coroner recorded the death as accidental; the inquest was told William was known to be clumsy. However, it was widely accepted as suicide, the result of his despair at the pending trial and not altogether unexpected in a man whose extreme mood swings were well known. Depression, even if the term was rarely heard, was not uncommon in the Foster family. Nor was suicide. An aunt of William's, who was also Kate's godmother, took her own life around the same time. '[In] our family . . . we go down into deep troughs & it's a hard fight to come up again,' wrote Kate, who even in old age considered herself an eternal '*malheureuse*'. By the time she and Greville were teenagers, suicide was part of their psychic landscape, no longer an unthinkable and awful taboo. Suicide had entered the realm of the possible and, as Kate wrote towards the end of her life, 'the more [suicide] there is in a family the more one is likely to think of it.'

William was buried in the family vault in Sedgley. In the wake of his death and the prurient local interest it generated (the slander case and its titillating back-story were widely reported when it came to trial in November of 1919), Mrs Foster sold The Limes and left Wolverhampton for London with her daughters.

William's death brought Greville's girlhood to a sudden and traumatic halt. But the rupture also transported her into a new world that – for a restless, refractory young woman – was full of opportunity. It propelled her from the provinces to the metropolis and into a brand new decade, one in which wartime austerity and communal sorrow would be drowned out by the sound of Edwardian conventions splintering. The hedonism of the Roaring Twenties has become the stuff of fable, but like all such cultural myths, it was grounded in truth. For Greville and others of her age and caste, the decade lay ahead like an unexplored pleasure ground. As one chronicler of the period has commented, enjoyment was to be 'the new currency – enjoyment spent as an unprecedented freedom to act, to experiment, to travel' and, for the first time, those freedoms would be available to young women of a certain class as much as their brothers.[11] Later, their excesses would be curtailed by the well-documented confluence of political crises and economic disasters that brought the decade to an end. But that was of no concern in 1920 if you were eighteen, well-off and desperate to wriggle free of middle-class provincial respectability. In readiness for her new London life, Greville cropped her hair, plucked her eyebrows into thin arches and took up smoking. Before long, she was drinking cocktails among the louche crowds that gathered at the Café Royal and dancing at disreputable clubs in Soho. As Sargeson would later write, in London she found herself at the vanguard of 'the generation which came to maturity in the twenties, for whom World War One was as much a liberation as a disaster'.[12]

Bright young things

The three Fosters lived first in Maida Vale and then Bayswater. Editha resumed her painting and her connections with old friends from her student days, and Kate followed her mother to the Slade as a student in 1921. Very quickly, the Fosters became part of an artistic circle that included the painters Richard and

Ready for her London life

Sydney Carline and their family, Stanley Spencer, Mark Gertler, Dora Carrington and Marjorie Hodgkinson (later Gertler). The evidence of these associations can still be seen in paint and charcoal. Mrs Foster lent the 'fancy nightgowns' worn by the women rising from the grave in Spencer's celebrated painting 'The Resurrection, Cookham' (1924–27).[13] Spencer also painted or drew Kate on several occasions, as did Richard Carline. She is one of the figures in Carline's 'Gathering on the Terrace' (1924–25), and the subject of a 1925 portrait now held at Museums Sheffield.

Greville, without artistic inclinations or talent herself, modelled for artists the Fosters knew – chancy, physically-tiring work that rarely paid more than a pound a day and usually much less.[14] Stanley Spencer's brother Gilbert may have painted her during the early 1920s, but no portrait has ever been identified. Greville certainly modelled for Sydney Carline, best known for his depictions of aerial combat while serving as an official war artist and later Ruskin Master of Drawing at Oxford University; his 1923 portrait of Greville has recently come to light.[15] And Greville was also painted by Mark Gertler on more than one occasion, most notably for *Head of a Girl* (1929) which is in the Glasgow Art Gallery's collection. Like Kate, she became close to Gertler's wife Marjorie; at one time, Gertler sourly described his wife in an 'ecstasy of happiness' at the prospect of a weekend with Greville.[16] But Greville's relationship with Gertler himself was strained – Kate speculated that he once made a pass at Greville and was shunned. They also quarrelled over *Head of a Girl*: Greville wanted her name included in the title, but the painter refused to indulge what he saw as self-promoting vanity. Years later, Greville would pillory Gertler and his friends in her 1949 novella *These Dark Glasses* (see chapter 4).

Both Kate and Greville were by now well-established habitués of bohemian London. It was a place with no particular geographical location, no fixed membership or manifesto; it was primarily 'a way of living and a state of mind' recalled a former denizen.[17] At any given time, there were multiple overlapping circles that considered

Portrait by Sydney Carline, 1923

themselves bohemian in temperament, and the Foster girls had links to several. Bloomsbury, once the apex of London literary and artistic bohemia, was still a force at this time and the Fosters are said to have met (and read) both Katherine Mansfield and Virginia Woolf. D.H. Lawrence was a family friend. But 'old' Bloomsbury was in a state of transition, as one of its scions, Quentin Bell, has described. The 1920s were its 'moment of efflorescence', he writes – a period when individual members were still making a mark, but the group's collective significance was 'slowly expir[ing] in still glowing fragments' with all the 'lazy scintillating splendour' of a firework.[18] By the time the Foster girls were venturing into London bohemian society, Old Bloomsbury's high priests and priestesses were almost of another generation. The Fosters' connections were thus with the younger fringes of Bloomsbury, 'young Bells, young Stracheys, young McCarthys, Slade students and many, many more'.[19]

This group intersected with a decidedly less high-minded cohort – the giddy Bright Young Things of the early 1920s, whom Evelyn Waugh depicted in *Vile Bodies* popping out of a car en masse 'like a litter of pigs, and run[ning] squealing up the steps'.[20] Their world was indeed very much as Waugh evoked, Kate confirmed years later. There were tête-à-tête lunches in private rooms at the Cavendish Hotel or lavish dinners at the Café de la Paix, fancy-dress parties where everyone dressed as 'savages' and even the most timid of guests might 'tear down her dazzling frock to her hips and dance like a Bacchante',[21] soirées in fashionably eccentric venues that had been commandeered for the purpose – a windmill, perhaps, or a swimming pool (in *Vile Bodies*, one takes place in a captured airship). In fact, Kate, who periodically worked as a fashion mannequin, told Sargeson she once met 'the original of [Waugh's character] Miss Agatha Runcible . . . the daughter of a socialist aristocrat who worked at Prince Yousoupoff's dress shop in Berkeley St . . . the same man who helped push Rasputin through the ice.'

Greville, meanwhile, was gravitating towards the colourful entourage associated with Augustus John. Now in his mid-forties,

John was Britain's best-known living artist. His popular reputation rested as much on his famously complicated domestic arrangements, hashish-fuelled excesses, flamboyant hats and gypsy earrings as on the work he had been producing with near-manic vigour for more than two decades. As well as virtuoso drawings and jewel-like landscapes, it included a growing number of portraits that ranged from 'bravura' studies of people who fascinated him, to 'dull and even incompetent' renderings of statesmen and soldiers.[22] Despite its varying quality, John's portraiture brought him a degree of wealth and prestige. By the 1920s, he had homes in Dorset and London which he shared with his companion and muse, the enigmatic Dorelia, and multiple children ranging from babies to grown men. In London, John could usually be found in his Chelsea studio or favourite haunts like the Café Royal, holding forth to a ragtag court that included not only artists, aspiring models and potential mistresses, but also 'decaying aristocrats, circus people, magicians and vagabonds . . . Social Creditors, practical jokers, picturesque anarchists of the Kropotkin school, flamenco dancers [and] Buddhists'. According to his biographer, John 'welcomed anyone stranded in a tributary off the mainstream'.[23]

Outside the mainstream was precisely where Greville yearned to be, and she had no hesitation in diving into John's circle. Exactly what role she occupied there remains unclear. At some point she was charged with opening the door to John's celebrity friends and sitters, including on one memorable occasion T.E. Lawrence (of Arabia).[24] She almost certainly attended John's legendary Chelsea parties, which offered everything a pleasure-seeking young woman from the provinces could wish for. They typically began at five in the evening and lasted until five in the morning, one guest remembered; there would be jazz and cocktails and exotic dancing and drugs, all the girls were 'wonderfully beautiful and young' and proceedings could end 'in the most dreadful orgy'.[25] Afterwards, John and friends might visit the oyster bar at Victoria Station, in those days 'the most exciting, the aristocrat of stations', Greville wrote later – 'John was very fond of Victoria and once spent a night

there after a binge (hashish) and astonished Mrs F by arriving at our
place. "Came straight from the station" [he said]. Mrs F seeing that
he was in no state for travelling was rather afraid he might have lost
his luggage.'[26] Although Greville has not been officially identified
in any of John's work from this period, she almost certainly
modelled for him then, as she would again in the late 1930s. It has
also been suggested that she was briefly one of his innumerable
mistresses,[27] and it was certainly not uncommon for John to require
his models to fulfil both functions. But in fact, Greville may have
been primarily drawn to John's circle by his son, David. Originally
and magnificently named 'Llewelyn de Wet Ravachol John' – the
first part of his middle name honouring an infamous Boer general,
the second an anarchist bomber[28] – David was exactly Greville's
age. He was Augustus John's eldest child from his marriage to the
artist Ida Nettleship, whose own considerable talents were rapidly
subsumed by marriage and child-bearing; she died after delivering
John's fifth son in 1907. As he grew up, David (like several of John's
sons) was careful to distance himself from his father's notoriety. A
1922 portrait by Charles Lamb shows an owlish, watchful young
man with a heavy fringe; Marjorie Gertler recalled him as serious,
rather reserved, dreamy, 'fine to look at and musical'. Greville fell
deeply in love, and later described pacing the street outside the
John residence, finally mustering the courage to knock on the door
with the intention of declaring herself. Unfortunately, David was
practising the oboe and she was told to go away.[29] Marjorie believed
David was 'the man [Greville] was most moved by in her life.
However, he didn't want her'.[30] David became first a professional
oboist and then a postman, evidently preferring a quiet life away
from the public eye and his father's celebrity.

But Greville was by now finding fulfilment elsewhere: on
the stage. As a chorus-line dancer, she began to establish an
independent life, separate (though never too distant) from her
mother and sister. She had a modest income of her own – perhaps
£3.10 in a good week – and an exotic new identity. She called
herself Margot or sometimes Marguerite Greville, a stage name

Photograph by Curtis Moffat © Victoria and Albert Museum, London

that not only endowed a certain cosmopolitan sophistication but also signalled a decisive break from Margaret Foster of Sedgley. As Margot Greville, she danced in shows at popular West End theatres like the Gaiety and the Winter Garden – *His Girl*, *The Cabaret Girl*, *The Beauty Prize* – as well as touring productions.[31] This was the heyday of the chorus girl, epitomised by the Ziegfeld Follies and the Tiller Girls, troupes of elaborately costumed dancers whose precisely-synchronised tap-and-kick routines featured in all the most popular revues and musicals. It was a decidedly déclassé world, where a working-class girl from Lancashire might dance alongside a girl from a respectable London suburb or even a rebellious daughter of an aristocratic family. Apart from talent and the right looks, what a stage-struck girl needed most was sufficient grit to survive the brutal audition and rehearsal regime; money and connections were irrelevant. Some chorus girls became celebrity actresses, especially if they could make the transition to movies. Many acquired large and ardent (mainly male) followings. Marjorie Gertler remembered Greville being sent bottles of champagne at the theatre by well-connected admirers like the aristocratic Lord Ilchester and his friend P.G. Wodehouse, both middle-aged and married. After shows, they would take Greville and other dancers out to nightclubs; on occasions, said Marjorie, Greville had danced with the Prince of Wales.

Lord Ilchester – also known as Lord Stavordale and, more affectionately, Stavvy – somehow overcame a highly conventional upbringing (Eton, Christ Church, the Coldstream Guards) to become in middle age a mildly eccentric peer. He owned Holland House, a grand estate with fifty acres of parkland in the heart of Kensington.[32] In the 1920s, all three Fosters would visit Holland House from time to time for lunches or intimate evenings, where Stavvy would serve them salmi (ragout) of swan sourced from his personal swannery in Dorset, along with the obligatory champagne. A sportsman and late-blooming scholar who went on to chair the British Museum and the National Portrait Gallery, he later re-appeared in Greville's life at a critical time when his connections and savoir faire proved invaluable. Greville considered him magnificent.[33]

Other friends were less helpful. According to Marjorie, Greville was introduced to drugs around this time, allegedly by the American painter, photographer and interior designer Curtis Moffat, first husband of Iris Tree. Drug use, both recreational and supposedly therapeutic, was then commonplace in fashionable London circles. Society beauty Lady Diana Manners – youngest daughter of the Duke of Rutland and later married to the conservative politician Duff Cooper – reportedly 'sent out' for choloroform during a particularly trying dinner party ('I must be unconscious tonight', she announced as it was about to begin). During World War One, she regularly injected morphine as a way of coping with the deaths or absences of friends at the front.[34] By the 1920s, there was growing alarm at the 'vicious craze' for cocaine, a habit-forming drug that London police maintained 'not only enslaves and ruins the whole constitution of its victim . . . but . . . directly promotes the committing of crime', including unspecified sexual vice. Women, especially prostitutes and those 'who haunt the West End at night', were said to be particularly susceptible, and the drug-ravaged young actress or dancer became a familiar character in popular novels. One, published in 1920, charts the sorry demise of a young actress who begins taking cocaine for stage fright, then uses veronal for her cocaine-induced insomnia and finally progresses to smoking opium. The author is particularly damning of the Soho nightclubs where drug consumption is rife and 'women entitled to wear coronets danc[e] with men entitled to wear the broad arrow, and men whose forefathers had signed Magna Carta danc[e] with chorus girls' – the very type of déclassé setting in which Greville thrived.[35] Marjorie Gertler believed Greville probably started by using marijuana (which was not criminalised in Britain until 1925)[36] but later progressed to harder drugs, including heroin.

Other novelties also captured her attention. In 1921, the press announced that out of 'one thousand of the prettiest young women of the British Isles', a panel of judges had chosen nineteen-year-old

Modelling for Mark Gertler; their relationship was founded on mutual dislike
Photograph courtesy Cristina Patterson Texidor

MOST BEAUTIFUL BLONDE AND
BRUNETTE IN ALL ENGLAND

Miss Winifred
Randall
and Miss
Margot
Greville

The All-England beauty queen
The Buffalo Enquirer, New York,
15 August 1921

Miss Margot Greville, 'a black-haired, brown-eyed maiden', as the most beautiful brunette in all of England. Along with her blonde counterpart, Miss Winifred Randall, Greville's photo appeared in national and international newspapers,[37] and part of her prize was a small role in a forthcoming movie. She was cast as the Countess of Chesterfield in the swashbuckling historical drama, *The Glorious Adventure* (1922), directed by J. Stuart Blackton. Set in the reign of King Charles II, it is an overheated romance featuring an attempted murder at sea, the Great Fire of London, a capricious Nell Gwynne and many dramatic sword fights. London audiences loved it, but it was more coolly received elsewhere, including in the United States where audiences found its storyline confusing and its execution ponderous. However it remains notable as the first full-length British film to be shot in colour, using the new Prizma technology just developed in America to sometimes spectacular effect, especially in the Great Fire scenes.[38] Its cast list also demonstrated the fledgling movie industry's allure to upper-class young women seeking careers and incomes of their own, or simply a way to upset their parents. The heroine, Lady Beatrice Fair, is played by Lady Diana Manners; Elizabeth Beerbohm, of the famous London theatrical and literary family, plays King Charles's mistress Barbara Castlemaine.[39] Two years later, both Greville and Kate (credited as 'Kitty Foster') appeared in another, much smaller, British film – *Moonbeam Magic* (1924), directed by Felix Orman, who had also worked on *The Glorious Adventure*. It too was a silent movie using ground-breaking colour cinematography, this time a British process invented by Claude Friese-Greene. Purportedly based on a biblical legend about an eastern prince, *Moonbeam Magic* was a self-referential fantasy telling how colour had been brought into the world through the intervention of a deity on whose command, 'flashing coloured moonbeams . . . painted beautiful colours over the face of the earth.'[40] No prints of this curious production remain today, which was one of a series Friese-Green made in an attempt to overcome technical problems associated with early screen colour (he unveiled the films before an invited audience of dignitaries, including Augustus John, in 1924, and later screened them in the United States). Surviving publicity shots show Greville (as 'Miriam') and other cast members resplendent in vaguely Oriental costume, although her precise role – deity, moonbeam, princess – is unclear.

By now, Greville was thirsting for more exciting adventures than England could deliver. It was now simply a 'jumping off base for the more exciting climates', she remembered with a characteristic lack of sentiment.[41] Over the next few years, she danced her way across Europe and the Americas with various troupes. She was not completely adrift: her mother Editha often travelled in her wake, sometimes for pleasure but probably more often for support – financial, practical and emotional. Beneath the nominal glamour, life on the stage could be rackety, uncertain and physically punishing – as Greville would later depict in the story 'Maaree'. The story's wretched English protagonist is a so-called Old Girl, an experienced chorus dancer who has remained behind in Barcelona after the rest of her troupe has moved on to another city. Maaree is now required to compete with younger, prettier newcomers for work and the attentions of a wealthy Spanish protector; she lives precariously 'on the edge of refinement' – not to mention in perpetual fear of pregnancy, poverty and eventual abandonment:

> The new girls were from the Jackson troupes and others of unknown origin, Sunshine, Coktel, or merely Les Girls. They kept arriving in batches from Paris. The agents said it was difficult to get nice girls from abroad, but after they had been in Paris it was easier to get them to go to places like Java or Barcelona. When the troupe moved on they always lost some of the girls in Barcelona. Those who stayed on were called The Old Girls.

Opposite page: As 'Miriam' in Moonbeam Magic, 1924: according to the publicity, Miss Margot Greville was 'a well-known member of the Winter Garden company' who had 'posed for a number of noted painters . . . Augustus John has exhibited several portraits of her.'
Photographer unknown

Some just hung about the Grill and got too bad . . . The others waited for the weekly visits of their *novios* [boyfriends] in furnished flats. They couldn't go to nice places, like the Ritz, because they might meet family girls there. That is to say, girls with a family, like the sisters of the *novios* . . . [T]hey could still work in the theatre, but only with the Spanish girls; propping up the scenery for three *pesetas* a night. The managers rated them with the Spaniards, the Consul turned his blind eye, the Old Girls had no status at all.

If they were to avoid getting 'too bad', young dancers had to know when to quit and when to move on, which Greville did frequently. She left few footprints, though she can be occasionally sighted in the official record as she swaps continents and stages (and sometimes identities). As Margot Greville, she's playing the role of Felice and dancing in the chorus when the musical play *Madame Pompadour* opens at New York's Martin Beck Theatre on 45th Street. It runs for eighty performances from November 1924 to the middle of January the following year. She's back in New York a few months later, disembarking from the SS *Carmania* as Margot Greville-Foster, late of the Boulevard Montparnasse in Paris. She dances in Oscar Hammerstein's hit musical *Rose-Marie* (famed for its show-stopping 'Red Indian' dance number, the 'Totem Tom-Tom') and in shows at the Winter Garden. In New York, she does some modelling and, according to a statement she later makes to New Zealand immigration officials, teaches gymnastics. She gets to know composers Virgil Thomson (he presents her with the score of a piano piece he wrote for Gertrude Stein) and George Gershwin, whom she becomes very keen on.[42] Back in Paris – which in 1924–25 is full of Americans seemingly intent on drinking themselves to death – she knocks about with a Finnish anthropologist, an American writer improbably called Lotus Zifather, and sometimes Kate, who is working as a mannequin for Mme Chanel. Marjorie Gertler is also in Paris, painting; she recalls Greville turning up at

her studio in Montparnasse late one night, 'definitely on some sort of drugs [and] in a very sick condition'. In 1926, Greville is back 'having a great time' in the United States with a travelling dance troupe, possibly the Tiller Girls, and sending postcards home from places like St Louis and Omaha. The girls are having many parties, 'but not too many', she assures her mother. Thanking Kate for her interesting letter 'about the Bloomsburys and your state of mind', Greville declares she is 'now more glad than ever that I am doing handstands in the state of Nebraska' and enjoying the scenic attractions of the Midwest: Kansas City is memorable for its 'very nice stockyards', she reports.[43] For a while, she's touring elsewhere in North America with a German or perhaps American contortionist who is also her lover. He wears a tight black bodysuit, reports Marjorie, and together they perform a wildly popular skeleton dance. It is the mysterious contortionist who gets Greville addicted to heroin, and Mrs Foster is said to have taken her away for treatment at a Parisian rehab clinic on at least two occasions.[44] From Paris, Greville tours other European cities with acts such as the 'Twelve Cocktail Girls'. At Barcelona's grand opera house, the Liceu, they perform the first Charleston the city has ever seen.

Most enigmatic of all during this period is a short-lived first marriage to a man Greville later referred to only rarely and pseudo-nymously. 'Mr Wilson' is understood to have been a Scottish army officer whom she met before leaving England. They married after he followed her to the United States, and honeymooned at Niagara Falls. The marriage lasted just two weeks because, said Greville, Mr Wilson 'had the nasty habit of reading the newspapers at breakfast'.

'Dancing on the edge of destruction'

Barcelona commanded Greville's affections as few other cities had done. In the late 1920s, the elegant grandeur of its tree-lined boulevards and the fantastic 'jazz architecture' springing up in the Gràcia quarter could not completely conceal older and murkier under-currents. Writer Ethel Mannin – a contemporary of Greville's whose life intersected with hers at various points – described Barcelona as 'passionate, sensual, vicious [and] reckless . . . a city of sailors, prostitutes, loafers, beggars, shoe blacks . . . and the smell of drains' as much as a showpiece for bourgeois prosperity. For a visitor strolling at night down the crowded Rambla, 'the great throbbing heart of the city', the inchoate sense of danger was unmissable:

> It becomes possible to feel then that under all that surface life of strolling and lounging and idling in the sun, there is violence and passion and bloodshed; that here are the people who instituted the Inquisition; that here is a city in which revolution smoulders like a damped-down fire, a city in which . . . anyone may throw a bomb at any moment, and her streets run riot with blood and destruction.[45]

It was in this febrile, exhilarating city that Greville met Manuel (Manolo) Texidor, a dashing local businessman, entrepreneur and motorcycle racer. He was from a wealthy and well-established Catalan family with homes in the city and at Sitges on the coast. The Texidors owed their fortune to the prescience of Manolo's grandfather who had established an art supplies shop in Barcelona in 1874, just as artists were starting to flock to southern France and the Costa Brava in search of quintessential Mediterranean landscapes and light. By the 1920s, the family's shop – La Tienda Texidor – on the Ronda de Sant Pere was a city landmark renowned for its exquisitely-detailed interior, the work of a well-known Catalan modernista architect.[46]

Manolo Texidor was handsome, elegant and full of life; he adored cars, parties and good times. When Greville met him, he was a salesman for the Lancia car firm who pursued a variety of private money-making schemes and dreams as well, some of decidedly dubious merit. Over the coming years, Manolo would deal in wine, cigarettes, cars and, with some success, cork. Less successful ventures included a plan to import sock-stretching machines from the United States. 'I think he simply works by impulses,' Greville

A young Manolo Texidor
Photograph courtesy Cristina Patterson Texidor

Manolo and Greville
Photograph courtesy Cristina Patterson Texidor

Kate and her then-husband Sherry Mangan at their home near Palma de Mallorca
Photograph courtesy Cristina Patterson Texidor

wrote later of her husband, 'some quite delightful others quite disastrous'.[47] Manolo may have been, in Kate's words, a thoroughly 'gay good-time type' and something of a wheeler-dealer. But he was also an intellectually-curious man with brave and independent convictions. His Jesuit education had left him with a passionate hatred of the clergy, and his politics were leftist; during the Civil War, he would put his motorcycling skills to account as a dispatch rider for the Republicans.

As a fashionable man-about-town in 1920s Barcelona, Manolo courted Greville with decidedly un-English élan. They would drive at high speed in his Lancia to the Costa del Garraf, just south of Barcelona. There they would picnic on roast chicken and champagne, then swim naked in the sea, delighting in the disapproving stares from the trains that ran alongside the coastline. They spent time in Paris with Kate and Sherry Mangan, the Harvard-educated poet and ardent Trotskyist to whom she was married for a period.[48] Years later, Manolo would remind Sherry ruefully of 'that winter in Paris in rue de la Cavalerie' when they were both hopelessly in thrall to 'les Fosters'. In middle age, the two men exchanged nostalgic memories of all they had endured as fellow vice-presidents of the 'Foster Sisters Alumni Association'.[49] How they had suffered, remembered Sherry fondly: 'These girls were sent into this world by le bon dieu for the disciplining of the male sex, and I hope we are both better for the (rather shattering) experience.'[50]

Unsurprisingly, Manolo's family disapproved of his romantic liaison with an apparently wayward English dancing girl. Their displeasure – in combination with a new business venture Manolo was developing, Greville's enthusiasm for the tango, and possibly an extra-marital pregnancy – prompted the couple to leave Spain for Buenos Aires, where they married in 1929. Their daughter Cristina was born there in 1930. But these were difficult times in Argentina; the economy in disarray, huge extremes of wealth and poverty, widespread industrial unrest. It was not long before the cork factory Manolo established in Buenos Aires failed and they were forced to return to Barcelona. In Europe, as in Argentina, it was now apparent that the late 1920s had been 'the Wild Party's crescendo, the final binge before the slump'; the decade ahead would have a very different complexion.[51] It was also apparent that Greville and Manolo's marriage was in trouble. Lingering family disapproval may have played a part, but Greville was also tiring of Manolo's endless money-making schemes that seldom came to anything – wary, too, that he might use (and lose) Foster money in some preposterous venture. Cristina remembered her mother's consternation when a beautiful leather handbag Manolo had delivered to her from an exclusive shop on the Passeig de Gràcia was repossessed almost as soon it arrived; it had not been paid for. Greville – whose values were still more English and middle-class than she may have cared to acknowledge – could see that Manolo 'was not going to be a good provider'.

Soon they were living apart much of the time; Manolo in Barcelona or Sitges, and Greville and Cristina in the coastal village of Tossa de Mar, north of Barcelona.[52] Dubbed the 'Blue Paradise' by Marc Chagall, Tossa was at that time a magnet for artists, writers and intellectuals from around Europe, including increasing numbers of refugees from Nazi Germany. Among the regular visitors were Chagall himself and fellow-artists Georges Kars, Lola Bech, Oskar Zügel and André Masson. They came for Tossa's beguiling terrain and light, the welcoming locals, and also for the extraordinary paintability of a working Catalan fishing village where people 'knew how to live . . . from the heart'.[53] Built on the site of an ancient Roman town, Tossa was flanked by great cliffs riddled with sea-caves and grottoes that could be explored by boat. A ruined Saracen fortress and a lighthouse overlooked one end of a turquoise bay; at the other, German and British émigrés were starting to build hillside hotels with commanding views, as yet too few to be an eyesore. In summer, bathers in bathrobes wandered a curving beach strewn with bright fishing boats. Small fish-salting and cork factories dotted the promenade. The narrow streets of the village were lined with the lime-washed white houses of the local fishermen, and on Sundays people danced the Sardana.

Tossa before the Civil War. Top left: With friends at the beach. Greville is to the right of the group, wearing dark glasses; Cristina sits in front of her. Top right: Greville with Cristina. Bottom: Exploring the local landmarks.

Photographs courtesy Cristina Patterson Texidor

In the wooded hills beyond the town walls, the scent of wild thyme, perfumed broom and charcoal fires hung in the air.

Just as Greville had loved the elegance and excitement of Barcelona, she was now enraptured by Tossa de Mar. She had grown increasingly besotted with the theatrical spectacle and mystical romance she projected onto Spanish life, and which she heard echoed back in the poetry of Federico García Lorca, in flamenco music, and in the songs of the gypsies (gitanos), the 'splendid and terrible people' whom she later recalled roaming the countryside 'as if [Lorca] had called them to life'.[54] To Greville, the gitanos lived life as it should be lived; fiercely and fatalistically, with passion and gaiety, apparently free of the crippling moral and religious codes that held sway elsewhere. It was all a very long way from Wolverhampton – perhaps also from the real lives of ordinary Spaniards, whether workers, peasants or the bourgeoisie (Greville would soon learn this from the anarchists she came to know in Barcelona; anti-romantic and pragmatic, they took a dim view of what they saw as Lorca's ersatz Spain).[55]

Greville was beguiled by the lyrical language and music of the gypsies and migrants from the south, but her daily life in Tossa was largely spent among left-wing locals and expatriates – the artists, writers, political fugitives and occasional freeloaders who had come there from every corner of Europe. The English contingent commonly congregated at places like the Marcus snack bar, famous for its excellent welsh rarebit, or in the American bar at the Hotel Steyer. In the evenings, they could be found in its lush red velvet lounge, where a painting by a recent guest, Frances Hodgkins, hung in pride of place, or dancing drunkenly under the plane trees at Emilio's beach café. Tossa's expatriate milieu was neither as exclusive nor as self-regarding as better-known artistic enclaves on the Riviera or the Côte d'Azur – places like Cagnes-sur-Mer or Cassis, villages transformed by an invasion of 'artsy flotsam and jetsam' into 'Bloomsbury-sur-Mer'.[56] Greville would later set her venomous novella *These Dark Glasses* (1949) in just such a place, populating it with lightly-fictionalised versions of Mark Gertler,

Kate, Richard Carline and others. Greville's fictional Calanques is an amalgam of Tossa and Cassis, where she holidayed several times. On one visit there, she encountered Gertler, whose description of their meeting was every bit as vicious as Greville's later fictional representation of him. While Cassis was undeniably charming, wrote Gertler to a friend;

> it is *filled* with the 'Bohemia' of London – absolutely packed – futile men and prostitute-like women. Mostly semi-acquaintances of a sort one tries to avoid like poison in London, and now Greville has turned up! Kate [Foster] and her 'boy' are coming . . . So that the whole place seems like a lunatic asylum.[57]

These Dark Glasses suggests that by the mid-1930s Greville was tiring of the bohemian pretensions and self-absorption of communities like Cassis and even Tossa. The intensity of the animus pervading her novella may have grown retrospectively, but something was undoubtedly changing in Greville – whether in response to Europe's darkening political climate, her own developing political consciousness (perhaps stirred by the grinding poverty she had witnessed in South America), or simply a consequence of growing older. It is the sensibility of this altered Greville – more reflective and politically aware – which inflects *These Dark Glasses*. In it, she vilifies her characters not just because they are unbearable (they are) but because they have chosen to insulate themselves from the impending European catastrophe, complacently dancing instead on what her narrator calls 'the edge of destruction'.

From a distance, Greville's transformation from pleasure-loving showgirl to political activist and militiawoman seems abrupt, inexplicable even. But it was not as precipitate as it seemed, and several conditions enabled it. According to Ethel Mannin, despite their apparent narcissism, not all the Bright Young Things were entirely indifferent to the miseries they saw writ large around them as the decade progressed; the hunger marches, the degradation of mass unemployment, the industrial unrest. Even the most feckless

Werner Droescher with his pupil Florian Steyer, 1933
State Library of New South Wales, ref. PXA 1210

*'One day we were all
in the café, Chagall
and Masson and Kars
and everyone ... and
the next day no one
was at the café and we
never saw any of them
again.'*
State Library of New
South Wales, ref. PXA
1210

were capable of seriousness and social responsibility, she insists. At some level, '[we were] critical of that very frivolity of which we were a part' and, while a mask of heedlessness was compulsory, 'with a part of ourselves we cared'.[58] Moreover, Greville's political consciousness, like Mannin's, had been well-primed by her upbringing. She too had grown up in a politically-aware, though far from radical, household in which people talked and cared about issues of social justice, even while they remained largely insulated from their effects.

But Greville's growing engagement with politics was also the product of a new relationship that began on the beach at Tossa.

Werner Droescher was a young German who had arrived in Tossa as a private tutor to the son of the German hotelier Ludwig Steyer and his wife Eva.[59] Werner had left Frankfurt for Spain in 1933, his first decisive break from a deeply conservative upbringing in Weimar Germany and the start of a global journey that would last more than four decades. Born in 1911, Werner grew up near Mannheim. His father, originally a civil engineer, had been an officer in the First World War. He was in many respects 'a typical product of the Prussian military ideology', his son recalled, but also a kind-hearted man completely lacking in arrogance. Werner's mother was devoted to her family, the privations and spiralling inflation of the post-war years instilling in her what Werner called 'an almost animal-like determination' to raise her children as best she could. As he grew up, Werner increasingly distanced himself from his family's reactionary values. By the time he was twenty, he was 'a left-liberal, vaguely socialistic', with strong interests in education, nature and the possibilities of communal living. In 1930–31, he attended the progressive teachers' training academy at Altona, known to outsiders as 'The Red Academy', where trainee teachers were encouraged to become not just purveyors of an official curriculum but 'socially conscious citizens' engaged in a shared enterprise with their pupils. When the government closed down Altona, Werner relocated to Frankfurt just as the Nazi regime began asserting its authority over all spheres of life. Out of curiosity, Werner attended a rally where Goebbels spoke, and sensed there the 'mass hysteria' that would soon be released. Once the first 'nauseating anti-semitic and militarist' school textbooks began appearing in bookshops, Werner knew he could not stay in Germany.

His task in Tossa was to coach young Florian Steyer for the Spanish high-school entrance exam. As more émigrés arrived, Werner acquired more pupils, including German Jewish refugees. He taught children of all ages together; on any given day, their classroom might be the beach, the town's Roman ruins or the forest. In his spare time, he offered open-air physical education sessions on the beach that attracted quite a following among émigrés and summer visitors. Among them was Kate Foster, visiting Tossa from Paris. Kate persuaded her sister to join her, and before long Werner and Greville – nine years his senior – were lovers.

Manolo still made periodic visits to Tossa. But Werner had already noticed an unexpected degree of sexual emancipation among British women abroad, and found Greville – still going by the name of Margarita or Marguerida Texidor – 'had no qualms about having an affair with the German tutor . . . I was quite happy to go along with her, content with not having to make a decision to enter a permanent relationship – that is, to marry.' They conducted their affair largely outside Tossa, where 'one could not make a move without the whole village knowing about it', meeting instead in Barcelona or 'romantic places' in the Pyrénées and Mallorca. By 1935, Werner was living in Barcelona, teaching languages and preparing to study at the city's university. Greville took a central city flat and visited regularly, leaving Cristina in Tossa with Mrs Foster. Once, Greville and Werner attended a reading of Lorca's poetry by the poet himself – a 'youngish, unpretentious man' who read from his collections *Romancero Gitano* and *New Poems*. His listeners were enthralled, Werner remembered, 'not only [by] the content of the poems, the simplicity of the diction, the poetic images, the insinuating rhythms, but also the manner in which he read . . . a completely natural manner, without pathos'. More than forty years later, Werner still had 'Lorca's way of speaking in my inner ear'. The imprint on Greville was equally profound. She would forever admire the enigmatic simplicity of Lorca's work, his affinity with the Spanish peasant tradition, his joyful resistance to the 'grey death' of fascism, and his insistence that his verse belonged chiefly to the people and not the intellectuals who lionised him. Once she herself began to write, the memory of this encounter with Lorca on a beautiful late-autumn afternoon in Barcelona remained a touchstone.[60]

The political volatility of pre-Civil War Barcelona intrigued Werner. But by his own admission, he did not yet appreciate the nuanced divisions between the city's anarcho-syndicalists and its numerous socialist and communist groups. His Spanish was not advanced enough to allow him to read local newspapers in depth, and he was in any event absorbed in his life as teacher, student and lover. Like most of their friends, Werner and Greville were delighted when a Republican government was elected in February 1936. That summer, Werner returned to Tossa and, while studying for his university entrance exams, worked as a gardener at Herr Steyer's new hotel. Greville meanwhile took the lease on a sixteenth-century farmhouse in a valley just outside Tossa. While it was renovated, she lived at the smallest and cheapest pension in town, the Pensión Delgado, whose proprietors Angeleta and Casimiro she later declared 'the best friends I ever had or will have'.[61] In their company, the distance between Greville and the expatriate community widened and she came to identify more with the local residents than the foreigners;

> I'd been living so long with Catalans that I'd come to share, at least in some degree, their feelings about the foreign visitors. . . . They were not impressed by Steyer's talk of prosperity for the village. Prosperity was having enough to eat and a house and they all had that and didn't fancy being turned out of the house to make room for lovers of the picturesque.

After several trying months overseeing renovations, Greville grew desperate to move into the house she had rented. It was

Can Sans d'Aiguabona
State Library of New South Wales, ref. PXA 1210

Anti-fascist poster on a Barcelona building
State Library of New South Wales, ref. PXA 1210

known locally as Can Sans d'Aiguabona – the house of saints and, reflecting its proximity to an ice-cold holy well, the house of good waters. From the moment she saw it, Greville felt what she called 'an almost unnatural affection'. The house was a short walk from town along a track that passed through woods and olive groves, following the course of a stream. Standing on a rocky rise with the black cork forest and the mountains behind, with views out towards the Mediterranean, it was (and remains) a beguiling site. When Frances Hodgkins visited Tossa in 1935–36, she joined Greville on several visits to Can Sans to check progress; the English novelist Ralph Bates, then living on a farm nearby, was helping lay pipes bringing water from the well to the house. On one occasion, Greville recalled walking there with Hodgkins in the cool of late afternoon and pausing on the bridge to gaze up at the house. 'Pepita had lighted the fire for the evening meal,' Greville remembered, 'and smoke from the chimney stood straight and white against the dark of the trees.' Can Sans was to be a proper home, her first – a symbol of the stability she had resisted during more than a decade of determined nomadism. Now she wanted nothing more. The house would tether her to the Spanish soil and peasant life; it would be the setting for the more settled, mature life she and Werner planned to build together. It would be the place that they would raise the child she was carrying.

But on the verge of fulfilment, her plans disintegrated. In July 1936, a group of Spanish Army generals led by General Francisco Franco, backed by right-wing factions including the Nationalists and the Fascist Falange, overthrew the recently-elected Republican government. Republican supporters of various political hues – centrists, communists, anarchists, syndicalists, socialists and others – rose up in opposition. Spain was engulfed by a civil war that quickly metastasised into something else; a proxy war between rival political ideologies and foreign powers, and a brutal rehearsal for the larger global conflict to come in 1939.

Werner admits that the outbreak of civil war took the couple by surprise. The first hint of trouble came when they were unable to make phone calls to Barcelona from Tossa. Next, the town's local police disappeared and an attempted military takeover in nearby Girona was rumoured. By then, Werner said:

> It was getting obvious that a fierce civil war was raging in Barcelona, however it was not clear whether it was a purely Catalan separatist affair . . . After a few days of great anxiety we heard on the radio a speech by the Catalan chief of government who, with a voice trembling with emotion, informed the people that the military rebellion had been crushed in Catalonia, with the aid of the trade unions, particularly . . . the CNT (Confederación Nacional de Trabajo), the anarcho-syndicalists and the FAI (Federación Anarquista Ibérica).[62]

Soon after, truckloads of armed anarchists arrived in Tossa from a neighbouring town. Proclaiming that 'God is dead', they damaged some churches but spared the priests. The anarchists met no significant resistance and soon took charge of the local police and civil administration, to the bewilderment of foreigners in the town. The change in Tossa was abrupt and absolute, Greville recalled: 'One day we were all in the café, Chagall and Masson and Kars and everyone sitting around the bowls of sugar and syphons while Emilio picked lemons for our lemonade, and the next day no one was at the café and we never saw any of them again.'[63] Alarmed at rumours of heavy fighting elsewhere in Spain and regular flyovers by military aircraft from Italy, many British and French nationals were evacuated by sea. Werner and others who chose to stay were adamant that the expatriate community was never in danger: 'I believe today that the British, afraid of Red revolution, did their utmost to foster the mood of panic', he wrote decades later. On a lovely July night, the foreigners remaining in Tossa watched 'the frightened village shr[i]nk behind its walls under the glare of searchlights from battleships, come to take away their nationals to safety', Greville remembered. It was a moment of collective shame that, in the years to come, she would commute into a moment of personal failure too.

Werner returned to Barcelona as planned, although now with a different aim: to 'join in the fight against fascism'. He found a tense, excited city, still bearing the mark of the Left's recent victory over Franco's rebels. After days of fierce street fighting, the city's workers (supported by the police) had prevailed and the Catalan Regional Government, or Generalitat, had now assumed the powers formerly held by the central government. While the Generalitat represented numerous leftist groups, real control lay with the anarchists. Workers had taken over the factories, hotels had been requisitioned for workers' organisations, churches had been burnt and their treasures destroyed. Buildings were pock-marked by bullet holes and bouquets of flowers still lay in the streets to mark where fighters had fallen. Armed workers with rifles slung over their shoulders walked the Ramblas and guarded important sites; they drove exuberantly around the city in late-model cars they had commandeered and daubed with the initials of various leftist factions. Barcelona's bourgeoisie were nowhere to be seen. Some, such as factory owners and certain professionals, were presumed to have been executed. Most simply lay low. It was a city engaged in two simultaneous conflicts: a civil war and a social revolution.[64]

Eager for action, Werner enlisted with the POUM (Partido Obrero de Unificación Marxista) whose headquarters was the Hotel Falcón.[65] There, a motley group of foreigners assembled and gradually formed themselves into a platoon or *centuria* – 'a little International Brigade in miniature' comprising four Frenchmen, two young Swiss, two Hungarians, an Italian and Werner. They were fitted out with the ubiquitous *mono* (overalls) and rifles, and told to wait for orders.

Werner later acknowledged he was still politically naïve and unaware of the deep tensions between the various leftist groups active in Barcelona at the time – the anti-Stalinist POUM, the foreign Trotskyists supporting them, the CNT, the FAI, the official Spanish Communist Party, the socialists. Forced to kill time at the Hotel Falcón, he found himself keeping company with anti-fascists of many allegiances. Many were young Britons who had come to Barcelona of their own accord or at the behest of the Communist Party – Ralph Bates, whom Werner already knew from Tossa; Hugh Slater, a former Slade student and old London friend of Greville's; the young poet John Cornford, soon to be killed fighting for the POUM; prominent British communist and journalist Tom Wintringham, subsequently commander of the British Battalion of the International Brigades. Werner did not initially distinguish between their various affiliations: 'I believed we all fought for social revolution and against Fascism and that it did not really matter to which party or political group one belonged', he remembered. But the mistrust, divisions and betrayals that would eventually tear the Left apart, recounted by George Orwell in *Homage to Catalonia*, were already in play. Before long, Werner was himself disenchanted with the communists, calling them 'knowalls who claimed the absolute truth of their political convictions . . . ambitious, powerlusting politicians'. Increasingly, he would be drawn to the anarchists' cause, finding in their beliefs 'everything that had been missing among the communists: a truly social behaviour of the individual, a form of organisation in which men were free but would agree voluntarily to restrictions limiting their freedom'.

Back in Tossa, Greville was eager to make her way to Barcelona before Werner's *centuria* left for the front. She arranged for Cristina, now aged six, to stay behind with the Delgado family, whose daughter was the same age. Despite the political upheavals, for the moment daily life in Tossa remained much as usual. Cristina remembered the two girls falling asleep under a table with the family dog while guests continued to talk, dance and drink late into the evening. Once, they watched the anarchist militias drag paintings and statues from the church and burn them on a bonfire in the town square. Later Cristina and her teddybear would be dispatched to stay with Texidor relatives in Sant Andreu de la Barca, where she witnessed the first bombs falling on Barcelona.

Once Greville had dispensed with all encumbrances (after months of separation, her divorce from Manolo was now formalised), she was free to commit fully to Werner and a more active role in the war. Most of what we know about her involvement is filtered through Werner's memoir, or drawn from her unpublished autobiographical novel *Diary of a Militia Woman*. As evidence of her motivations for embracing the anarchist cause and taking up arms, neither source is altogether satisfactory. But Greville's daughter Rosamunda Droescher confirms what both sources suggest: her mother was no mere adventurer or camp-follower, far less the 'stupid society girl' despised by Mark Gertler. She became a genuine anarchist with a sound intellectual understanding of the movement's principles and history. She was well-schooled in the writings of Kropotkin and Bakunin (the nineteenth-century theorists whose work strongly influenced the Spanish anarchist movement) and had ties to prominent Barcelona anarchists. They included the Conejero brothers, printers of mixed Andalusian and Catalan background whom Greville had met when doing translation work before the Civil War; it was through their influence that she was able to join the anarchist militia, even though women were by that point in the war technically banned from enlisting.[66]

At the same time, it is clear that Greville's political commitment was shaped by her aesthetic sensibilities too. The undeniably romantic traditions of Spanish anarchism – whose roots lay among the Andalusian peasants and revolutionary brigands of the eighteenth century, as well as the Catalan proletariat with their age-old hatred of Castilian domination – proved as persuasive as, if not more persuasive than, Bakunin's rigorous analysis of capitalism. Like Lorca's poetry, Spanish anarchism seemed to her imbued with an innate theatricality, emotional energy and deep spirituality, all powerful attractions. Austrian journalist Franz Borkenau, whom Greville met several times in Spain, wrote in his account of the Civil War that the Spanish proletariat were anarchist revolutionaries 'by heart and instinct', their politics compelled not only by high idealism but also distinctive morality and deep emotion:

> Anarchism *is* a religious movement . . . [It] does not believe in the
> creation of a new world through the improvement of the material
> conditions of the lower classes, but in the creation of a new world out
> of the moral resurrection of those classes which have not yet been
> contaminated by the spirit of mammon and greed. At the same time
> anarchism is far from being well behaved and pacifist . . . One result
> of the peculiar type of anarchist anti-capitalism is its emphatic belief
> in direct action.[67]

Strong passions, bold actions, a refusal to be well-behaved;
the creed of anarchism might have been tailor-made for Greville.
She had always been ruled by fierce and unequivocal affections,
and equally fierce enmities; now they inflected her politics too.
She regularly expressed her political judgements as matters of
taste, as if someone's decision to join the Communist Party or
become an anarchist was analogous to a preference for lapsang
souchong over Earl Grey. 'It is nice to hear that you are [no
longer] a communist,' she wrote to Sherry Mangan after the Civil
War, adding, 'We had a terrible time with them in Spain.'[68] In
Barcelona, she found the foreign communists who had flocked to
fight for the Republic doctrinaire and austere; their disagreeable
manner seemed to distress her as much as the near-certainty they
were being manipulated by Moscow. By contrast, she sensed in the
company of the anarchists – as she had among her local friends
in Tossa – something that seemed authentic, indigenous and
unmistakably *alive*. Notwithstanding her genuine intellectual
grasp of their ideology, the decision to fight with them was bound
up in the strong emotional connection she felt with the Spanish
people – people to whom, in Borkenau's words, 'beauty [was] more
important . . . than practical use; sentiment more important than
action; honour very often more important than success; love and
friendship more important than one's job'.[69]

But Greville was also a pragmatist. Unlike Werner, who
maintained an idealistic belief that anarchism could defeat fascism
almost until the end of the war, she recognised early on that the
anarchist revolution would almost certainly fail – at least in part

because of the intervention of foreign powers. The Nationalists' strength was built on the German and Italian weapons, aircraft, troops and expertise at their disposal; the Republicans increasingly relied on Russian specialists and materiel, as well as the international brigades backed by the Comintern (the Moscow-controlled association of national communist parties). But even when it was patently clear that outside forces were co-opting the Spanish war for their own ends, Greville still chose to fight under the anarchist banner. Regardless of the likelihood of failure, 'you nonetheless had to take sides and to act', she told Rosamunda. In this sense, Greville's actions conformed to the norms of her culture and class, even though she had spent the past fifteen years in flight from both. 'She had that very British conviction that you had to do your bit. You didn't shirk responsibility or run away,' said her daughter.

Greville reached Barcelona in late July. While Werner and his POUM comrades sat in cafés waiting for their orders, she had personal matters to deal with. Within days of arriving, she had an abortion, performed even more covertly than usual by a doctor clearly fearful of the city's anti-bourgeois mood. Then, with Werner about to be dispatched to the front, the couple married in an anarchist ceremony; even if such marriages were not recognised legally, they had now declared themselves life-companions, *compañero* and *compañera*. The next day, Werner's *centuria* set off for Aragón to help defend the village of La Zaida from the fascist forces dug in nearby. Greville remained in Barcelona where she too enrolled in the militia. With some difficulty, she managed to track down Werner's whereabouts and made her way to the front, joining him at La Zaida beside the Ebro River. By this stage, his POUM *centuria* had disintegrated, and the couple now committed themselves fully to the anarchist cause. They became part of a newly-formed anarchist *centuria* whose members were mostly tram drivers and conductors from the Barcelona suburb of Les Corts. As the only English speakers in the group, they were invited to meet the legendary American anarchist activist Emma Goldman when she visited the front; they would meet her

With Werner and Spanish friends in Barcelona, 1936–37
State Library of New South Wales, ref. PXA 1210

again later in Barcelona and London.[70] But apart from feigning an attack on the Nationalist-held town of Quinto, they saw little action. According to Werner, their time was mostly spent standing guard, digging defensive trenches and trying to persuade the local peasants to form an agricultural collective. Before long, the couple was sent back to Barcelona to become part of a new militia unit. They boarded with an anarchist family in Les Corts and were impressed by the spirit of voluntary cooperation they found there, Werner said – especially the 'tranquil cheerfulness' of the women who dispensed services and aid to other residents.

Equipped with 'new' weapons (in fact, ancient Winchester rifles supplied by the Mexican government), their *centuria* was again dispatched to the northern sector of the Aragón front in August 1936. They were driven in absolute darkness into the middle of an apparently empty landscape close to the fascist lines; fortunately, they were rescued by Italian anarchists who gave them hot food and shelter for the night in a deserted barn. The next day, Greville and Werner took part in the attack on the town of Almudévar. Despite a half-hearted aerial bombardment and the destruction of their two armoured cars by anti-tank guns, the *centuria* managed 'to creep up within sight of the elaborate barbed-wire defences of the fascists who defended their positions with rifle, machine-gun and artillery fire'. But the anarchists lacked sufficient troops to break through and were forced to take shelter in caves dug into the hillsides. After several wet, cold weeks, it was clear they had no hope of moving forward. They subsequently learned that a communist militia was supposed to come north to support their advance but had failed to turn up. Years later, a prominent Italian anarchist who also fought at Almudévar recalled bitterly that 'the communists had misled us with their promise of a thousand men, who they had decided not to send, since such reinforcement would have assured success and boosted the anarchists' prestige, when they really wanted to see them discredited'.[71]

Along with their *centuria*, Greville and Werner were sent back to Barcelona. Borkenau, who also returned to the city from a tour of the battlefields around this time, was struck by how empty and quiet it had grown; already, he wrote in his diary, 'the revolutionary fever is withering'.[72] Outside Catalonia (and even to some extent within) the communists increasingly controlled the struggle against the Nationalists; in Barcelona too, the nascent social revolution had been subordinated to the military campaign and the anarchists were losing influence.

Disheartened, Greville and Werner returned briefly to determinedly non-interventionist England, where they wrote propaganda and raised funds for organisations working under the 'Aid to Spain' umbrella. But they found scant satisfaction stuffing envelopes and drafting pamphlets in smoky offices in South London. Young English poets, intellectuals and militant workers may have been 'exploding like bombs' in their fervour to support the Republic, as Auden put it in his poem 'Spain' (1937). But the bulk of the English population remained indifferent, content to linger in what Orwell called the 'deep, deep sleep of England'.[73] As one Conservative politician observed cynically (and not entirely truthfully) of the Civil War's impact; for the English public 'it's just a lot of bloody dagoes killing each other'.[74]

To Greville and Werner, the progress of the war in Spain seemed even more depressing from a distance. The savagery of the fighting seemed futile, and the conflict and betrayals between leftist groups increasingly disheartening: 'As time went on, it was sad to read how the revolution was being watered down . . . [and] finally liquidated by the communist government,' Werner recalled. Nonetheless, like many other Republican sympathisers, they felt they could not abandon Spain even if the cause now seemed certain to fail. They decided to return in late 1937 – not to fight, but to care for children evacuated from Madrid, which had been under heavy bombardment by the Nationalist rebels and their European fascist allies since October 1936. Their appointment was arranged by the Society of Friends and the Joint Committee for Spanish Relief, both of which played a key role in coordinating British and international aid to Spain.

Greville and Werner were sent to Cantonigròs, a village in the mountains north-west of Barcelona. There they took charge of one of two hostels established by an aid agency of opaque provenance, the Paris-based Commission des Enfants. In an almost-grand villa on the outskirts of the village, Can Rifa, they became house parents to some twenty 'high-spirited and affectionate' children ranging from toddlers to teenagers, including some orphans. They sent for Cristina to join them from London, where she was living with her grandmother downstairs from the Gertlers; Marjorie Gertler accompanied seven-year-old Cristina as far as Paris, where she boarded a train and completed the journey alone.

The evacuees' schooling was the responsibility of the teachers who had accompanied them from Madrid – vain Spanish schoolmasters, according to Werner, who shirked their duties, intrigued against the 'foreigners' and were quite possibly fascist sympathisers as well. Everything else fell to Greville and Werner. They ensured their charges were warm and well-fed through the tough winter months: local villagers provided whatever food they could spare, and other supplies were brought by truck over the French border. They wrote potted life stories of every child to send to sponsors and hosted a procession of sympathetic foreign visitors. They organised outdoor activities: vegetable gardening, river swims and long bracing walks that alarmed the streetwise young Madrileños, more comfortable with footpaths than forests. At night, the children slept in dormitories named after local flowers and wildlife – Lilies, Roses, Mariposas. If they were woken by the unfamiliar silence of the countryside, by homesickness or troubled dreams, when they cried out for their dead mothers or missing fathers, it was Greville and Werner who would tuck them in and soothe them with a cough lozenge, small comfort against nightmares of incendiary bombs and headless corpses but the only palliative they had to hand.

Greville kept a couple of photographs from her time at Cantonigròs. In one, the hostel children pose en masse for the camera. At the centre stands Werner, calm and sad-eyed, his hands clasped before him. Around him swarm girls in cotton frocks and

Greville and Werner with their charges, Cantonigròs. Right: The kind Señora – Greville helps Cristina and other children with their sewing.

Photographs courtesy
Cristina Patterson Texidor

boys with close-cropped hair and monkey grins, ready to bolt as
soon as the shutter is pressed. Some exude insouciance and easy
confidence, like Cristina's friend Consuelo, a lithe, smiling girl who
stands with one leg cocked and a hefty slice of bread in her hand.
Other children have retreated to the margins of the group where
they stand, still and watchful. Like small feral animals, they know
to anticipate danger even in a place of apparent safety. Greville is
absent; perhaps she is behind the camera. Of Cristina, there is no
sign. But the other photo from Cantonigròs brings them together.
They are sitting on a window ledge at Can Rifa, their heads bent
over some sewing, close but not touching. Cristina is a story-
book English schoolgirl with neat plaits, pinafore, knee socks and
lace-up brogues; she concentrates on her task, pleased to have her
mother's attention at last. Greville, though, is tightly sprung, ready
to be diverted at any moment by the squabbles or tears or neediness
of the girls sewing in the room beyond, or perhaps by treacheries
and troubles brewing out of sight. At Cantonigròs, Greville has
assumed the unfamiliar role of protector, but she is a protector to
many. As a mother, her presence is contingent; another withdrawal
from Cristina and the burden of her needs is already imminent.

Greville revisited these precarious months in 'Jesús Jiménez',
a short story she wrote a few years later in New Zealand.[75] The
eponymous narrator is a six-year-old evacuee, sent from Madrid to
the comparative safety of a children's home in a Pyrénées village –
unnamed, but clearly Cantonigròs. He quickly becomes a favourite
of the pretty British Señora in charge. (Jesús may be modelled on
one of Greville's favourites at Can Rifa, Robertito, described by
Werner as 'a charmer, with all the coquetry of a Spaniard'.) The
boy's mother is almost certainly dead, last seen lighting a candle
in a bombing raid; his father is purportedly fighting fascists in the
siege of Teruel. Jesús's narrative is a sequence of disjointed, guileless
reports on daily life at the hostel – naïve, eloquent, capricious,
cruel and funny by turn. He records the arrival of the heroic 'uncle
comrade' who drives across the mountains with food and warm
clothes, the rice at dinner-time that crawls with semi-cooked snails

the children have gathered from the garden, the well-meaning *extranjero* who comes to do his bit for the Republican cause:

> *A man from England comes*. He wears a white helmet like a jungle explorer. He is going to make a vegetable garden. The flowers are all uprooted: the boys stand around him waiting for his commands. War is very wicked and cruel, he says. Then he gets diarrhoea and goes to bed.

There is grotesque comedy, too, in the boy's reply to a solicitous visitor who asks if the children have enough to eat: 'I say, *When the meat is all eaten we shall eat the flesh of the Fascists*.' This and similarly bloodthirsty descriptions of comrades 'eaten by wolves and fascists' go untranslated. The visitor departs, her well-rehearsed sympathies intact. While Jesús's apparently artless reportage is a source of uncomfortable humour, it also unwittingly illuminates the tragedy unfolding beyond the hostel. Jesús describes the little girls crowding around the Señora, 'fighting and biting each other' in their desperation to hold her hand – a slight but violent image into which all the brutality of a war waged against civilians seems concentrated. When he recalls stealing turnips at dusk, we are told only that 'the sky is turnip colour. A bell is ringing and over the cold fields people are calling. The turnips, washed in a muddy pool, taste bitter.' The economy of the description matches the limits of the child's vision, but it's also freighted with a deep, proleptic sadness, the weight of accumulating tragedies beyond his apprehension. And in the dormitories at night, there are screams as the children 'dream their mothers are dead or we are surrounded' while the strangely silent boy Helmuth – the most unfortunate of all the refugees, the Señora says, because he alone 'was born one' – is tormented by nightmares. The Señora 'tries to lift [him] from his cot; he lies like a stone, he doesn't want to wake. Once awake, he fights and scratches her, screaming words that nobody understands. Then he falls on her shoulder; his tears fall.'

Set alongside the 'true' version of the Cantonigròs hostel documented in Werner's memoirs and contemporary newspaper reports, 'Jesús Jiménez' is in many ways a faithful record. But it is also a revisionist one. The kind, pretty Señora – high-minded, compassionate, politically astute – can be read as Greville's fictional better self. The author bestows on her the gift of prescience: a sage understanding of the reasons for the Republicans' failure that Greville would have only acquired later. Other details have also been revised, including the circumstances of the Señora's departure; she leaves abruptly after attracting the unspecified suspicions of the local civil guard. In reality, Greville and Werner's assignment at Cantonigròs ended, equally abruptly, in late 1938 after a visit from the Commission des Enfants that had engaged them. Some foreign aid agencies working in Spain were widely suspected to be backed by Moscow, their activities camouflaged under neutral names that allowed them, in Werner's words, 'to infiltrate into the organisations of state'. Unwittingly, Werner and Greville had ended up working for one. The Commission's openly disdainful representative ('a narrow minded, stolid communist', remembered Werner) made it clear that the organisation did not wish the children's home to be run by non-communists, and Werner and Greville were dismissed.

Again, Cristina was sent back to England while Greville and Werner returned to Barcelona. There, they endured a few weeks of aerial bombing that left the population 'in a state of nervous hysteria'. As the Nationalist forces gained more territory, Italian bomber squadrons repeatedly attacked the city's port and surrounding neighbourhoods, unleashing as many as fourteen air-raids a day.[76] The couple heard reports of personal tragedies and sorrows suffered by people they knew elsewhere, tragedies that enacted in miniature the political disaster now engulfing the whole country. Lorca was long dead, executed by the Falangists near Granada and dumped in an unmarked grave.[77] Back at the *pensión* in Tossa, the Delgados' beloved pet dog had long ago been eaten. The whereabouts of the Cantonigròs children was unknown, including smiling Consuelo; she would simply disappear into the dark fog of Franco's Spain – perhaps to Madrid, perhaps to be reunited with her family, perhaps orphaned, imprisoned, exiled or dead. Exhausted and profoundly disappointed, Greville was evacuated aboard a British cruiser while Werner remained to secure the documentation he needed to enter Britain.

Rats in a trap

Werner made it as far as Newhaven, where officials found his papers unsatisfactory and, without allowing him to disembark, sent him back across the Channel to France. Not long after, he was picked up by the Dutch police and forced to return to Nazi Germany. In Hamburg, the Gestapo questioned him closely about his time in Spain; he managed to downplay his involvement in the militia, emphasising instead his work with the Quakers. Satisfied that Werner was foolish rather than subversive, the authorities sent him to do military service in the Signal Corps alongside a few other 'elderly' conscripts. Training was minimal, he recalled: his most demanding mission was participating in a grotesque *tableau vivant* on Hitler's birthday. Then, after firing exactly three shots on a rifle range and being taught to lay cables, Werner was allowed to leave the army – evidently, he was not seen as soldier material. He secured an exit visa under the pretext of taking up a teaching job in the United States and, soon after Kristallnacht, again made his way to England.

In Werner's absence, Greville had joined her mother and Cristina in the basement flat of the Gertlers' home in Highgate. There, she acquired 'many interesting friends, artists and writers, who helped her come to terms with the Spanish trauma', Werner reported. Most had been, and remained, active supporters of the Republican cause. They included members of the musical Goossens family, the Harley Street specialist Dr Andrew Morland (who a few years earlier had cared for D.H. Lawrence in his final illness) and his wife Dorothy Morland, who helped run a fostering organisation for Spanish orphans. Greville rekindled her friendship with Marjorie Gertler, judging her a 'good anarchist by nature' even if she also saw her reading Trotsky.[78] At one stage, Augustus John – no longer quite the scourge of respectable society he had been more than a decade earlier – hired Greville as a model.

Being back among London's sympathetic intelligentsia may have offered Greville a degree of comfort, but she no longer felt at home in their company; her experiences in Spain had sealed her off from them at some fundamental and unalterable level. Her growing distance from this milieu emerges in her story 'Reconstruction', which savages the London elite with 'their Jaeger pullovers, pipes, and enlightenment', the smug drawing-room radicals who are content to let refugees 'sell their wretched antifascist rags on the street, or even . . . be invited to private parties at Hampstead' and precious little else. However familiar, Greville found this world was neither substitute, salve nor release for her recent experiences. She was also reunited with her sister Kate, who had likewise been active in the Spanish war. Kate had worked as a correspondent for the *Toronto Star* and as a propagandist for the Republican Government in València. However, through her partner Jan Kurzke – a German Marxist who fought with the International Brigades – Kate had allied herself with the Communist Party for the duration of the war. Back in London, 'differences of political opinion' now further strained the sisters' already complicated relationship, Greville told Sherry Mangan.[79]

Despite Werner's breeziness, by the time he joined Greville in London, she was in fact far from 'coming to terms' with what had happened in Spain. Like Magda, the protagonist of her unfinished Spanish Civil War novel, the strain of war was imprinted in her every movement and on her skin; like Magda, there was 'something abnormal in her excitement . . . [Spain] was all she lived for. She wanted to live it all over again. . . . "I did wrong" she used to say over and over'.[80] This is the troubled, watchful woman we see in Augustus John's sombre *Portrait of a Woman*, which almost certainly dates from 1938. John may have engaged her as a sitter through a combination of sympathies, for Greville herself and for the anarchist cause in general (in the 1890s, he had frequented

Augustus John, Portrait of a Woman, c. 1938
© National Museum of Wales

London's anarchist clubs with his sketch book, enthralled by the 'foreign desperadoes . . . [and] sinister celebrities' who gathered there, including Kropotkin himself, 'dressed in a frock coat and radiating goodwill', and he remained a critic of Franco throughout his long life).[81] But as an artist, John was perhaps more intrigued by the challenge of capturing such a naked embodiment of war trauma, especially in someone who had so recently seemed to epitomise the blithe 1920s. The circumstances surrounding this portrait of Greville were later described, with certain inaccuracies, by Albert Meltzer, a British anarchist who knew John. Meltzer recalled the painter taking pity on the 'English girl friend' of a German anarchist who had been sent back to Nazi Germany by British officials. Apparently Greville (whom Meltzer misleadingly calls a member of the 'Carrington set') had 'wept' her story to John as she sat for him. At the time, John also 'had the ear' of Queen Elizabeth, whose portrait he was trying to paint. Obligingly, the queen agreed to speak to the Home Secretary, an intervention that Meltzer claims led to Werner's sudden release – something Werner himself verified when Meltzer met him in London thirty years later.[82]

In Werner's absence, Greville had also been working for various Aid for Spain organisations, including helping to write, produce and sell a regular anarchist newspaper. The newspaper office in South London was 'a place where anarchists or people who think they are air their ideas' in an atmosphere of near-total chaos, she told Mangan:

> [T]he editor is an engineer with very little time to spare and I can't spell and Maria Luisa Berneri doesn't know English and the printer doesn't know how to print. . . . [It] is absurd for me to be doing anything like this but no one better can be found. All our people are really workers from Stepney and places like that and they are so enthusiastic about selling the paper that one can't disappoint them.[83]

It was clear that this work had little practical impact on the course of the war. But the only alternative was to do nothing, which Greville would not countenance. Doing nothing meant effectively abandoning Spain to Franco and admitting that the armed struggle had been futile. 'Spain must be supported, being all we have,' she was still insisting defiantly in 1938. Meanwhile the London anarchists engaged in endless debate about why the social revolution and the military campaign had both failed. Notwithstanding the anarchist hero Durutti's undoubted capabilities, would a different leader have better anticipated the disintegration of the Left? Did the anarchist volunteers, who had proven themselves superb street-fighters, lack the training needed to be effective soldiers? As to the future, 'we never get farther than [agreeing] that a mass movement must be moral before it is political,' Greville despaired. In Spain, the anarchists were like the early Christians, she declared: 'when they get a foothold they will become political like the Church and cease to be libertarians as the Pope has ceased to be a christian'. It all seemed absolutely hopeless.

After Werner's arrival in London, the couple moved to a flat in Charlotte Street and continued working for the Spanish cause as best they could – assisting refugees and supporting Emma Goldman's efforts to secure asylum for Spanish anarchists fleeing their homeland. But by now they were weary of war, physically and psychologically. Apart from Greville's allowance, they were virtually broke. Their only income came from selling belts and designs for buttons, produced by a German refugee friend in Paris, to small factories in the East End. Another war was imminent. Even the ever-positive Werner admitted disillusionment was setting in. They began thinking of breaking altogether from Europe, which now seemed in its death throes:

> After the disappointment in Spain where we – like so many others – had thought that a new, socially just order was beginning, we were inclined now to 'flee the world'. We felt that we had had 'our' war, and that we could not bear to be involved or to participate in another civil war – or the world war that we saw looming up. There was little hope that [it] would create a new social order. We believed

that it would be another imperialist war, in which the nations would fight for self-preservation or gain of power.

As news reached them of Franco's final victory, they investigated emigration options. America looked promising, but Werner unfortunately 'bungled' their visa application. Mexico was also attractive; it welcomed with open arms anyone who had worked for the Spanish Republic. But it was also politically unstable and civil war threatened. New Zealand, where Mrs Foster had connections and a few Prideaux relatives, was another possibility.

But at the beginning of 1939, the Society of Friends offered Werner a job running a reception centre for the German refugee children now reaching England in growing numbers. The centre was initially housed at Dovercourt, near Harwich, in an off-season Butlins Holiday Camp. Hundreds of children aged between four and eighteen – many Jewish and nearly all distressed or traumatised – passed through such centres en route to English foster homes or other countries where family members had already settled. When Butlins needed the camp for the summer season, the residents had to move. Greville and Werner were sent south to Westgate, not far from Margate, where they were put in charge of a group of orthodox Jewish boys. This meant learning how to prepare kosher food (once an entire heap of plates had to be smashed after coming into contact with the wrong food) and improvising ways for the children to observe their religious rituals. But there were also lessons and sea swims and football matches against a nearby home for Basque refugees. As war with Germany became an inevitability and the night sky filled with defensive balloons, Greville and Werner distracted themselves and their charges by adapting the opening chapters of *Great Expectations* for the stage. In May 1939, they were married in a civil ceremony in Thanet – it had been made clear to them that a 'proper' marriage was essential to their emigration prospects. And in August, they received permission to emigrate to New Zealand.

Werner with boys at the refugee hostel in Westgate, 1939
State Library of New South Wales, ref. ON 400

Their marriage may have helped secure them entry to New Zealand, but it could not have come at a worse time. When war was declared in September, Werner immediately became an alien – and, as his wife, so too did Greville. Both were required to appear before hastily-convened classifying tribunals. Werner was so confident of being declared a 'friendly' alien that he went to his hearing in Ipswich without any luggage. But despite testimony from the couple's well-connected London friends, he aroused suspicion on multiple, if contradictory, grounds; the tribunal was determined 'to prove at the same time that I was a Nazi, on account of my recent sojourn in Germany, or a dangerous Red on account of my life in Spain, or a Pacifist who would not support the war,' he remembered. Defending himself strenuously against all three claims, Werner managed only to give 'the impression that I was a slick young man and could not be trusted'. The judge considered him a danger to national security and ordered him to be interned.[84] He was taken by train to London (accompanied by Greville and a detective; Werner remembered the trio enjoying an incongruous afternoon tea together in the restaurant car) and then to the Seaton internment camp in Devon, another Butlins resort commandeered by the government. Behind a barbed-wire fence patrolled by armed sentries, some four hundred German and Austrian men – Nazis, Jews, communists, Oxford professors, tradesmen, travellers – were held in three-man huts. The Seaton regime was not unduly punitive; inmates could earn money making camouflage nets, and they played sports or took classes on an unexpectedly broad range of topics. But Werner had no inclination to spend the war in captivity, especially with an entry permit to New Zealand in his pocket. He immediately appealed his internment.

When Werner was packed off to Seaton, the judge gave Greville the chance to leave for New Zealand with Cristina as she was entitled to do. But she refused to leave and, in December, it was her turn to appear before the tribunal. The hearing did not go well. According to Kate, Greville 'made a point of declaring that she was an anarchist' – a rash declaration that the more prudent Werner most likely avoided. Moreover, the judge considered she had 'no real ties to this country, and [was] dominated by her husband'; he noted that she had threatened to take her life when Werner was interned. Much to her shock, Greville too was classified an enemy alien and interned in Holloway Prison in December 1939.[85]

Even though her imprisonment did not last long, Greville was devastated – not only by incarceration itself but also by the collective opprobrium the sentence represented. Margaret Foster from Wolverhampton – a Cheltenham girl who had once consorted with earls and danced with the Prince of Wales! – was being decisively cast out of her tribe. Giddy Margot Greville was being punished for her transgressions; militia-woman Greville Texidor was condemned for backing a lost cause. Imprisonment was not just punishment but proof of personal and political failure. And to Greville, it was yet another betrayal; Churchill and the British establishment now joined Stalinist Russia, Franco and fascism in the catalogue of those she blamed for the fate of the Spanish people and her own predicament.

Unlike the low-key internment camp at Seaton, Holloway Prison in north London was a grim and formidable symbol of state power. During the early months of the war, several thousand women were interned there, many for short periods pending transfer to other detainment centres, such as the Isle of Man. The internees were a varied group: domestic servants who had entered Britain recently as refugees (including Sigmund Freud's Austrian maid, Paula Fichtl), long-term British residents of German or Austrian origin, some genuine Nazi supporters, a group of German Jews who had escaped Holland in a lifeboat the day the Dutch surrendered and were picked up in the Channel by a British destroyer.[86] Regardless of background, all were subjected to searches, allowed only thirty minutes daily exercise in the prison yard, and required to prop open their cell doors – on which the words 'Enemy Alien' were emblazoned – when they used the toilet. One of the Jewish refugees rescued at sea recalled being 'locked up for twenty-three and a half hours a day' and fed nothing but 'slop'.

Many were shocked by their treatment at the hands of a nation renowned for its sense of fair play, she said; 'I used to stand by the bars of my cell and when anyone went by I used to shout: "I done nothing! I done nothing!"' Some from sheltered or highly religious backgrounds were alarmed to find themselves among criminals: 'We used to ask them, "What did you do?" and they would answer things like "I poisoned my husband".'[87] Some internees may have even crossed paths with the handful of fascists held at Holloway, including Diana Mosley – one of the Mitford sisters, a self-declared Nazi and intimate of Hitler – who was sent there in 1940.[88]

Greville was held in Holloway for little more than a month. She spent Christmas there, sending Cristina a sketch of herself behind bars in lieu of a present. Later, she drew on the experience in her story 'In Fifteen Minutes You Can Say a Lot' (about a jailed conscientious objector) and in an unfinished play, *Truth is Stranger*.[89] In the latter, a disparate group of women – refugees, pacifists, uprooted aristocrats, Spanish Civil War veterans and a lone 'crazy old woman' – endure imprisonment in Holloway as best they can. Passionate political arguments pass the time, but when they are alone, the deep horror of confinement and solitude weighs heavily on even the boldest. Yet it also binds them to each other, and to the suffering of other unknown prisoners:

> I never get used to being locked in. As soon as they shut the door I begin to read like mad. . . . And when you're finally shut in the dark. All the prisoners shut in the dark. . . . In here it is as quiet as the grave. Outside the war goes on. In the death silence of camps the prisoners wait. The Spaniards who were not afraid of death in the open are waiting for the end. In camps in France the refugees who walked into the trap. Everywhere prisoners waiting. The war getting nearer – nearer. We are caught like rats in a trap.

But even as Greville suffered in her Holloway cell, people on the outside were engineering her release. Werner reported that the Home Office was bombarded with letters from friends and acquaintances, all willing to vouch for the couple. Ultimately, the combined intervention of some particularly influential individuals and groups – the Society of Friends, Wilfrid Roberts of the National Joint Committee for Spanish Relief, Dorothy Morland, Sidonie Goossens on behalf of the BBC, and Greville's old admirer the Earl of Ilchester – allowed them to appeal their internments. Both succeeded. However, the Appeals Tribunal made it clear that the couple was no longer welcome in England and they should make their way to New Zealand without delay. Mrs Foster had already gone. At the beginning of April, Werner, Greville and Cristina were finally able to leave as well, escaping what Werner called 'the menacing imbroglio'. They knew next to nothing of the place to which they were headed and which, for Greville, would be the setting for another reinvention.

State Library of New South Wales, ref. PXA 1210

2. Not so much as a moo

Mrs Foster, hat and hairpiece in place, was the one familiar sight when Greville, Werner and Cristina disembarked from the RMMV *Rangitata* in May 1940. The ship had made slow progress from England, zigzagging across the Atlantic to avoid U-boats. An engine failed mid-Pacific, leaving the ship vulnerable to attack by a German raider rumoured to be nearby. En route, the passengers heard that the Nazis had invaded Norway; just after the ship reached Auckland, it was the turn of the Low Countries and France. They had left behind a 'phoney war' but, by May, the conflict was an abstraction no longer.

The machinery of wartime bureaucracy had also caught up with them, and Greville and Werner's battles with British officialdom were now transposed to New Zealand. As the dominion was at war with Germany, Werner was an enemy alien from the moment he stepped ashore. So too was Greville, who became a German national when she and Werner married in 1939 (although, thanks to the vagaries of German law, Cristina remained British). While Greville's recent imprisonment had intensified her antipathy towards her homeland, it was clearly in her interests to be British in wartime New Zealand. Within days of arriving, she was writing to New Zealand's Department of Internal Affairs about regaining her British nationality. Yet again, the timing was poor. On 1 August, Greville's application was firmly but sympathetically declined by the Under-Secretary of Internal Affairs Joseph Heenan (with

Cristina and Mrs Foster in Auckland
Photograph courtesy Cristina Patterson Texidor

whom she would later have happier dealings): the New Zealand Government had just resolved to stop granting naturalisation for the duration of the war.

And so both Greville and Werner became enemy aliens again, subject to the Alien Control Emergency Regulations. For the duration of the war, their lives in New Zealand would be constrained by restrictions ranging from the petty to the sinister.[1] They would be investigated and classified by yet another alien tribunal. They would need to register with the police and obtain police permission to leave home for more than twenty-four hours. Their correspondence would be read with extra vigilance by the official censor. They would be prohibited from living in so-called sensitive locations – places where they might observe troop movements, for example – and banned, at least initially, from contributing to the war effort. They could not own certain items deemed potentially subversive: maps, firearms, even cameras. Unpleasant and intrusive as these restrictions were, Werner at least avoided internment on Somes Island, a fate that by mid-1940 had already befallen around thirty Germans. Incarcerated on an island in the middle of Wellington Harbour, there they formed an almost comically incongruous community – Nazi sympathisers rubbing shoulders with Jewish refugees and declared communists like Frank Sargeson's exuberant young friend Odo Strewe.

Greville's wish to regain her British nationality was well-founded. Most New Zealanders in 1940 were unused to foreigners. Theirs was a small, deeply homogenous colonial society still emerging from the Depression, the Pākehā majority largely united in their desire 'to refashion in these islands' the British homelands from which nearly all their forebears originated.[2] Only a few years earlier, the sensational trials of Eric Mareo – a Sydney-born musician and impresario of Austrian descent, twice sentenced in 1936 to hang for the drug-fuelled murder of his actress wife in Auckland – had graphically demonstrated the community's suspicion of outsiders. In passing judgement on Mareo and the dissolute artistic lifestyle he seemed to personify, the juries had also very publicly reasserted 'a clear boundary between New Zealandness and foreignness'.[3]

And New Zealandness meant Britishness. In 1939, out of a population of 1.6 million New Zealanders, all but 0.5 per cent were British subjects.[4] Anyone else was, in official parlance, an alien. The alien population included some Chinese but was largely made up of continental Europeans. Many were descendants of much earlier immigrants and had married New Zealanders of British origin, learned English, and become more or less invisible in a country that remained determinedly British in character. More conspicuous were the recent refugees from Hitler whom the New Zealand Government, with considerable hesitation, had been accepting since 1936.

Once war was declared, New Zealanders looked anew at the foreigners among them, and not always favourably. Certainly, many of the refugees from Nazi Europe met with numerous individual acts of generosity and kindness. Some local business-owners spoke out on behalf of their foreign workers, expressing dismay at the prospect of losing them to internment camps. Whether motivated by ethical, religious or commercial concerns, compassionate voices could be heard urging the authorities to take a measured approach in their treatment of aliens. But anti-alien rhetoric was equally voluble. Ignorance was widespread; some New Zealanders could not or would not distinguish between long-established foreign residents and new arrivals, between migrants and refugees, between Nazi sympathisers and those fleeing Nazi persecution. They all had strange names, they all spoke with accents and ate strange food; the newly-minted label 'enemy aliens' served to confirm this shared strangeness and fundamental untrustworthiness. 'Whether they are innocent or not, the best place for them is a cell,' wrote an incensed Southlander to his local newspaper in June 1940.[5] And suspicion of foreigners could go hand-in-hand with anti-Semitism, sometimes from unexpected quarters. A.R.D. Fairburn, a loyal admirer and friend of the exiled German-Jewish poet Karl Wolfskehl, was also a devoted follower of the anti-usury Social

Credit movement and given to anti-Semitic outbursts. Even Frank Sargeson, known for his anti-fascist views, lost a friend 'because of [Sargeson's] open offensiveness to a Jew'.[6]

Heightened by the apparently unstoppable advance of the Germany army across Europe, anti-foreigner sentiment was gaining traction at the very time Greville and Werner reached New Zealand. Elements of the press, the Returned Services Association and other interest groups were howling for aliens to be locked up immediately and indiscriminately; a 'Fifth Column surprise must *not* happen here,' declared the newspaper *New Zealand Truth* after the fall of France.[7] News that Britain was taking a hard line against its alien population added to the xenophobic mood, as did the sinking of the *Niagara* by a German mine in the Hauraki Gulf just a month after Greville and Werner arrived. Groups ranging from the Farmers' Union to the Medical Council expressed outrage at the prospect of aliens holding well-paid jobs, buying land and establishing businesses while 'real New Zealanders' fought overseas to protect them. Predictably, *Truth* warned readers not to trust the foreigners among them, claiming that despite their 'plausible, fulsome manners', their goal was nothing short of infiltration.

In this agitated climate, Greville and Werner saw it was prudent to keep their heads down. They moved into temporary accommodation in Mt Eden with Mrs Foster, sought advice on Greville's naturalisation prospects and, with increasing urgency, looked for work. Like all aliens permitted to enter New Zealand, they had been required to bring with them savings of £200. But after the hurried departure from Spain, months of low-paid social work in Britain and then imprisonment, that was probably about the limit of their immediate resources.

Yet again, they set about reinventing themselves for their new circumstances. As an enemy alien, Werner knew school teaching was out of the question.[8] Besides, he reasoned, wartime New Zealand 'needed hands, not brains'. He found odd jobs as a manual labourer, including with Len Salter, a builder and carpenter who also ran a general store in Takapuna with his wife Gladys; both

were good friends of Sargeson, who occasionally helped out in their
shop. Meanwhile Greville worked at the Summit Shirt Factory,
supplementing her income by modelling for artists in the evenings.
But Auckland's artistic milieu was decidedly different to London's.
It was not to Augustus John's gaze that she now submitted, but the
inexpert scrutiny of students at a commercial art school.

Enemy aliens at large

After two uncertain months in Auckland, the Society of Friends
once again handed the couple a lifeline. A job was found for Werner
with an elderly Quaker farmer, Josiah Hames, who lived at Paparoa,
a remote and sparsely-settled spot on the Kaipara Harbour north
of Auckland. Werner jumped at the offer of a permanent job, with
the bonus of a cottage for the family; it was the perfect setting for
a self-confessed 'bookish' European to transform himself into 'a
versatile, practical "colonial"'.

Whether or not Greville shared Werner's optimism, the prospect
of life as an enemy alien in Paparoa could scarcely have seemed
worse than their precarious existence in Auckland. Repeatedly, she
had shown herself to be adaptable in the face of physical hardship.
Living in the backblocks of Northland, whatever that entailed,
would scarcely faze someone who had recently slept in cells, caves
and under aerial bombardment. Like the central character in her
early story 'Home Front' – Rex, a one-time Civil War combatant
visiting a fallen comrade's parents on their isolated Northland farm
– Greville was well-used to being stranded in alien surroundings.
She knew too what it felt like to bed down uncomfortably in yet
another strange room, surrounded by things that were not her
own, listening to the sounds of an unfamiliar night. Indeed, the
experience had become so frequent that its very strangeness was
reassuring. As Rex reasons in his icy bedroom, 'this one would be
no worse when it had been lived in. Someone must have slept in
the bed once, and sat at the dressing table doing their hair, and
looked through the window over the fields when it wasn't raining

like this'. Greville had learned the same lesson: dislocation could be denied simply by adjusting expectations. If you did not expect to feel at home anywhere, you did not feel homeless. If you did not yearn to belong somewhere, you could belong anywhere.

As Paparoa could not be easily reached by road from Auckland (Kaipara people often travelled between settlements by punt), Greville, Werner and Cristina went north by train – the same journey Rex undertakes in 'Home Front'. As it approached the Kaipara Harbour, the track ran alongside small sharp hills. Once they had been covered in dense virgin bush growing all the way down to the shoreline. But now the bush was gone, burnt off for pasture; all that remained were the bleached stumps that Rex registers as 'white bones. . . . Little green calvaries topped with tall dead trees.' When the train reached Paparoa station, some distance from the settlement itself, there was 'only a long shed with an iron roof, standing alone in the middle of the green'. Like Rex, Greville had reached her destination, a desolate place 'where there is not so much as a moo' she wrote later, affecting a jauntiness she almost certainly did not feel.[9]

Paparoa was a curious place for Greville to have washed up in, but not a wholly hostile one. It lay within the area originally known as Albertland, where a group of optimistic English non-conformists had tried to establish a utopian religious settlement in the 1860s. According to the settlement prospectus, Christian men 'united by common sympathies and aspirations' would create a substantial colony on the shores of the Kaipara Harbour; there, their children could 'grow up amid all the influences of a preached gospel and practical religion'.[10] Some three thousand people, mostly from Birmingham, signed up to emigrate to this promised land. However, their high hopes were quickly extinguished by harsh conditions, poor soil and acute isolation. A few made a go of it, clearing the bush to establish dairy farms and apple orchards. But Port Albert – a city the settlers hoped would eventually rival Auckland in importance – never eventuated. The area remained sparsely populated by Europeans, most of them farmers or engaged in the timber trade. The Māori population was even smaller. In pre-European times, the Kaipara's rich resources had made it an attractive and highly-contested area, as evidenced by numerous pā sites. But inter-tribal clashes in the early nineteenth century had dispersed many of the original Te Uri o Hau inhabitants (kin to Ngāti Whātua) who lived around Paparoa. By the early decades of the twentieth century, much of their land had been alienated and most Māori, now significantly outnumbered by Pākehā settlers, had retreated to their remaining lands.[11]

Over time, the original European inhabitants' ardent faith and spirit of independence had given way to sober rural respectability. Paparoa became a small service town whose residents embodied 'the devotion and singleness of aim' which their pioneering forebears had brought to the area, even if the original radicalism of that aim had been diluted. It was home to 'men and women who stand for all things worthy and true in community life', a local history recorded approvingly.[12]

But 1940s Paparoa also harboured pockets of non-conformity and independence, as Greville and Werner discovered. Josiah Hames himself, then aged eighty-five, had caused a stir many decades earlier by abandoning his family's Methodist faith to become a Quaker – and, by consequence, a pacifist, a decided irregularity in wartime New Zealand. His farming practices were old-fashioned and considered somewhat peculiar. Werner describes an 'idyllic' small farm with only a dozen cows that were milked by hand. With its abundant orchards and gardens, the Hames property stood in sharp contrast to the neighbouring farms – heavily stocked, chemically-fertilised and almost completely devoid of trees. Josiah himself was a small 'gnome-like' man with 'an extraordinarily sweet disposition', remembered Werner, and despite his advanced years, he remained impressively active. Greville wrote him into her story 'Home Front' as Isaiah Chapman, an elderly farmer who speaks with the biblical cadences and distinctive idiom still found among older Quakers. In a narrative suffused with intimations of death, Isaiah's apparent vigour and 'meek insistent smile' is a veil for his impending mortality. He is already halfway to another world, Rex thinks; 'a wave of milky pallor' passes across the old man's face 'like the first waves of death lapping over him, and receding so gently that he was unaware'. Josiah Hames too was somewhat other-worldly. He spoke little and seldom explained farming matters to Werner, once leaving him to kill a maggot-infested sheep unaided – Werner had never slaughtered an animal before and had no idea what to do. Before meals, Josiah would kneel to say prayers that could go on at some length; if there were guests, it was not unknown for his wife Emma to interrupt him with a surreptitious kick.[13]

Paparoa's general store – which sold essential provisions and electric appliances, as well as housing the public library – was something of a magnet for the community's more free-thinking members. It was run by Lily and Ernest Crowley, a conspicuously non-religious couple with 'an interest in the left and humanitarian causes', recalled Gladys Salter (who farmed and taught in the area before moving to the North Shore). The Crowleys were committed to several progressive causes, running the local Left Book Club and helping organise Workers' Educational Association (WEA) activities. During the war years, a small group of committed locals would gather at the Crowleys' home or the community hall for WEA discussions on current issues: politics, the international economy, the arts. Such self-directed study groups flourished in New Zealand during the war, in towns and rural communities alike. According to a WEA volunteer in another rural district, discussion often 'drifted from the point, sometimes becoming irrelevant, while all too frequently it relapsed happily into local gossip'. Pedagogical standards were not always high, but that was hardly the point. Study groups like Paparoa's embodied the ideals of the WEA's founders: to equip people otherwise unable to access higher education 'to understand and to learn and to think for themselves' about the crucial economic, social and political issues of the day.[14] Occasionally, visiting speakers delivered lectures, although these were not universally popular. University of Auckland English

Professor Arthur Sewell lectured at Paparoa on drama and poetry in 1940 or 41.[15] It was not a success, recalled Gladys Salter, who drove Sewell up from Auckland. Locals complained afterwards they hadn't understood the talk, and they remained distinctly 'cagey' about their distinguished guest. Whether Greville attended is unknown, but she certainly knew enough about the occasion to mine it for comedic effect. Her caustic story 'You Have to Stand Up to Them' skewers both the 'progressive professor' delivering his lecture 'enthroned on the Kosyback chair', and the earnestness of his audience – 'all those [locals] who didn't want to get in a rut'. The lecture concludes with a ragged communal singing of the Internationale, but it is not repeated.

Another enclave of non-conformity lay further north from Paparoa, at Rawene beside the Hokianga Harbour. This was the domain of the maverick Scottish physician Dr G.M. Smith, yet another friend (and frequent source of vexation) to Sargeson. By 1940, Smith was known in Northland and nationally as a scourge of the medical establishment, staunch advocate of Māori health and tireless promoter of social and medical causes from the enlightened to the downright wacky. Among many crusades, he campaigned for the release of Eric Mareo, drawing on his own clinical experience with barbiturates to argue the musician's innocence. Greville and Werner came to know Smith through Sargeson, who regularly visited the doctor in Rawene. Later, Greville would submit herself to another of Smith's enthusiasms, the practice of 'twilight' childbirth.

Despite such pockets of eccentricity, it was hard to be outsiders in wartime Northland. Werner's geniality, his enthusiasm for the outdoor life and his eagerness to learn proved to be assets. He turned his hand willingly to all kinds of farm work, Josiah sometimes loaning him out to neighbours who taught him how to operate milking machines, put up fences and use dynamite. He confounded the suspicions of more narrow-minded residents by joining the Ambulance Unit of the local Home Guard – 'my third experience of being a soldier in the course of a few years!' he noted

wryly. But unlike the Wehrmacht in which he had so recently
served, the warriors of Paparoa 'practised warfare in the spirit of
World War I'. Werner found their preparations for a Japanese
invasion nothing short of ludicrous. Still, by participating, he
showed a willingness to fit in and contribute to his new homeland.
By the time Sargeson dropped in at the Droeschers' cottage on his
way home from a visit to Rawene, Werner seemed thoroughly at
home on the farm, very much the 'versatile, practical colonial' he
had imagined becoming. Sargeson recalled him arriving for lunch
on a motorbike, the milk billy handle 'securely held in his excellent
German teeth':

> A large man, 'Aryan', yet a good deal more dark than fair, he was
> smiling and communicative, the most open-natured of the [family].
> Clearly too he was a good deal younger than his wife, and proud to
> be the husband of a very beautiful woman.

As for Greville herself, Sargeson was smitten:

> At home in the decayed old house there was the remarkable (not
> to say remarkably beautiful) woman who was to become known to
> discriminating New Zealand readers as Greville Texidor. . . . How I
> wished that [Augustus] John could have been there that day to paint
> her again – bare-footed, with a kind of smock covering sub-ample
> proportions. Her manner was enchantingly friendly (how well she
> knew her dark eyes were not just for seeing with!)[16]

But for all her enchantments, Greville was considerably more ill
at ease in Paparoa than Werner. She had always worked, but now
she had nothing to throw herself into other than domestic chores.
Ten-year-old Cristina was away at school all day; Paparoa's was
the thirteenth school she had attended. After Cristina boarded
the school bus each morning – with her mother's injunctions to
buy more cigarettes before coming home ringing in her ears –
Greville was alone for much of the day. The family's cottage had no
electricity and a limited water supply.[17] Werner may have considered
it 'almost fun to re-live the conditions of older pioneer families',

The second cottage at Paparoa.
State Library of New South Wales, ref. PXA 1210

Versatile, practical colonials: Werner, Cristina and Greville outside the first Paparoa house.
State Library of New South Wales, ref. PXA 1210

'I can't tell you how cut off we feel living so far away and so long ago'
State Library of New South Wales, ref. PXA 1210

but if Greville found any pleasure from washing the family's clothes in a stream full of eels, it would have been short-lived. According to a former schoolteacher who lived in the area shortly before the family arrived, 'anyone with [Greville's] life experience . . . who had lived in civilised countries . . . and travelled to New York and Paris, would have found this farming area "dreadful and primitive"'.[18] This overstates Greville's taste for luxury; as her sister Kate once observed, Greville had earlier put up with a succession of 'wretched' pensions in Spain and elsewhere, so uncomfortable 'that it was a mystery how anyone bore them for more than a week, seeming indifferent to food, baths, heating or privacy'.[19] But it was true that day-to-day rural life in Paparoa lacked many rudimentary comforts, let alone sophisticated pleasures of the kind Greville enjoyed. 'I can't tell you how cut off we feel living so far away and so long ago', she wrote to her former brother-in-law Sherry Mangan (now in Portugal), beseeching him to post a copy of *Partisan* or other up-to-date reading material.[20] Even the landscape seemed to resist human engagement. As the narrator of her story 'Elegy' observes while visiting her friends' Kaipara farm:

> There wasn't much I could say about the view. It was strictly neutral. There were the rich wet paddocks, there was the white water and the grey sky and the tin-roofed house that should have made the centre. It was worse since the [pine] tree had gone. Eyes wandered. There wasn't any place they wanted to rest. [Jim and Jess], though they lived right off the land . . . didn't seem to belong. Even the child and the few flowers round the house didn't make them belong.

More uncomfortable still was the burden of difference Greville felt at Paparoa, something that the 'enemy alien' tag both confirmed and amplified. That burden is almost visible in the few photographs recording this period. Posed with her husband and daughter beside a water tank, Greville hunches apprehensively, watchful and aware of being watched. The couple walks hand in hand across a paddock, Werner revelling in the pioneering adventure. But Greville lacks all conviction. She is guarded, all too painfully aware of what she is: an unwelcome alien in an alien landscape. When Gladys Salter visits for the first time, she is warmly welcomed by Werner and finds Mrs Foster (on a visit from Auckland) sitting serenely outside, painting with watercolours 'as if she were in the home country'. But Greville is hiding, claiming a sore throat; later she tells Gladys 'she thought someone had come to feel sorry for her'.

In Paparoa, Greville's outsider status was repeatedly confirmed in ways both large and small. However much she tried to dress down, she stood out, remembered the local schoolteacher. She was 'a very striking woman with beautiful bearing' and her conversation, however carefully she calibrated it to her audience, showed she had clearly led a 'travelled, freer life'. Despite her respectably British origins and vowels, there was something disturbingly foreign about 'Mrs Droescher', said the teacher. Perhaps it was the open physical affection she and Werner shared, 'something not usual in a country district of this nature', or the family's occasional naked swims in the estuary, which they were accustomed to doing in Europe. To the residents of Paparoa, Greville seemed decidedly 'Bohemian and more brittle than the typical New Zealander'.[21]

Anticipating there was no place for bohemianism in wartime Paparoa, Greville tried hard to fit in. She sent Cristina to the local Sunday School, perhaps more to get some time alone with Werner than out of concern for her daughter's spiritual wellbeing. She kept chickens, or rather encouraged Cristina to – instead of paying her daughter pocket money, Greville instilled habits of thrift and enterprise by buying eggs off her. She made an effort to get to know the local women. They were helpful, practical farmers' wives who could turn their hands to anything; their manifest capabilities, suggested Gladys, compensated for 'other shortcomings'. These Greville observed and filed away, later bestowing them on an array of fictional characters – Mrs Withers whose endless talk is 'like something left running . . . seeping colourless from a wound' ('Anyone Home'); Mrs Chapman with her doilies, her disdain for dirt and her stifled grief at her son's death ('Home Front');

Joy's mother whose ferociously well-organised Boxing Day picnic collapses beneath the weight of a lifetime's disappointments ('An Annual Affair'). Greville found the brisk competence of such women intimidating and their unvarnished demeanour dismaying. Years later, she described an Australian acquaintance as looking 'like a Paparoa housewife[,] that is to say as if she'd just been run through the mangle'.[22]

But for now, the world of Paparoa housewives was Greville's milieu and she had to learn its codes. The morning or afternoon tea party was the crucial proving-ground; scones, sponges, dainty cakes and sausage rolls were its currency. But Greville's repertoire was all wrong. Rather than mastering melting moments, she baked bran muffins – which Cristina would fling into a gully on her way to school to avoid having to reveal the contents of her lunchbox – and made her own yoghurt. Greville's conversation was all wrong too. Over boiled fruit cake and cups of tea, she tried regaling the Paparoa women with the racy stories she had already shared with Gladys – of touring America in the Roaring Twenties with the German contortionist, of her dancing days 'when if you were good looking and had admirers [who] would give you jewellery, you could move up the theatrical ladder accordingly', Gladys remembered. 'How corker!' perhaps her neighbours chorused, like the well-mannered Miss Masseys in 'Anyone Home' who listen politely to returned soldier Roy's account of bare-breasted Melanesian dancers, before taking their leave – outraged, yet a little thrilled as well.

In Paparoa, Greville was surrounded by the conventions of kindness and hospitality but suspected the worst. She was sure she was not liked or, worse, that she was pitied. The attentions of the local police and other government authorities further confirmed her marginality. In November, under the scrutiny of the local policeman, she and Werner wrote statements to convince the Aliens Authority in Whangarei they posed no risk to public safety.[23] Greville's emphasises her thoroughly English pedigree; her professional background as a dancer, dancing teacher and gymnastics instructor; the circumstances in which she met and married Werner. She notes her earlier marriage to 'a Spaniard', but neglects to explain what happened to him. She is likewise opaque about Spain ('I left in 1938 and went to England') and altogether silent on the subject of Holloway Prison. She and her family have come to New Zealand with the aim of settling here, she says, and because of family connections; an admirable Lieutenant Colonel F. Prideaux ('now in Egypt') gets a mention, as do other relatives in Auckland and Whakatane. Greville asserts she has most certainly never belonged to a political organisation, nor possessed any forbidden items. Werner's statement proceeds along similar lines, though he is somewhat more forthcoming, if selectively, about his time in Spain. He says he taught languages in Barcelona before the Civil War and 'was afterwards assisting to evacuate children on behalf of various bodies . . . I was never engaged as a belligerent.' A careful account of his deportation to Germany avoids any mention of military service. Although his parents and siblings still live in Germany, he no longer corresponds with them, he declares. Indeed, virtually his only recent overseas correspondence has been to request a publisher's catalogue from Mexico. (Greville admits to receiving a letter from Sherry Mangan; she refers to his credentials as a journalist, but not his Marxism.) Werner is emphatic that he is 'a voluntary exile from Germany for political reasons'; namely, 'that I do not believe in Hitler's doctrines of Nazism'.

These declarations satisfied the Aliens Authority. Greville was deemed 'an English woman of British outlook and sympathies [whose] loyalty is undoubted'; Werner was 'a sincere upright young man' opposed to the Nazis and wholeheartedly backed by the Quakers. He was 'extremely desirous of throwing in his lot with the British Empire and settling in New Zealand,' noted the Authority approvingly. Both Werner and Greville were deemed 'Class D' aliens – in other words, to be regarded as essentially harmless although still subject to certain restrictions.[24]

Official approbation did not save the family from ongoing scrutiny, however. Towards the end of their time in Paparoa, the Under-Secretary for Justice Berkeley Dallard wrote in alarm to the director of Security Intelligence about 'the presence of an Aryan German of military age in what I believe to be an area of some military importance' and urged him to investigate Werner's background in more detail. Eventually information obtained from England reassured the intelligence services that Werner was indeed 'a genuine political refugee'.[25] Meanwhile in Paparoa, the local policeman insisted on checking their home for concealed electronic devices, including up the chimney. Greville told Sargeson that the policeman and local postmaster, who knew Morse code, had hidden outside their cottage at night after neighbours reported the couple signalling to enemy craft at sea. In reality, the flickering lights came from their kerosene lamp as they moved from room to room; they could not even see the sea from the cottage. Sargeson recounts the incident comedically, taking the chance to again rhapsodise Greville's physical charms. Instead of uncovering espionage, he records gleefully, the policeman hiding under a macrocarpa tree received 'an excellent view of a lovely woman taking off her clothes as she went to bed'.[26] In his memoir, Werner treats the episode more seriously – he says it showed the family's tenuous position in a community that, for all its superficial hospitality, viewed them with mistrust – but ultimately dismisses it.

But if Werner could shrug off such ludicrous incidents as evidence of communal paranoia, Greville could not. Sargeson, for one, was adamant that she never fully recovered from the years of official scrutiny and casual suspicion she experienced as an enemy alien: 'How could the intelligent but unstable Texidor cope with a world in which forces of this kind could at any moment be let loose?' Moreover, he argued in his autobiography, she somehow convinced herself that such suspicions were deserved. Brilliantly (though crazily), she came to believe that 'what many New Zealanders might think about her was after all *right* – perhaps quite unknown even to herself, she *was* a spy!' According to such perverse logic, Sargeson continued somewhat unconvincingly, 'She was[,] had been and always would be guilty, and nothing and nobody was ever going to alter her intolerable situation.'[27] It is

debatable whether Greville's treatment by the authorities in itself
triggered quite the depth of existential despair Sargeson suggests –
her sister Kate certainly disagreed with Sargeson's diagnosis – but
there is no doubt of its psychological impact on a woman already
traumatised.

At the time, though, Greville's response was defiance. She
painted the floors of the family's cottage bright blue to remind her
of the Mediterranean. And she began to write short stories.

A cause of her own

Greville had never tried her hand at fiction in any sustained way
before coming to New Zealand (although years later, she recalled
an early attempt to draft what became 'Santa Cristina', presumably
in the early 1930s; as she 'couldn't write' at the time, the result had
been 'a stupid story').[28] But the decision to do so was not wholly
unexpected. She was extremely well-read, in several languages,
and her voracious reading undoubtedly fuelled her writing.
She had mixed with writers in England and Europe. She was an
excellent raconteur, her storytelling instincts polished by years of
stage experience. And she had always done other kinds of writing
– teenage diaries, propaganda for the Republican cause in Spain,
biographical portraits of the evacuee children she and Werner had
cared for at Cantonigròs. But all that had been what she called
'hack work for the cause of humanity'. Now, in New Zealand, she
declared it was time to embark on 'a cause of my own'.[29]

Sargeson's account of his first visit to Paparoa recalls the
excellent dinner Greville produced and lively conversations about
the present war, the Civil War in Spain, and the possibility of
establishing a kind of commune or artist's colony in Northland
(an idea that Sargeson flirted with intermittently for years, with
and without the Droeschers). But he does not refer to Greville's
writing. She may well have hesitated to present herself as a writer
on his first visit: after all, by 1940 Sargeson was New Zealand's
acknowledged master of short fiction, already hailed as creator

and sentinel of a new literary tradition.[30] But Greville's first stories were almost certainly already taking shape by the time Sargeson visited. She set up her typewriter first at the kitchen table and then in the garden, where Werner put up a tent for her. There she wrote for much of the day, the tent filling with an ever-thickening fug of cigarette smoke.

It is impossible to know exactly where Greville's impulse to write came from, why then and why fiction. Her few remaining diaries and letters offer little insight. Sargeson had his theories, speculating that – adrift in the alien backwater of Paparoa – writing became a surrogate for the intense and sometimes visceral existence Greville had left behind in Europe:

> [F]inding herself unable to establish with this country relations which could be in any degree thought of as a serious love-affair, she substituted literary endeavour for the many-sided involvement of day-to-day living which had been her habit in environments that appealed to her as more congenial.[31]

But the course her writing took suggests it was compelled by something beyond a simple need to occupy herself in an unsympathetic setting. Writing fiction became a way for Greville to see her new environment and fit it, with all its manifest limitations and disappointments, into the pattern of her past, to meld Paparoa with the vanished world of pre-war Europe. Before long, she was also using fiction as a tool with which to excavate her Civil War experiences, perhaps even to find expiation for the sense of personal and collective failure that burdened her. Even when her stories attend to Northland's physical and social landscape, Spain and the failed cause she had embraced are never far away. It is an over-simplification to say that a sense of guilt compelled Greville into fiction, but it undoubtedly animated much of it and, perhaps, finally curtailed it too.

Greville's aversion to dating her drafts and letters makes it hard to be certain exactly which of her stories were written in Paparoa, and which later in Auckland. But those she at least *began* in

Paparoa probably include the strongly autobiographical 'Maaree', 'Jesús Jiménez' and 'Santa Cristina', and perhaps also some parts of her unfinished, much-reworked Spanish Civil War novel, *Diary of a Militia Woman*. When it came to raw material, it seems that 1930s Spain was still more real and urgent to her than the empty Paparoa farmland she could see through the window. 'Why do the war stories seem much more immediate?' she wrote in an undated note. 'Can't a story be written about NZ?'[32] With Sargeson's encouragement, she found it could and began producing stories in which a distinctly Sargesonian New Zealand – populated with semi-articulate men, embittered women, wowsers and hypocrites – is overlaid with a distinctive cosmopolitan sensibility and voice that is by turn sardonic, arch and occasionally mystical.

Her first story to appear in print was 'Home Front'. Written in Paparoa, it was published in *New Zealand New Writing* in 1942 and, a year later, in *Penguin New Writing* in Britain as 'Epilogue'. It was quite a coup for a novice writer to earn a place in New Zealand's only 'serious' literary publication of the period, let alone in English publisher John Lehmann's progressive journal (the issue that featured Greville's story also included new work by Roy Fuller, Stephen Spender, Laurie Lee and Sargeson; other recent contributors were Jean-Paul Sartre, Lorca, W.H. Auden and Dylan Thomas). Hers was almost certainly the only piece of fiction written in Paparoa that Lehmann would ever publish. 'Home Front' was also a salutary introduction to the hazards of publishing fiction, which would dog Greville again a few years later. Sargeson told a friend soon after the story's New Zealand publication, 'Poor Greville Texidor has had endless trouble over [the story]. . . . Apparently some people in her district recognised somebody in it. There's hell to pay. Of course the somebody was told.'[33]

To local readers, the setting of 'Home Front' and other Paparoa stories may indeed have seemed familiar, but they were far from comfortable reading. Without exception, they register moments when an insular New Zealand sensibility is disturbed by tremors from the world beyond, or when a foreign gaze falls upon local reality for a brief, uncomprehending and discomforting moment. Reading the date on the grave of a long-drowned Kaipara settler, an English visitor realises with a start that she would have been alive at the time ('Elegy'). Unbidden, 'some paths in my life converged' at that moment. But the tenuous connection brings her no comfort; she remains unmoored in a place where 'you could sleep, of course, but there wasn't any place you wanted to rest'. A radio is switched on in an isolated farmhouse; immediately 'the shell of the house [is] filled with world echoes', but they cannot fill the nullity that lies all around. Years later, Greville would describe the colonial landscape as 'beautiful but dumb'.[34]

Greville's New Zealand has been described as an alien land seen through alien eyes – imagined, it has been said, 'with an intensity of emptiness that *only an alien* can see' (my italics).[35] Certainly, if we turn to Anna Kavan's wartime essay and some of the stories by Christchurch-based German Otti Binswanger (published in 1945 as the collection *'And How Do You Like This Country?'*), we find other alien writers registering similar responses. The New Zealand they see is likewise a place that, for all the energetic toil of its pioneers, remains curiously vacant – its original inhabitants extinguished or invisible, the European population still uneasy tenants. 'Here in these islands,' the protagonist of Binswanger's 'An End to Pioneering' observes, any compassionate and sensitive person must 'suffer the pains of loneliness and . . . fight hard against incomprehension and despair'.[36] But it was not only aliens who were imagining local reality in those terms at the time. The so-called nationalist writers were also bearing witness to an isolated and tenuously-inhabited land in which, memorably, there was 'never a soul at home';[37] indeed, apart from the occasionally awkward syntax, the words of Binswanger's protagonist might almost be Curnow's. Greville's fiction is part of the same project. In her Paparoa stories especially, the vision of the alienated outsider and the alienated native blur as they do in Binswanger's, whose soul-searching narrator is in fact no estranged exile but a taciturn 'son of his country'. In neither woman's fiction do we encounter many refugees or exotic outsiders, though there are some; their stories are largely populated by recognisable Sargesonian types, men and women adrift in a place they nominally inhabit but universally fail to understand. Both are exilic authors refusing to write from the outside 'about' the New Zealand scene in which they find themselves; with varying degrees of success, they are stepping into it and trying on the sensibilities of its people. At the same time, they also step beyond the belonging/estrangement, insider/outsider, Old World/New World binaries expected of exilic writing. They are writing from a position that is familiar, local and distinctly of its time and in doing so, they are writing themselves into the mid-century literary project.[38]

But by the time Greville's first stories were appearing in print, her days in Paparoa were nearly over. In the winter of 1941 the family enjoyed what she called 'a grand holiday in town' when Werner was offered a short-term building job in Auckland. Staying with the Salters on the North Shore, they met up again with Sargeson and were introduced to more of his friends – 'all the writers and people who are interested in anything (not many)', Greville reported to Mangan. Sargeson's circle was clearly trying very hard 'to create a NZ atmosphere', she said, but was there any other country 'so difficult to write in'?[39] Nonetheless after the wilderness of Paparoa, Auckland seemed 'quite gay'– despite its astonishing liquor prohibitions, early closing hours and absence of stimulating cultural life. When Len offered Werner a permanent job, the couple immediately sought official permission to move to the city, supported by a statement from their lawyer Frank Haigh that 'Mrs Droescher's state of health requires her removal from the country'.[40] Quite what constituted or precipitated this health crisis is unknown, but it certainly helped bring their exile-within-an-exile to an end. Back in the city, Greville could apply herself in earnest to her latest role – a published writer of literary fiction.

Aliens at large: Greville, Cristina and Werner on a visit to the central North Island
State Library of New South Wales, ref. ON 400

3. In the leper colony

Greville's mood lifted immediately when the family returned to Auckland. For all its limitations, she saw the city as a potential gateway to other places; if nothing else, it boasted a decent railway station. Even more promising attractions were rumoured to exist: cabarets (regrettably teetotal), a public library (whose holdings of foreign books amounted to a single translation of Rilke), a Chinese restaurant in Grey's Avenue.[1]

The family moved to a house Mrs Foster had bought at Sheriff's Hill on the North Shore, not far from Torbay and just a few miles from Sargeson's bach in Takapuna. The villa was on a rambling, partly-overgrown section which could be reached from both a side-street, Stanley Avenue, and the busier East Coast Road. There was a large vegetable garden, which Cristina unwillingly weeded, with a wilderness of gorse and mānuka beyond. Eventually a caravan was installed at the back of the section, variously serving as Greville's writing bolthole, accommodation for lodgers, and a venue for parties and more intimate encounters. Later, the caravan made way for a small house designed by the North Shore modernist architect Vernon Brown; Mrs Foster and Cristina would live there for a time after Greville and Werner left New Zealand.

Before long, the Droeschers' house at East Coast Road was something of a magnet for what has become known as the 'North Shore Group' of writers, artists and intellectuals. At various times, residents of the wider neighbourhood included Sargeson; poets R.A.K. Mason, A.R.D. Fairburn and the exiled Karl Wolfskehl;

artist Terry Bond; writer Anna Kavan and her pacifist-cum-landowner partner Ian Hamilton; the sculptor Molly Macalister and her Hungarian builder husband George Haydn; and budding authors like John Reece Cole and Maurice Duggan. Alongside the artists and writers were various convivial, curious-minded people from other walks of life – physiotherapist Barbara Platts who married Duggan in 1946, the Salters, Vernon Brown, the refugee physician Dr Alfred Dreifuss, lawyer Frank Haigh and his wife Honey, surgeon Douglas Robb and Helen Robb. It was a shifting, contingent assortment of loosely like-minded people far more than it was a coherent 'group', but they undeniably shared tastes, prejudices, causes and habits. The critic and art historian Eric McCormick gently mocked it as a community 'whose bodily ailments are diagnosed by Mr Douglas Robb, whose habitations are designed by Mr Vernon Brown, whose legal affairs are disentangled by Mr F.H. Haigh'.[2]

For Greville, the North Shore 'bibble-bobble' – the term she, Werner, Sargeson and Duggan coined for the local literary set and its chatter – provided the closest available approximation to the social environments she had always thrived in. Certainly it was small and inward-looking. But it was also unconventional, free-thinking, politically-attuned and creatively stimulating. Importantly, it allowed release from the sometimes stifling confines of family life. The motto of the Droescher household might well read 'No emotional complications', she once wrote bitterly to Duggan, because 'except for an occasional spiteful yelp from me . . . not a sound is heard not a funeral note. Talking upsets Werner & he is the stabilizing agent that keeps the family temperature normal (sort of emotional chaud-froid or air conditioned cauchemar)'.[3] While Greville undoubtedly needed domestic equanimity as a bulwark against tumult, she also craved escape. Now – surrounded by literary and political arguments, personal intrigues and regular 'grog' parties – she was back on familiar ground.

Werner meanwhile was working as a labourer and carpenter for Len Salter. He earned enough to support the household (supplemented by Greville's allowance from her mother) and learned practical skills that would last a lifetime; into old age, he remained proud of his ability to 'build a simple house of the New Zealand pattern, perhaps not so well finished as by a tradesman, but liveable'.[4] At the same time, he was preparing to resume his teaching career post-war. Encouraged by Professor Sewell, Werner studied extramurally for a BA in German and, with characteristic industriousness, earned his degree in three years. Briefly, he became involved in an ambitious project with Ian Hamilton, who owned land at Separation Point in the Bay of Islands. An advocate of organic gardening and farming long before it became fashionable, Hamilton had recently established a fledgling commune on the site, the New Life Colony. Various friends from the North Shore had visited, including the Droeschers, but none had committed themselves; Sargeson for one was decidedly sceptical of Hamilton's idealistic venture.[5] Now Hamilton and Werner decided to establish a school at Separation Point. Werner would take charge of the curriculum and teaching while Hamilton would be responsible for growing the community's food, entirely without fertilisers and chemical sprays. It was an excellent proposal, Werner wrote in his memoir, combining 'progressive methods of education with progressive production of food; there would have been untold possibilities of relating the work in the gardens and orchards to the work in the classroom.' Hamilton started making enormous compost heaps at Separation Point in preparation. But the idea proved to be 'a little ahead of the times', said Werner; the proposed school attracted little interest and few prospective pupils. The scheme was abandoned altogether when Hamilton, to his considerable surprise, was interned as a conscientious objector in 1943 and sent to a central North Island detention camp.[6] Werner also found time to work on some fiction of his own on the North Shore, not for the first time. One of his stories had already been published in *Book*, a Caxton Press miscellany published in 1942 (curiously, he called it 'Epilogue', the same title Greville's 'Home Front' had appeared under in Britain). And in Spain in the early

1930s, Werner had written a novel which he abandoned at the outbreak of war – astonishingly, he was able to retrieve it when he returned to Tossa de Mar twenty years later.[7] Now as he tried his hand again in Auckland, Sargeson was ever-supportive, telling Denis Glover about the German refugee he was helping – a 'nice bloke' who was 'beginning to write nicely'.[8]

But it was Greville who benefited most from Sargeson's attentions. As his protégé, one who was already internationally-published and cloaked in enviable glamour, she found she had a certain status among the North Shore intellectuals. It was not only the young and impressionable who were dazzled. Karl Wolfskehl – scholar, poet, friend of Rilke, Thomas Mann and Franz Kafka – thought her 'charming' when they met at a North Shore gathering, but was even more impressed by her literary achievements; 'beautifully polished short stories printed all over the world', he enthused in a letter to a German academic colleague.[9] Whenever work in progress was read aloud at parties or the conversation turned to writing, Greville had an eager audience and a new stage to perform on. 'I like talking at length on things – my own and other people's,' she enthused, especially when the wine was flowing freely (even if the only available option was usually Lemora, 'a stinking drink' according to the beer-loving Duggan).[10] Some in Greville's new social circle were wary of what they saw as her 'penchant for malicious indiscretion'.[11] However her quick wit, storehouse of stories and skills as a raconteur also made her irresistible company. She was willing to play the 'batty 1920s showgirl' on occasion if that was what her listeners wanted. But it was her cool, clever sophistication and evident acquaintance with the trappings of European high culture that most entranced them. After meeting 'Mrs Droescher' for the first time, Duggan penned a polite letter thanking her for her hospitality. He had spoken little as he soaked up the heady literary conversation and confessed to feeling 'a little strange' throughout the visit. Greville, he wrote shyly, had 'helped remove this strangeness. Perhaps it was the coffee, perhaps the ice water, or more possibly the conversation'.[12] One senses that coffee and iced water, perhaps even stimulating conversation, were relatively new discoveries for Duggan. But equally eye-opening had been Greville herself, with her 'brittle and inventively sardonic' manner and high-culture connections. Duggan's biographer says she and Werner were at this time 'by far the most exotic people [he] had ever met'.

Probably less impressed after his first meeting with Greville was Glover, whom she famously encountered – drunk and in belligerent mood – at a party at Bob Lowry's home: 'Denis across the kitchen table from Greville offered some opinions on the conduct of the war in Spain, "Too many of the Republican side fought with their fountain pens and not enough with their rifles . . ."' Greville responded by brandishing a carving knife, and 'fisticuffs' ensued: according to Sargeson, the fists were not the pugilistic Glover's but Greville's.[13]

The stimulating social and intellectual climate of the North Shore was an acceptable simulacrum of the world she had left behind in Europe and, after three years in 'the Methodist backblocks', Greville embraced it.[14] The prime attraction, though, was her proximity to Sargeson. To anyone interested in literature, his status at this time was near-mythic. But he was also unexpectedly accessible, a distinctive figure who could be occasionally glimpsed in the Auckland Public Library or on the respectable streets of Takapuna with '[h]aversack, tweed jacket, knitted tie – a living writer, in disguise'.[15] He had already been captivated by 'the beautiful Texidor';[16] now he was to become the enabler of her writing life.

Il Miglior Fabbro

At the time he met Greville, Frank Sargeson was at a personal and professional turning-point. Writing in the 1930s, he had sought 'to deal with the material of New Zealand life'[17] as he saw it, and with his own peculiarly conflicted sense of being both at home and an outsider in his own country. To do so, he claimed to have 'discovered

Sargeson at home, c. 1947.
'The gas gave a morbid light
that showed only the dirt on
things. The gas stove was very
black, the camp beds sagged,
my books looked dilapidated,
the pictures pinned on the wall
curled at the edges. But I'd
lived here for ten years, I liked
it . . . It was my place. I didn't
want anybody else to like it.'
(The unnamed narrator in
'Goodbye Forever')
Alexander Turnbull Library,
PAColl-7624

John Reece Cole in Auckland,
1940s
Photograph courtesy Cristina
Patterson Texidor

Bibble-bobble: Greville with Maurice and Barbara Duggan at Red Beach, Auckland
Photograph courtesy of Nick Duggan, supplied by Ian Richards

a new way of writing'. Its hallmarks were a deceptively plain literary idiom and a highly compressed narrative form, qualities he had first encountered in the work of American and Australian post-colonial writers such as Sherwood Anderson, William Saroyan and Henry Lawson. The stories and sketches Sargeson produced in the thirties ('Conversation With My Uncle', 'A Man and his Wife', 'Good Samaritan' and many more) seemed slight, but they carried a strong charge. They confronted local readers with an unsettling representation of New Zealand and New Zealanders that felt both disturbingly radical and utterly familiar.

His work was not universally popular. Indeed, many middle-brow New Zealand readers recoiled from his unvarnished realism, preferring the rollicking adventures that filled the *New Zealand Railway Magazine* or the gentle humour of Frank Anthony's *Me and Gus* stories. Some critics likewise resisted Sargeson's apparently inconsequential plots, the prosaic or downright unsavoury settings of his stories and the unappealing premise that lay behind them – '[s]omeone not very bright is going to tell us about somewhere not very nice'.[18] A *New Zealand Truth* reviewer accused Sargeson of presenting an 'impossibly brutish concept of New Zealand life'.[19]

But Sargeson's work had a profound effect on some, particularly aspiring writers such as the playwright Bruce Mason. Looking out from his bedroom window at 'the cardboard and pinex spires' of the 1940 Centennial Exhibition then underway in Wellington, the teenaged Mason intuited a prophetic message in Sargeson's stories:

> 'Look! Listen! Mark! This is all it has amounted to. Against your growth, your progress, I place these bleak and stunted lives; against the blare of self-congratulation, the tiny music of the numb and spiritless. I offer you a people sealed off by shock from all that is brave, creative and joyful.' It was quite a shock in itself.[20]

Readers like Mason found in Sargeson's work a sense of authenticity and shared experience they had never before encountered in fiction, and which accorded perfectly with the awakening consciousness of an indigenous national culture. To R.A. Copland, raised on a diet of English fiction ('villages and copses, footmen and squires, Baker Street, the Punjab, yard-arms and keel-hauling'), here at last was someone who had 'put the real world into a book'.[21] And Sargeson had done more than merely reproduce that world; he had validated it and given it literary status. Milking sheds, road gangs, the corner store and domineering mothers in floral aprons claimed their place on the page. To emerging writers especially, this legitimisation of the local was exciting, liberating, yet strangely unsettling: 'It felt very queer, like having an auntie in the First Fifteen', remembered Copland.

By the 1940s, Sargeson had attracted a following of young admirers eager for his advice, opinions and support. To those yearning to write, stuck in a country that seemed utterly inimical to literary activity, Sargeson was a symbol of hope. At a time when probably no one else in New Zealand was surviving solely by imaginative writing, he was a dedicated professional, almost fanatically committed to the writing life regardless of the material or personal costs. To his followers, his was the first local fiction to really matter; the parsimonious narrative form he had developed 'the only possible kind of short story and his people the only true New Zealanders', declared one ardent acolyte.[22] As Vincent O'Sullivan has commented, 'Sargeson's personal fable became the assumed fable of his country'.[23]

Sargeson's role as mentor to a generation of writers was at its height at the time he met Greville. He was in regular contact – in person, or in response to their painfully polite letters – with many of the country's up-and-coming writers: Maurice Duggan, A.P. Gaskell, G.R. Gilbert, David Ballantyne and John Reece Cole among them. With a few later additions, these were the writers later dubbed the 'Sons of Sargeson'. It is an ambivalent epithet suggesting both devoted loyalty to the man and the tradition with which he was associated, and also a certain familial 'sameness'.[24] At his invitation, young writers would pass nervously through the famous hole in the hedge to enter his Esmonde Road bach

for the first time. Inside, they found not only a stimulating new
world of bookish conversation, organic vegetables and Lemora,
but also a place of possibility – a place where being a writer was
as normal a vocation as being an accountant or a shopkeeper (and,
in fact, considerably more worthy). Seated amidst piles of books
and manuscripts, the self-described 'god father-midwife'[25] would
engage them in an intellectual disquisition, drawing on his own
wide reading and literary contacts. Eventually they would show
him their work and Sargeson would respond with practical and
positive encouragement: technical advice, suggestions for possible
publishing outlets, tips on craft and practice. He insisted they
read widely and critically. He could be overweening and dogmatic
but also determinedly light-handed. 'Leave a bigger left hand
margin, and always put your name and address at the end of your
typescripts' was about the extent of his criticism when Duggan
sent him a story in draft in 1944.[26] His reluctance to give adverse
criticism that might silence a tentative writer frustrated some. But
it also instilled confidence, discipline and determination in those
who lacked application or self-belief. When he considered his
protégés ready, Sargeson would promote their work to publishers,
critics and reviewers – both local and overseas – with whom he
had leverage. And thus his Sons were launched into the world.
Some prospered, outgrew his influence and developed enduring
writing careers. But others faltered and fell silent, hamstrung in
some cases by their devotion to the literary tradition Sargeson
had inaugurated in the 1930s but which was already becoming
moribund by the time they mastered it.[27]

Undoubtedly flattered by the attention, Sargeson nonetheless
had misgivings about his mentoring role. He feared imitation,
distraction, competition, the exposure of his own limitations.
When first approached for advice by the young Duggan at the
beginning of 1944, he reflected:

> [S]hould I say: 'you intelligent young hound go ahead, but forget you
> ever read Sargeson'. . . . If I get to know him will he have enough

native grit bounce resilience independence to take what good he can
from me & reject the bad. Or should I be an old devil & claim him
if I can as an enslaved disciple, a sycophantic prop for my old age, a
perpetual feeder of my pride conceit & arrogance.[28]

Such doubts added to a raft of other professional and personal
anxieties that were burdening Sargeson in the 1940s. Perhaps most
significantly, he was feeling increasingly constricted by the material
and method that had become his signature. Like other *Phoenix*–
Caxton writers, the work he had produced in the 1930s had been
attuned to that particular historical and cultural moment – the
material and spiritual deprivation, the totalitarian drift of what
Auden had called 'that low dishonest decade'.[29] By the 1940s,
had Sargeson exhausted all this particular seam of material could
offer? In the post-war world, would it prove irrelevant or, worse,
irredeemably dull? The critical realist method and semi-articulate
idiom Sargeson had so painstakingly developed was also beginning
to feel like a straitjacket. It depressed him to find his work lauded
primarily for its documentary naturalism rather than its revelation
of what he called a 'truer reality',[30] or for its stylistic sophistication,
its use of symbol and its psychological depth. Had no one noticed,
he complained to E.P. Dawson in 1944, that he was 'a complicated
crafty blighter . . . as arty as hell beneath my plain exteriors'?[31]
Even as he was critically feted as 'the exponent of a local tradition
that has hitherto been inarticulate',[32] Sargeson was convinced
he had reached an impasse; in the post-war world, he could no
longer keep writing as he had. Thus the 1940s marked the start of
a long journey towards reinvention. Wanting to free himself of the
'constipated perfectionis[m]' and pointed morality of his earlier
work, he began experimenting. He started producing discursive
and increasingly opaque stories, among them 'The Making of a
New Zealander' (1939), '"Gods Live in Woods"' (1943) and 'The
Hole that Jack Dug' (1945). He became hell-bent on writing a
novel, although his attempts to do so were poorly received by many
readers and reviewers. In fact, Sargeson's efforts to produce fiction

that unashamedly 'use[d] more words and presuppose[d] a slightly higher level of intelligence' would not really bear fruit until the publication of his picaresque novel *Memoirs of a Peon* in 1965, the start of a remarkable late-career flowering.

While Sargeson pursued creative reinvention, his personal life was also in transition. Throughout the 1940s, he was loosening his connections to the fellow-writers who had been his chief allies in the preceding decade, especially Fairburn and Glover and the macho literary 'gang' gathered around them. Sargeson's homosexuality – undeclared and unacknowledged, though hardly unknown to most acquaintances – meant that belonging to their world required him to adopt a careful strategy of concealment and over-compensation.[33] Hence his crude but also camouflaging remarks about women writers, many saved especially for his correspondence with Glover. Robin Hyde was a 'silly bitch' and her poems 'a sort of orgasm in 3 stanzas'.[34] Other women writers were 'just frightful nuisances', he told Gaskell in 1944, 'unless they're more than half men'. Even Greville with her 'lovely dreamy grace' was not immune. After Glover had described Anna Kavan as 'one of those blondes who get round the world with their knees behind their ears', Sargeson sniggered that Greville's knees too were 'inclined to be behind the ears, Kavan-like', although 'the attitude [was] different'.

Despite such conspicuous displays of misogyny, Sargeson's place in the old gang was becoming harder to sustain as the 1940s progressed. When he showed Glover a draft of his short novel *That Summer* (1943–44), his friend reacted violently against the homoerotic undercurrent and refused to publish it. Glover was later equally vitriolic about the 'cunning little red herrings' and 'sniggering shithouse humour' he detected in *I Saw in My Dream* (1949). The two men remained friends, but their relationship was never quite the same.[35] Sargeson's split with Fairburn was even more decisive. Nominally, disagreement over the merits of state patronage was the catalyst, but Fairburn's homophobia and his conviction that a 'Green International' was covertly promoting the interests of homosexual writers like Sargeson – and thereby capturing 'the literary tradition' – was behind the rift.[36]

Increasingly, Sargeson's most important and sustaining literary relationships would lie elsewhere. There were his London contacts, like the publisher John Lehmann and the South African-born writer-critic William Plomer, and Charles Brasch from Otago, who would become founding editor of *Landfall* in 1947. Plomer and Brasch could be described as colonial cosmopolitans; all three men were homosexual. There were the wartime immigrants and refugees then establishing clusters of cultural influence on the North Shore and elsewhere, including the legendary poet and scholar Karl Wolfskehl, who had arrived in Auckland in 1938. To Sargeson, the elderly, near-blind Wolfskehl represented the full force of European culture; an extraordinary literary giant whom Thomas Mann had once called the 'last European man',[37] now absurdly stranded in suburban Takapuna like some kind of 'intellectual porpoise'. Initially, Sargeson was utterly enamoured, telling Glover in 1943, 'intercourse with [Wolfskehl] is so damned attractive I'm losing my grip. I'm degenerating into a second-rate European'. But he later abruptly withdrew his friendship, 'overpowered, weighed down by so much civilisation' and leaving Wolfskehl hurt and bewildered. Sargeson later admitted that, along with others, he had 'let Karl down in his last years'.

It is not hard to see why Greville would have seemed such an attractive addition to Sargeson's expanding circle. She offered access to the cosmopolitan sensibility and cultural tradition that had so distressingly eluded him when he had travelled to Europe as a young man, and towards which he still harboured such complicated feelings.[38] She was experienced in every way imaginable. Janet Frame once wrote that Sargeson always liked to identify in his friends the 'personal marvel of nature, talent or experience' that they alone possessed 'like a dazzling lure'. Greville's unique attraction, said Frame, was the sheer performative spectacle of her life; 'where she had been, what she had seen, and what she had done – with her contortionist husband!'[39] But for all her exotic allure, Greville was

not as discomfitingly foreign as Wolfskehl. With her tweed skirts
and public school education, she looked and sounded familiar, a
recognisable representative of 'the upper reaches of the English
middle-class'.[40] Greville's modernity also appealed to Sargeson and
again distinguished her from Wolfskehl, with his lingering fin-de-
siècle associations. She was the quintessential modern European
woman – mobile, financially independent, transgressive, twice
divorced, trailing artistic and political connections that were
decidedly 'modern' too. She counted D.H. Lawrence among her
friends; she had talked art with Georges Kars and music with
George Gershwin; she had borne arms in the decisive conflict of
their generation. She was, without a doubt, the real deal – and she
was here, in Sargeson's own backyard! Importantly, Greville was
also someone who seemed to have chosen a life of 'homelooseness'[41]
– a condition very different from the enforced exile that burdened
Wolfskehl, with all its connotations of irreparable dislocation and
loss. Greville's condition was familiar to Sargeson. By virtue of his
vocation and covert homosexuality, he too was homeloose in his
own way, inescapably set apart from his community even as he gave
voice to it. In Greville's rootlessness, as well as her disdain for the
social and cultural landscape of her new homeland, Sargeson saw a
reflection of his own marginality.

And of course, Sargeson saw in Greville yet another emerging
writer whose unmistakeable talents he could develop and shape
– and perhaps learn from too. When she began refashioning
her European experiences into stories like 'Santa Cristina' and
the novella *These Dark Glasses*, Sargeson saw – beyond their
occasional imperfections and unrealised potential – an enviable
appetite for modernist experimentation and lush verbal play.
Likewise in the stories she wrote about New Zealand, he saw that
modernist literary practices (symbolism, the disruption of linear
time, interiority) could serve alongside critical realism as tools
with which to inscribe 'New Zealandness' – a strategy that would
increasingly find its way into his own fiction. This particular
mentoring relationship would be more than a one-way street.

To say Sargeson enabled Greville's emergence as a writer seems, in the twenty-first century, to rob her of personal and artistic agency. But, for better or worse, that is how both parties seem to have viewed the relationship. Sargeson always claimed Greville would have been lost without him and, with studied disingenuousness, described how he made her into a writer:

> No doubt it would be rash on my part to say that without my encouragement, my suggestions and proddings, not to say occasional scornings, and even downright condemnings, Greville Texidor would never have become a name to add to the list of distinguished literary people who have visited our country.[42]

Sargeson was never averse to reminding Greville of his role in her success. In 1951, she told Duggan of receiving a disagreeable note from 'our one and only Frank' inquiring 'if you ever have time to remember that without me Greville you never would have been worth a damn?'[43] But, essentially, she agreed with him. 'I haven't written any more stories lately,' she told Sargeson regretfully after leaving New Zealand for Australia. 'Probably because you are not there to run your pencil through it or whatever you did. Anyway it worked.'

Exactly what it was that Sargeson 'did' for Greville is hard to assess now; there are no marked-up drafts showing his interventions, and only a few letters in which he offers direct feedback on her work. Greville's younger daughter Rosamunda Droescher says Sargeson sometimes sat literally at her mother's shoulder as she wrote, ransacking her storehouse of pre-war European stories, coaxing them onto the page sentence by sentence. Memories of her dancing days, of Tossa's bohemian expatriates, of superstitious Catalan peasants with their dreams and portents, of passionate anarchists and dour Party apparatchiks – Greville had the stories, recalled Rosamunda, and Frank brought them out. '"For Christ's sake, write it down", he'd say.'

As with all his protégés, Sargeson doubtless had mixed motivations for encouraging Greville's writing – some explicit, some unacknowledged, some altruistic and others personal. He was an unreformed Europhile, for all his dedication to the local literary project. Her European stories gave him access to the larger, more cosmopolitan life he had craved ever since escaping 'the Grey Death' of his Hamilton boyhood, with its 'puritanism [and] wowserism gone most startlingly putrescent.'[44] Her work conveyed him to places imbued with Lorcaesque poetry, where people argued over ideas and art, where they fought and died and drank from wine skins in the midday sun surrounded by the 'exuberant smell of flowers and frying' ('Home Front').

But Sargeson recognised that Greville's writing had more to offer than exotic armchair travel. He quickly saw her capacity for sharp observation, her powerful visual imagination, her sensitivity to atmosphere and keen ear for New Zealand speech.[45] Why, then, should she not set herself to deal with what he called 'the material of New Zealand life' that lay around her, using the distinctively New Zealand idiom that sprang from it? Thus, while her evocations of 'the Spain she loved so much' would always transport and delight him, he urged her also to mine material from 'the New Zealand . . . for which she felt almost no love at all', as she had already done in 'Home Front'. And so she produced the 'New Zealand' stories that, more than her European fiction, brought her to the attention of a New Zealand audience. After 'Home Front' came 'An Annual Affair' (1944), 'Anyone Home?' (1945), and 'Elegy' (1945), all published locally soon after they were written. Apart from the last, they would also reach later generations of readers through their inclusion in anthologies of New Zealand short fiction.[46]

From the available evidence, Sargeson's mentoring of Greville seems to have been largely concrete and practical. He tried to instil in her the habits, techniques and discipline she needed to become a working writer: persistence, a regular routine, rigorous self-editing. He corrected her notoriously abysmal spelling and would probably have agreed with Sherry Mangan's verdict: 'They may have taught you to think and feel and write delightful prose at Cheltenham, but oh my dear they certainly didn't emphasize such elementary matters as spelling and punctuation (or perhaps they did, and yours is the product of a revolt against same).'[47] Sargeson even gave her paper, which was in short supply in 1940s New Zealand. Several of her early stories are typed on the same green paper Sargeson favoured, some even on the back of his own drafts (the juxtaposition of passages from Greville's surreal, unpublished 'Trees and Days', an elaboration of intensely remembered childhood sensations, with extracts from Sargeson's *When the Wind Blows* is particularly striking). When it came to critique, Sargeson clearly saw his role more as coach than scalpel-wielding surgeon. As other novice writers also found, their mentor would readily identify and comment on technical problems but leave it to them to find solutions. Thus, when Sargeson read the first draft of Greville's 'An Annual Affair' – a New Zealand story, in which she maps the treacherous undercurrents of a community picnic through the eyes of a teenage girl, Joy – he thought it a fine story marred by an unconvincingly sophisticated narrative voice:

> [I]t immediately struck me as unfortunate that she had written in the first person, using for her narrator a young country girl . . . It seemed to me that the various and difficult problems of first person narration had not been solved, hence much excellent material had not been fully realized . . . I think I unkindly said, 'Look, you make it appear that this girl must keep a copy of Chekov in the cowshed – which she reads instead of doing her share of the milking'.[48]

Before long, Greville had produced another version in which the painful comedy and incipient tragedy of the community picnic is revealed through free indirect discourse, a sophisticated authorial voice now mediating Joy's convincingly guileless and partial impressions. Writing decades later, Sargeson predicted 'An Annual Affair' would be remembered as 'her most beautiful piece of New Zealand writing'. As much as Greville's technical accomplishment impressed him, so too did her evident attentive-ness to the social and physical environment. In fact, 'An Annual Affair' relied less on Greville's observational powers than on her elder daughter's.

Cristina remembers her mother 'pumping' her for details of a Boxing Day picnic she was taken to near Paparoa but which Greville herself refused to attend. Cristina's obliging descriptions of the women mixing soft drinks in old kerosene tins, the disappointing Christmas cake, the kids pretending to fish on the jetty; it is these details that create the texture of authenticity that clearly delighted Sargeson.[49] Even if their source was second-hand, Greville's responses to 'the material of New Zealand life' struck him as both accurate and a gratifying echo of his own. Perhaps more than anything else she had written, 'An Annual Affair' assured him that Greville could be successfully drawn into the national project with which his own work was so closely associated.

But Frank and Greville's relationship throughout the 1940s was not simply a literary one. It was a real friendship, warm and affectionate for much of the time although with a vein of malice that eventually became more pronounced. They had been born only a year apart at the very beginning of the twentieth century and, despite the different paths their lives had taken, they found themselves with much in common. They were depressed by the apparently unstoppable spread of fascism across much of the world and also by its smaller-scale local manifestations. They fumed about the obtuseness of wartime bureaucrats, and the narrow-mindedness of their North Shore neighbours – those who told Sargeson that 'there was no place in the neighbourhood for a man who was . . . well known to have "shirked doing a stroke of serious work in twenty years"' and the housewives whose insistent kindness Greville found so suffocating.[50] They shared books – Proust, Malraux, Hawthorne, Olive Schreiner's *The Story of an African Farm* – and went to the movies in Devonport. A contemporary remembered them 'walking together and ha[ving] fun making up parodies of the Georgian poets'.[51] Greville helped Sargeson bottle tomatoes and cook capsicums from his garden. They visited disreputable Auckland pubs where they ate oysters, and they holidayed together at Mount Maunganui. Sargeson even invited her along on a trip to his 'most truly spiritual place', his beloved Uncle Oakley's King Country farm, but the visit was called off at the last minute.[52] Sargeson addressed her as 'La Texibubble' or 'Dearest Greville you lovely Thing', writing her gossipy and even tender letters whose tone differed markedly from the bluff masculine manner he used with his younger male protégés.

But of course what distinguished Greville most obviously from the other emerging writers he had taken under his wing was her gender. Along with her foreignness, this ensured she always occupied a different category of significance from the (male) writers who consumed most of his attention. Sargeson's relationships with women during this period were important – many of his closest friends were female – yet also riddled with contradictions. As well as Greville, they included Jean Bartlett (formerly part of the *Phoenix* editorial team) and Elizabeth Pudsey (E.P. or 'Peter') Dawson, the English-born pacifist, novice writer and generous supporter whom Sargeson sometimes visited in Mount Maunganui. Another friend was Una Platts, a teacher, artist and writer who lived near him in Takapuna and was the model for the central character in his 1954 novel, *I For One . . . .* The publisher Christine Cole Catley and Janet Frame would soon become important friends and colleagues too. Despite the significance of these relationships to Sargeson, they were always qualified and constrained by the fact that these friends were women, whose sexuality both intrigued and repelled him. 'In all his conversation there was a vein of distrust, at times hatred, of women as a species distinct from men,' Frame remembered. 'I listened uneasily, unhappily, for I was a woman and he was speaking of my kind'.[53] G.R. Gilbert's wife Joy recalled the particular delight Sargeson took in goading Greville, Anna Kavan and other women in his circle:

> They would say deeply philosophical things and then he'd question them a little bit, as if to make them prove what they were saying . . . I think he was being very naughty. . . . In the end the woman would . . . get terribly heated and start bursting out crying . . . and Frank would think he'd won. He was very difficult like that.[54]

To the extent that Sargeson belonged to any tribe, it was emphatically male. Its members might be diverse in sensibility – they ranged from rural working men like his beloved Uncle Oakley, to cosmopolitan sophisticates like Lehmann, Plomer and Brasch – but it admitted only men. While women could visit, they could never join. In this respect, Sargeson's relationship with Greville foreshadowed his later one with Frame. Frame, however, emphatically rejected Sargeson's attempt to mentor her in the way Greville seems to have willingly accepted, and the writing careers of the two women followed very different arcs.[55] But there were affinities. Both were mature women with opaque and complicated pasts by the time they entered Sargeson's world; both were distinctly less malleable than the earnest and awestruck young men gathered at Sargeson's feet at Esmonde Road. Lacking the opportunity to become Sons (even had they wished to), both Greville and Frame were thereby freed of the burden of Sargeson's expectations. He did not look to them to deliver the great New Zealand novel, despite both women writing their first novels virtually under his nose, nor see them as heirs who would 'carry right on where I & others will never be able to go'.[56] They were thus free to follow literary inclinations that diverged from Sargeson's own. Greville moved away from her mentor's model more cautiously than Frame. She could certainly 'do' Sargesonian realism, but it quickly bored her – 'so much time is spent in getting everything out of the drawer and then it all has to be put away again', she complained.[57] But while the more imitative of the Sons continued recycling the Sargesonian model, Greville (like Frame) became increasingly intent on what the critic W.H. New calls 'animat[ing] the independent life of language on the page', and using non-realist techniques and modes to distort or defamiliarise the material world.[58] If Greville's writing life had continued longer, her fiction might well have moved further in this direction.

Sargeson may have made Greville into a writer. But their relationship was not simply that of apprentice and mentor. It was an *exchange* between two writers launching themselves on very different literary trajectories – one intent on turning herself into a writer, the other embarking on a lengthy period of reinvention, both personal and literary. If what Sargeson mainly offered Greville, professionally, was his craftsmanship and his contacts, Greville brought to the relationship her acumen as a reader and critic. Sargeson greatly respected her literary judgement, even once her own output was faltering. When he showed her extracts from *When the Wind Blows* (1945) in draft, she wondered if his concentrated, stripped-back prose style was appropriate to the longer form; 'in a long work this glittering simplicity is apt to attenuate to slickness', she commented, precisely articulating his own self-doubts.[59] She was even more direct in her critique of *I Saw in My Dream* (1949), again identifying with deadly precision one of the literary sins that Sargeson roundly despised: authorial condescension. 'I feel you are writing down to your characters by spinning subtleties about them which they . . . are really quite unable to carry off', Greville wrote from Australia. 'That most of the points you make are so much beyond them that you have to do a fair amount of winking behind their backs to someone [an imagined reader] who is probably overseas.' More welcome to Sargeson would have been Greville's unprompted appreciation of the homosexual understory running through the two books (the second of which grew out of the first). She was one of the few New Zealand readers to recognise its presence, and the fact she did so without remark confirmed her as an ideal reader for the writer Sargeson was seeking to become.

'Someone who knows exactly what one is trying to do'

There was another dimension to Greville's productive literary exchange with Sargeson: Maurice Duggan. This was a three-cornered relationship whose hierarchies and allegiances were constantly reconfiguring. Sometimes, Greville and Duggan closed ranks against Sargeson's more unreasonable demands. On occasion,

it was Duggan and Sargeson who allied themselves in mutual
exasperation at Greville's capriciousness. Sargeson and Greville
shared doubts about Duggan's more extravagantly experimental
early drafts. Eventually, this triangular relationship came apart
altogether. But at its height, between 1944 and 1946, it was
significant – not only because it was so fertile but also because it
seems so contemporary. At times, what was going on in Takapuna
in the mid-1940s looks very much like a more informal and non-
institutional version of today's university-based creative writing
workshop. 'Isn't it strange how easy it is to see what's wrong with the
other's writing?' Greville exclaimed to Duggan after his particularly
brutal dissection of a draft she had sent him. 'I wish I had let you see
it before. That is where criticism can be so helpful. But it must be
someone who knows exactly what one is trying to do.'[60]

When Duggan met Greville for the first time in 1944, he
was just twenty-one years old, still living in the family home in
Mount Eden (his parents had recently moved to Wellington),
still struggling with the trauma of having his left leg amputated
because of osteomyelitis. His stump refused to heal, and he would
be repeatedly hospitalised over the next few years. He had only
recently met Sargeson after sending him a fan letter that included
a perceptive critique of the grotesque ending to 'Sale Day' ('I was
left with a feeling as if I had been on a train & had seen the most
horrible accident, & yet the train wouldn't stop', Duggan wrote).
He also sought advice on his own hesitant attempts at writing,
and Sargeson had invited him to lunch, curious to meet this
'intelligent young hound'.[61] Sweating and overdressed, Duggan
found the visit nerve-racking. However, he retained his composure
sufficiently to show Sargeson a manuscript he 'just happened' to
have with him, and Sargeson promised to read it.[62] After lunch, his
host insisted they catch a bus to East Coast Road to visit Greville.
Duggan was overawed not only by her sophistication and glamour,
but also her literary accomplishments; she was a published author
whose work had already appeared in London, and Sargeson clearly
held her in high esteem. Duggan's first, carefully-crafted letter to

Greville compliments her on 'Home Front', which he has clearly been discussing with Sargeson:

> To my, as yet immature, judgement there were certain outstanding points in it. With Frank, I see the effectiveness and life of that scene where Jim is drinking from the wine-skin. I had never thought of it but wine does 'flood the teeth' doesn't it? The paragraph where Rex breaks the news of Jim's death, and the shock of the Quaker couple on hearing [how their son died] are well done and seem strong with feeling.

Soon, Duggan dropped his endearing attempts at critical sophistication, and his exchanges with Greville became less forced. Before long, he was her favourite conversational sparring partner. John Reece Cole remembered typical Saturday night gatherings at the Droeschers' home often ended in what he called a 'Jabberwocky session':

> Maurice and Greville usually stuck it out to the last. They often moved into a small room adjoining the lounge and the kitchen. Here for hours they would communicate in what was to me a convoluted verbal free association. Werner, making what he sometimes called one of his 'English Chokes', referred to it as Jabberwocky.[63]

They enjoyed more than wordplay, briefly becoming lovers too. But their literary relationship outlived the affair; for a few critical years, as their regular correspondence reveals, each was the other's reader, student, teacher, colleague, rival, most trenchant critic and most ardent admirer. After that first meeting, Greville sent Duggan some recent translations of Lorca by Stephen Spender and Joan (John) Gili.[64] She also showed him some of her own Lorca translations, which Duggan professed to like even better, and introduced him to the work of other Spanish writers: Ramón Sender ('the greatest prose writer now living', Greville declared) and Arturo Barea, which Duggan diligently sought out in translation. 'Do come and see us again', she urged, and Duggan – after an enforced hospital stay – did so eagerly. He began sending

her his own as-yet-unpublished stories, usually after he had
worked on them with Sargeson; increasingly, though, he showed
them first to Greville. Always encouraging, her feedback was
nonetheless searching and tough-minded, qualities that Duggan
welcomed after Sargeson's studied neutrality. Unlike Sargeson, she
found the smatterings of Joycean language throughout Duggan's
'Faith of our Fathers' ill-matched to the narrator's consciousness:
'Frank says it doesn't matter . . . But I feel that in a short piece
unless one is a very experienced writer it is safer not to step out of
the characters (I hope you know what I mean).' Greville's verdict
on Duggan's 'St Louis Blues' was similarly to the point: *there is
too much in it*. . . . It is like a cake made entirely of raisins – it ceases
to be a cake if you know what I mean'. However, she added, 'I can't
tell you how I envy you. I have the greatest difficulty in finding
"stories" [that are] any sort of framework for the feelings I have.'
Duggan's story 'That Long, Long Road' – which Greville heard
Sargeson read aloud one Saturday evening – was another over-
fruited cake, she thought, 'so overloaded with words as to be quite
opaque in places'. Although she was partial to such verbal excesses
('I can take more of this kind of thing than the average reader'),
Greville felt Duggan had not yet mastered the art of integrating
'sensationary writing' with exposition.

Increasingly, each writer's stories responded to and reflected
back the other's; the work itself was in conversation as much as the
writers. In 1944, Duggan wrote 'Dream of Dreaming', an extended
dream sequence in which a man bludgeons his wife to death. A
year later, he wrote a sketch entitled 'Insistent Anaesthetic' in
which he sought to recreate the sensation of anaesthesia. Neither
piece survives, but they clearly drew on Duggan's repeated spells in
hospital and amputations under anaesthetic. It is also clear that he
discussed these formative experiences with Greville, and that she
drew on them in turn in her 1945 story 'Anyone Home?', whose
protagonist Roy recalls an anaesthetic-fuelled descent 'down in[to]
wicked silence'. When she showed Duggan a draft of this story,
he questioned the adequacy of 'rubbery darkness' as a metaphor

Cristina with Maurice Duggan in Auckland
Photograph courtesy Cristina Patterson Texidor

for the sensations he had patently described to her: 'I know we did talk about this,' he wrote, 'but as an adjective [rubbery] loses its exactness. . . . I suppose my feelings were of hemming/closing/ encircling *rubber* darkness'.[65] In the final version of the story, Greville has deferred to Duggan's first-hand experience, with Roy now recalling the 'the sweet-frigid Godspeed of a false friend on the journey through ether' as a descent into 'rubber', not 'rubbery', darkness.

Greville insisted Duggan treat her as a fellow apprentice, despite the disparities in age and experience. She was, she insisted, a collaborator rather than an expert adviser. After offering a hard-hitting critique, she added: 'Don't pay any attention to this of course. If I really knew anything about writing I wouldn't be where I am. . . . Your writing is so visual (like mine) but I daresay you'll be much better as you won't be in such a muddle.' Another trait they shared, Greville noted, was a fondness for a dense and sometimes over-ripe lyricism – something that clearly set them apart from their mentor Sargeson. When she sent Duggan her (never published) story 'Aller Retour' – an assemblage of intensely-felt memories and moments, snatches of conversation in French and English, unexplained leaps in time, place and narrative perspective, all drenched in the inescapable odour of Jean Rhys's Paris[66] – he found its uncompromising difficulty both attractive and familiar. 'You demand as much from the reader as I do,' he wrote admiringly, describing it as 'really specialist writing . . . in that it will have a special reader.' Greville agreed, but said their demands were different:

> Mine is full of hiatus lagoons lacuna. You just gorge [your readers].
> Reading you I really do begin to understand about this arrangement
> Freud speaks of (in the brain or somewhere) that operates simply to
> shut out sensations so that what comes through can be dealt with
> before it flattens you out. I think yours must be seriously impaired.
> Perhaps it is this defect that makes you such an interesting writer.
> . . . However . . . you should watch out that [in] wallowing in all
> this lovely stuff you don't fall into utter garrulity. Take that dreadful
> little paragraph at the top of page three.

Despite Duggan's admiration, Sargeson was troubled by Greville's susceptibility to unfathomable 'hiatus lagoons lacuna' and her own moments of 'utter garrulity'. Privately, and perhaps as a coded warning to Duggan about the young man's own predilections, he told him there were 'two Grevilles'. One was evident in the 'private' symbolic language and interiority she deployed intermittently and which, to Sargeson's dismay, figured so prominently in the anaesthesia passages of 'Anyone Home?'. The other Greville was on display in the leaner, more naturalistic, less 'feminine' (and, implicitly, more estimable) stories like 'An Annual Affair'.[67] The mere fact that Sargeson considered the coexistence of these two modes of writing to be problematic points to the challenges he was confronting in his own work – he claims to be receptive to the experimental and the non-naturalistic, but still prefers the particular form of realism he has made his own, that signature 're-arrangement of reality which is accessible to everyone'.[68] Finding a way to integrate the two approaches would preoccupy him throughout the next two decades.

Late in 1944, Greville's 'Santa Cristina' appeared in *Penguin New Writing*. If, as Sargeson believed, 'Home Front' showed she had 'assimilated [this country] remarkably well considering', this new story confirmed Greville 'could be relaxed and at her ease only when the New Zealand scene was absent from her work'.[69] In an undated note, Greville later indicated the idea for 'Santa Cristina' had been following her around for some time: fifteen years earlier, she had written an unsatisfactory version which she had shown to a 'writer of boys adventures'. The response of this unknown author was discouraging, prompting her to abandon the draft (and, for the time being, fiction altogether). Now in New Zealand, with Sargeson and Duggan close at hand, she finally worked out 'what it was I couldn't write about. I think nothing much stayed in [from the earlier draft] except a corpse and a coastguard whistling like an owl.'[70]

Set in a village near Barcelona at the outbreak of the Civil War, the story's protagonist is the gypsy-like Cristina. Little more than 'rags and bones walking, and a desolate monkey grin', the old woman survives by begging and telling fortunes, tolerated and taunted in turn by the locals. Near the hut where she shelters at night is a church housing the relics of the village's patron saint, Santa Cristina. From her vantage point, the contemporary Cristina observes the comings and goings in the village, including the periodic visits of a slick young man to his mistress, a foreign blonde. He is a revolutionary from Barcelona, known to Cristina only as a far-off place of 'clanging trams and factories and manifestos'; he is also a harbinger of the bloodshed that will inevitably spread from the city. The story ends with a violent struggle, the flight of the local priest, a death and the certainty of more killing to come. At the last, the figures of Cristina and her holy namesake are brought together when she is attacked in her hut. Falling to the ground, her rags

> gave way without a sound, like cobwebs, and she lay quiet, a heap of pale bones on the ground until a finger of moonlight entered the hut. Then she gathered her bones together and covered herself with a sack.

This conflation of the outcast and the saint, the living and the long-dead, the symbolic and the everyday, is one of several surreal moments that punctuate the story. Dreams and premonitions are commonplace, and the landscape is filled with omens – the owls who call from 'nests of darkness', the red sky, the afternoon wind 'that lived behind the hills and panted down the valley and fluttered the shutters with hot, heavy breaths'. The inanimate world brims portentously with life:

> on nights when the moon and the tide of nightingales rose the watchers were silenced, for now the valley was boiling with light and life. Then if a cloud crossed the white life of the valley Cristina would step outside to curse it away, and sit in the doorway keeping an eye on things, till a grey breeze lifted the night and a bird called with a soft human voice.

Horror and cruelty are always at the margins. The hotel-keeper's small son shouts abuse at Cristina as he skips past to trap birds in the wood, a 'sick smell' rises from a pit where bound rabbits wait to be killed for the celebratory feast, while in the church the skull of the titular saint grins beneath its wreath of orange blossoms. Greville's attention to the heat and uncanny stillness of the location – Cristina's hut smelling 'of stale sunlight and earth', the sandy courtyard with 'the trees and the rocks standing so still in their shadows', the semi-deserted church in which light 'pour[s] like wine over the rough stones' – serves to foreshadow and intensify the shocking explosion of violence at the story's climax. Throughout, Greville demonstrates a sure-footedness that belies her relative inexperience and clearly impressed both Sargeson and the publisher John Lehmann.

To the young Duggan, 'Santa Cristina' was sheer poetry. Lyrical and suggestive, it was 'utterly different from anything else I have seen', he told her:

> I felt the imagery to be so accurate that I wondered why I had never realized it before . . . That part – 'the Blue Line bus drove right through the church shattering it like an eggshell, and then right over the cliff with all the holiday-makers still in their seats' [a dream told to the central character] – appealed to me, although perhaps I *read* the symbolism into it. . . . What matters is that I like it, I am impressed with it . . . I am envious, and I know it's a bloody fine thing.[71]

Sargeson likewise considered 'Santa Cristina' to be 'extraordinary'. But initially, he was worried by the apparently unregulated lushness of the writing. It suggested a worrying absence of narrative control, he told E.P. Dawson:

> She's like Father Christmas in the way she pours out a succession of brightly coloured striking images. She may be a genius. I don't know. But whether her vague easy-going topsy-turviness is a species of surrealism or just plain carelessness I've never been able to decide.[72]

Sargeson eventually overcame his misgivings, later calling the story Greville's 'finest achievement'.[73]

Despite his initial deference to Greville's accomplishments, Duggan became increasingly unafraid to flex his own critical muscles when reviewing her work. In mid-1945, she sent him drafts of two new stories, both set in Europe in the aftermath of war (both later collected in *In Fifteen Minutes*). The first, 'Reconstruction', earned his ultimate accolade; it was another 'bloody good' story, he declared. But he was less sure of the other, 'Time of Departure'. A young woman, formerly a combatant in the Spanish war, now waits in an unnamed port city for the ship that will convey her to a new life. But it is the events that have brought her to this point of departure that preoccupy her: a suicide attempt, a spell in a sanatorium, a journey into Spain with her now-dead lover Jan, a crucial encounter with a sinister railway official who may or may not have hypnotised her. While being questioned at the border, it seems a momentary slip of the tongue 'changed the rational world [she] knew to chaos' and condemned Jan to death. Now, the narrator is numb and alone, possessing only her 'patient tragic suitcases', her shame, and an abiding fear of persecution by a nameless 'Them'. The workings of the narrator's disordered mind texture the story, forming a mosaic of dreams, memories and snatches of conversation occurring both in the story's present and in a remembered past. Sometimes we are in Switzerland, sometimes in Paris, sometimes on the Spanish border. Tenses switch; speakers change mid-sentence; language sometimes breaks down completely – 'It snapped . . . a voice broke . . . it began to groan and gabble'. Chronology and exposition are deliberately suppressed in a jagged narrative that both enacts and describes a nightmarish post-war world glimpsed 'through the smoke of burning Europe'. A couple of repeated motifs – a doomed insect trying to crawl up the side of a cracked basin, the banal wallpaper in the narrator's studiedly neutral hotel room 'that does not change with my travels, that does not belong to any climate or country' – are the only clues that signal the passing of time.

Confronted with what was perhaps Greville's most stylistically experimental story to date, Duggan was unsure. Here, and in other stories she later abandoned, she was exploring the formal questions that had preoccupied modernist prose writers since the end of the First World War: how to give narrative form to fragments, to the chaos of modern warfare and its messy detritus? Could the passage of time or the elasticity of individual consciousness be fixed on the page? Could the intrusive scaffolding of plot be dispensed with altogether? But Greville's responses to such problems did not convince Duggan; something had been 'extended too far', he wrote, and the story lacked momentum and coherence. He suggested cuts, including the struggling bug in the basin, but seemed unconvinced that they would address the fundamental flaws. The story 'is in some way too thin', he concluded, 'stretched beyond the point where it is still whole'. Duggan's own work revealed his appetite for experimentation and difficulty. But when wearing his reader's hat, he had more conventional expectations; he wanted understanding as well as sensation, to grasp a meaningful whole as well as marvel at brightly-coloured fragments.

Apart from appraising one another's work – its merits, its shortcomings, its superiority to anything they had themselves written – Greville and Duggan tried to help each other get published. For Greville, getting her work in print was, among other things, validation that she had become someone she wanted to be, and she emphasised its importance to Duggan. Whatever you write, she told him, just keep sending it out:

> If the editors (and as [Henry] Miller said, 'Who are these shits anyway?') don't like the woozier ones try them with the others and vice versa. Stories should be aired I think and it's rather fun when everyone has conflicting opinions about them. I think the important thing is to get a few published – then you have the excuse to go on writing. At least in my case – I used to meet with some opposition from my family but now I seldom clean the lavatory and let things boil over and so on and nobody says a word.

Initially Sargeson had been their route to publication but Greville and Duggan increasingly identified their own opportunities independently of their mentor. For Duggan these included publications associated with Auckland University (he became editor of the student magazine *Kiwi* in 1948), while Greville turned to her literary contacts overseas. After reading Duggan's 'Man Alone' (she greatly admired it, despite objecting to his unsightly neologism 'sheloins' which she put in the same etymological category as 'teasets'), she urged him to send it to James Laughlin, editor of the American journal *New Directions*. *Angry Penguins* in Australia was another option; its editor Max Harris was 'the only person this side of the equator at all likely to publish anything experimental', she advised, adding that he was sure to be 'mad about' the story. When Duggan hesitated, Greville simply slipped a copy of 'Man Alone' into her own letter to Harris, along with another story Duggan had shown her, 'Sunbrown' ('so hot, so full of sunshine . . . like something seen through a heat haze' she wrote admiringly, even if Sargeson thought it 'overloaded'). 'No harm done', she assured Duggan breezily, although she knew Sargeson had his eye on 'Sunbrown' for the anthology of contemporary New Zealand writing he was then compiling (*Speaking for Ourselves*). However, the timing was not propitious. Harris and his co-publisher John Reed, recent victims of the infamous Ern Malley hoax, were at the time embroiled in the legal proceedings that led to the demise of *Angry Penguins* and had been forced to abandon several planned publications, including Greville's own novella *These Dark Glasses* (see chapter 4). There was another failed attempt at international publication in 1945 when Duggan showed her his story 'Mezzanine'. Greville offered to send it to the New York poet/editor/art critic Nicolas Calas (whom she knew through Sherry Mangan) along with a Spanish story of her own, 'The View from Mount Calvary'.[74] But this plan fizzled out too, this time because of her inability to resolve the problems Duggan had spotted when he read an early draft of 'Mount Calvary'. Parts were 'almost pure poetry', he said cautiously, including the lavish

SPEAKING
FOR
OURSELVES

EDITED BY FRANK SARGESON

THE CAXTON PRESS

Greville's stories appeared in several
New Zealand anthologies in the
1940s and later

NEW ZEALAND
NEW WRITING
1

ISOBEL ANDREWS, CYNTHIA ASTON, MARIE
BULLOCK, ALLEN CURNOW, A. R. D.
FAIRBURN, A. P. GASKELL, G. R. GILBERT,
IAN A. GORDON, A. JACKSON-THOMAS,
J. R. HERVEY, M. H. HOLCROFT, ANNA
KAVAN, JOHN O'SHEA, FRANK SARGESON,
GREVILLE TEXIDOR, ANTON VOGT

EDITED BY IAN A. GORDON

KIWI BOOKS

religious imagery that appealed to his Catholic sensibilities. But he felt 'the thing stumbled somewhere'; the whole was 'faintly unsatisfying'. Eventually, in what would become a regular pattern, Greville abandoned the story. 'I am always ready to cut out redundancies or any parts where I haven't communicated what I intended but structural alterations are rather hopeless. It doesn't seem worth while,' she told Duggan glumly.

Periodically, the politics of their respective relationships with Sargeson required delicate handling. Duggan feared something he had written and sent to Sargeson for comment was too obviously based on one of Sargeson's own ideas; Greville reassured him it wasn't, and urged him to publish it anyway (though noting its rather graphic violence made it unlikely to be accepted by the *New Zealand Listener*, in which 'there hasn't been a spot of blood . . . in [all] the years I've been reading'). Later, Greville sensed 'a little edginess in the atmosphere' when Sargeson discovered that Duggan had sent his story 'Man Alone' to *her* for first comment. It briefly occurred to her that such resentments might form the basis of a novel – two middle-aged writers jealously competing for the attentions (and manuscripts) of a brilliant young 'discovery' – but nothing came of it. Sargeson was clearly very protective of 'his *young* genius', she told Duggan with heavy emphasis, worried about 'the wrong kind of critic butting in and knocking the bloom off' his protégé. She was *not* that kind of critic, she assured Sargeson when finally handing over the Duggan manuscript, adamant she had not interfered in her 'clumsy feminine way'.

The pressure-points in the Sargeson–Texidor–Duggan relationship were particularly exposed by the anthology *Speaking for Ourselves*, which Sargeson compiled in 1944–45. The anthology's gestation was difficult. It was originally commissioned by the Progressive Publishing Society as a showcase for New Zealand writing of the 1940s. A general call for contributions went out, and Sargeson was asked to make a final selection. But the Society collapsed in 1945, leaving the publication in limbo until the Caxton Press agreed to take it.

Sargeson's foreword declared his only aim was to select stories of 'the greatest possible variety' from those submitted. He was being more than a little disingenuous about his editorial methods and motivations. Nearly all the unsolicited submissions proved to be unpublishable, and wading through them brought Sargeson to the point of despair. There were rollicking romances with titles like 'The Pearl of the Pacific' (evidently a 'true love story', he told E.P. Dawson, 'so bad that it almost becomes good'), and feeble domestic sketches like 'Jane's Birthday'. There was enough material in the reject pile for him to publish an auxiliary collection, he complained to A.P. Gaskell, which would be 'packed with every sort of fantasy from masturbation to identification with God'.[75] So awful did he find the task that he enlisted Greville's help; she was similarly dismayed. Ultimately, only five unsolicited stories made the cut, four by women. They included Helen Shaw (also known as Hella Hofmann) and Lyndahl Chapple Gee (mother of the novelist Maurice Gee). The dearth of quality writing forced Sargeson to shoulder-tap others for contributions. Seven of the final fifteen stories were by authors he was actively mentoring and had asked directly for submissions: Roderick Finlayson, A.P. Gaskell, G.R. Gilbert, David Ballantyne, John Reece Cole, Greville and Duggan. He asked two other writers for contributions because he either owed them a favour (his friend E.P. Dawson, who had bankrolled the anthology) or wanted one (Max Harris; by including his story, Sargeson hoped to enhance the prospects of the anthology being published across the Tasman). The fifteenth story was Sargeson's own 'The Hole that Jack Dug'.

Overall, his selection policy was generous and catholic, perhaps surprisingly so. The anthology showcases a post-war literary culture that he suggests will be more inclusive and diverse than before. It is young and more sharply attuned to the larger world beyond the isolation of pre-war New Zealand – a world that, at the time the anthology was produced, was exerting political, social and cultural pressures both exhilarating and terrifying. The anthology also reflects an unexpectedly feminine sensibility. More than a third of the authors are women, considerably more than appear in the next substantial anthology of New Zealand fiction, Dan Davin's *New Zealand Short Stories* (1953), where only seven women feature among the thirty contributors. And – despite a cover drawing of rural New Zealand by Eric Lee-Johnson that seems straight out of an early Sargeson story, complete with empty paddocks, gnarled macrocarpa trees and outdoor dunny – *Speaking for Ourselves* is also, in places, modestly experimental. Certainly there are some decidedly imitative Sargesonian contributions from A.P. Gaskell, Audrey King and others which reprise all-too-familiar tropes: the Teds and Georges with their easy-going New Zealand idiom, the careful drip-feeding of information as the narrative unfolds with the apparent artlessness of a fireside yarn, the compact between an offstage narrator and an assumed reader who is more sophisticated and emotionally alert than the characters. But other stories sidestep the Sargeson model entirely, including the self-consciously avant-garde 'The Papeye and The Molacca' by Max Harris (who Sargeson considered 'an awful fool and a shockingly bad writer most of the time'[76]) and an erotically-charged fable by Sargeson's protégé G.R. Gilbert. Sargeson disliked Harris's story intensely and found Gilbert's strange (he confessed to choosing it mainly for its 'lavish pulp story atmosphere'[77]) but their inclusion made an important editorial announcement. Just as this anthology made space for women writers and youthful talents, it was also accommodating modernist experimentation – and, by implication, so too would New Zealand's post-war literary culture.

Nonetheless, when Greville and Duggan forwarded their contributions, Sargeson was dismayed. He was willing to accommodate writing that was not to his personal taste, but the book also had to generate sufficient sales to pay its backers. He asked both writers for more accessible stories. From Duggan, he got 'Notes on an Abstract Arachnid'. It may have been an improvement on the young writer's first (unidentified) submission, but Sargeson still disliked it – although he later reconciled himself to it somewhat. Like Gilbert's, Duggan's story owes something to the conventions of pulp fiction, with its lurid depiction of a woman murdered by a brutish man who then contemplates her corpse in the company of the eponymous spider. But the situation itself is simply a vehicle for Duggan's energetic linguistic experimentation. The dense, feverish prose is saturated with would-be Joycean wordplay and neologisms – 'Jumbly-wurben I kerkreekras on your crinite shadow. Gigantic I rear-sneer above your night-jingling bed . . . And I shrink until I am a pulp-slug on the carpet . . .' – that anticipate the more successful linguistic inventiveness of 'Along Rideout Road That Summer' and later stories. Duggan himself later called 'Arachnid' 'embarrassing crap'. Certainly, it frequently falters and is sometimes laughably pretentious ('I am the reason growing like hair on the hands of your memory' has been called one of the worst sentences ever to appear in New Zealand literature).[78] But as a declaration of intent – by an emerging author, and by an editor announcing a new and more accommodating literary era in which even writers who don't sound like him have a place – the story is a striking inclusion.

Sargeson also struggled with Greville's contribution, 'Anyone Home?', dismayed by what he saw as its unsuccessful flirtations with surrealism and stream-of-consciousness narration. Paradoxically, though, the story also reveals the extent of her debt to Sargeson. All the strategies she has learned from her mentor are in evidence: economy, suggestiveness, a delight in dark social comedy, a disdain for what Sargeson himself called the 'petty hell' of rural New Zealand.[79] Her central character, Roy, has returned from war service in the Pacific and is visiting the family farm of his fiancée, Lily. Roy initially presents as a stock Sargesonian character, speaking to himself and others in the familiar clipped, affectless idiom: 'He was good and brown. He looked good in that shirt. Lily would like it.' Greville's treatment of the ghastly celebratory afternoon tea organised by Lily's parents is an excoriation of the same New Zealand puritanism that Sargeson had repeatedly denounced – the pompous local schoolteacher who inflicts on the gathering his old photos from the Islands; wretched Mrs Withers, her endlessly apologetic conversation leaking out of her like a broken tap; her disagreeable husband with his joyless laughter and derisive silences. Throughout, we are privy to Roy's unspoken resentments and his aggressive conviction that it is '[o]ur innings now', the start of a new era of pleasure, spontaneity and freedom for his generation. He and Lily will be moving to the city, he tells Mr and Mrs Withers; they want to go dancing and have fun. But it is clear that Roy's future is unlikely to unfold along these lines. Prim, perennially-disappointed Lily – who has sensibly prepared for Roy's return and impending marriage by having her teeth pulled out in readiness for dentures – is as repressed and unimaginative as her parents, almost certainly destined to drain Roy's vitality.

But there is more going on here than ruthless social vivisection or Sargesonian moral critique. War has left Roy physically and psychologically damaged in ways he can scarcely acknowledge to himself, let alone divulge to others. Greville renders his psychological state through narrative techniques which her mentor Sargeson would never have used, at least not in the early 1940s. She collapses time: when Roy's train enters a tunnel, he instantly returns to the 'anaesthetic darkness' of his wartime stay in hospital where 'down in the wicked silence' he saw death, 'the dream that is no dream and lasts for ever'. She distorts words and syntax to express her protagonist's shattered psyche ('no Roy, no me, no life, no dying, no rest. Only the suffering speck not-I') and introduces a symbolic language to render the horrors that Roy's wartime experiences have laid bare. Like the enigmatic hole dug by Jack in Sargeson's own story, a defiantly unfathomable void sits at the heart of 'Anyone Home?' too; here, a pool on the Witherses' farm becomes Roy's personal abyss, a monstrous darkness where his fiancée's reflection floats like 'an angel in dark ice. The blue space behind the skull was staring through eyes like crystals'.

After Greville was 'hauled over the coals very hot coals by Frank', largely due to the anaesthesia passages in the first draft, she turned to Duggan for help. His critique was practical and specific. He identified a mismatch between Roy's 'ordinary colonial'

character and the 'sharp and visual and apt' impressions that
Greville attributed to him, and suggested she instead show Roy
'struggling but unable to express his reactions and condition'. She
followed this advice, and the nearest Roy gets to disclosure in the
final version is his muttered admission that 'I haven't got the war
out of my system'. Though Duggan described the redrafted story
as 'really amazing and accurate', Sargeson remained unconvinced,
referring to it as a 'chunk of Greville's private soul-writing' and
telling Duggan she had over-reached herself. Sargeson pleaded with
her for a different story for the anthology, but Greville remained
adamant that it was 'Anyone Home?' or nothing.

In fact, despite Sargeson's antipathy, 'Anyone Home?' embodies
much of what his anthology stood for. It expresses an anxiety about
the destabilising effects of the recent war and a sense that a new
dispensation is emerging in which social and gender relations will
be subtly recalibrated. It is a story that both honours the Sargeson
tradition and casts it off, demonstrating that there are other ways
to articulate the local. 'Anyone Home?' also stands as an emblem
and product of a short-lived but extraordinarily fertile triangular
literary relationship. The story's provenance shows that this was a
relationship not only between writers, but also between the work
Greville, Duggan and Sargeson were simultaneously producing.
Their texts were engaging with one another as they came into
being, products of a three-way conversation as well as acts of
individual invention.

A private Belsen

By the time *Speaking for Ourselves* appeared in print, Greville's life
on the North Shore was souring. The change in her relationship
with Duggan since his marriage was one contributing factor. The
Droeschers had always considered their own marriage an open one,
reflecting the mores of the Catalan anarchist world of the 1930s in
which it had begun.[80] They each took lovers at times throughout
their twenty-odd years together. Sometimes the entanglements were

spontaneous and short-lived: Greville's sister Kate had an English
male friend who, meeting Greville immediately after her release
from Holloway Prison, found her 'so exhilarated and bubbling
over with life . . . that he promptly went to bed with her though he
had never done so before'. But predictably, such liaisons came at a
cost; raised voices and 'weeping in the night' were not uncommon
during the years in New Zealand.[81] Duggan's biographer describes
the young man's relationship with Greville as 'the briefest of sexual
encounters', which ended when Duggan met his future wife.[82] But
Greville's letters to Duggan suggest something of more significance,
at least to her. One letter – decidedly incoherent in places and
undated, but probably written around 1946 or 1947 – recalls a
drunken encounter in the caravan or perhaps a garden shed. At
the time, an affair with Duggan had seemed simply 'convenient', a
diversion. Now, though, she wants something more. She yearns for
him to visit – not as a family friend wanting to chat with Werner
or drink tea with Mrs Foster or give Cristina a driving lesson, but
simply to be alone with Greville. Of course now he is married,
though, and whatever kind of relationship he and Greville once
had, it is clearly no longer 'convenient' nor 'allowable' for them to
be together, à deux:

> [Y]ou come & go which is nice but . . . there never is any time & there
> is always Werner & Barbara. So I think oh well it is like that in N.Z.
> no-one ever is alone with anyone unless they are married or sleeping
> with them or just about to. So I think *ahí va* that's how it is but it
> makes everything rather strange & rather romantic because when
> you are old it is like when you were very young – you don't know just
> what is allowable or where you are in the world. . . .
>
> So you're often asking me to have dinner & a pleasant evening
> & I back out of it as often as I can and W[erner] says What is the
> matter? When we could all have such a nice time. So I go & it is nice
> the atmosphere is heavy with goodwill but I have to talk all the time
> to keep away the evil spirits . . . . And Barbara is so very kind – she
> is thinking everything is all right & quite convenient Greville is one
> of Maurice's old bibble bobbles & will never cause even a ripple in

the family rockpool. Then you are so kind about putting up shelves
& things & I look at your innocent smiling face I think really I am
a beast. There are no evil spirits. But they come out again at night in
a dark shed. So I will never really like anyone again. Who will ever
want to be liked by me [when] I can shanghai them into a shed or
caravan.[83]

The companionship and affection she had enjoyed with
Sargeson was cooling too. He was 'incredibly bitchy', she told
Cole in 1946, adding that though she could 'take a lot from Frank
because he has been so good to me at times', she was disinclined to
visit him. She seems to have found the combination of Sargeson
and Ian Hamilton particularly aggravating. Together, they were
pure malice, she confided to Duggan, a pair of 'rather sinister old
Aunties' sowing disharmony with their 'slimy little secrets'. Yet
they were also 'the only people of my own age who would speak
to me (let alone tak[e] me out anywhere which they seldom did)',
she recalled later. 'I used to sit down, when I ever had time off
from my household duties, and wonder which of them I disliked
the most.'[84]

Sargeson's myriad health and financial worries over this
period doubtless made him difficult company. In the mid-1940s,
his physical complaints included not only the ongoing effects of
tuberculosis but also a fistula, dermatitis, 'a sort of shingles of
the backside' and back pain. He was under distressing official
pressure to rebuild his dilapidated Esmonde Road bach.[85] Such
anxieties were burdensome distractions from the demanding
project of artistic reinvention to which he had dedicated himself.
Greville's 'almost pathological' outbursts and tendency to over-
dramatise were further sources of exasperation. On one occasion,
he was dragged in to help with a brief foreword (to her own Lorca
translations) that Greville had been asked to write for *Angry
Penguins*. Faced with this straightforward task, she had broken
down completely and 'declar[ed] that it can't be done', Sargeson
complained to Dawson. All that was needed was for Greville 'to be
temporarily sensible, come out of her dream, use her commonsense,

be lucid'. But this seemed beyond her.[86] Sargeson later vented his frustrations to the Under-Secretary for Internal Affairs Joseph Heenan, from whom he later successfully secured state funding enabling the publication of *These Dark Glasses*. Greville was certainly 'trying', he told Heenan with characteristic man-to-man misogyny, 'but women in their forties, you know. One must give them time to settle down for the last few furlongs'.

Undoubtedly, Greville's behaviour could be challenging. Her daughter Cristina remembered her mother's 'tremendous highs and lows' and frequent rifts with friends, family and lovers. This exhausting cycle of mania and deep depression had probably patterned Greville's life for years, as it had her father's. But since Spain and her subsequent imprisonment, depression seems to have become an even closer companion. She told Duggan that Werner had arranged for her to receive unspecified injections from 'Dr Dryfuss' to deal with her 'delusions' – this was probably Dr Alfred Dreifuss, a Jewish refugee doctor from Germany who practised as a specialist radiologist and general practitioner in Auckland during the 1940s.[87] But it is uncertain what kind of treatment, if any, she received, nor exactly what condition it was meant to address.

In her letters, especially to Duggan, Greville was both open and analytical about her depressive episodes, erratic outbursts and moments of paranoia. At their root lay a primal fear of ageing, social isolation and irrelevance – the torment of confinement in what she called her own 'private Belsen'. She knew she could be difficult, acknowledging only half-mockingly that people had become 'scared to be alone in a room with me'. Some days, 'I am just not fit for human consumption & really cannot be put right with a drink or an excursion or holiday'. She suspected she was becoming a local joke, the neighbourhood 'manic depressive reach-me-down', the very embodiment of the sensitive literary Englishwomen she had always loathed: 'Very dull. Almost as dull as being dead'. Sometimes she blamed herself. Writing apologetically to Duggan after a Christmas party, she attributed her bad behaviour to 'a touch of ennui and claustrophobia' and quoted Baudelaire's description of ennui: 'a delicate monster [that] preys only upon the finest natures'. At other times, she blamed her unhappiness on friends and family – bitchy Sargeson, dissembling Duggan, imperturbable Werner – or her North Shore neighbours, all so 'terribly interested in Art & Culture', all masking their disapproval with relentless displays of kindness. She accused Duggan of emotional dishonesty. If he were truly 'the good warm hearted chap we all think you', he would be more honest about her manifest failings, she wrote – he would tell her plainly that she could be unkind to people, that she was 'a neurotic erotic old party who suffers from delusions & persecution mania'. Instead, she said bitterly, he would probably laugh at her behind her back with Barbara and send a piece of poetry.

Greville's increasing struggle to write was another dimension of her 'private Belsen'. In 1945, publication of her novella *These Dark Glasses* seemed imminent and she told Duggan that the publishers Reed and Harris wanted an option on 'all [her] work for three years novels and everything (I don't know how many they think they're going to get) fifty fifty with the proceeds if any!' But she was finding it increasingly hard to start or indeed complete anything. She struggled on with what she called 'the Spanish novel', her first long-form work, which Reed and Harris wanted her to 'sen[d] over in hunks as it comes out of my unconscious, Caramba!' It was 'all there', she told Duggan, but she needed a month or two to complete it (in fact, the novel was still unfinished when Texidor left New Zealand three years later, and remained so when she died nearly twenty years later). Greville tried adopting a more regimented routine, rising early to write because '[David] Ballantyne was here yesterday & he & Werner were solemnly assuring me that all writing problems would be solved if I would get up at 5. So here I am'. But soon she was confessing to Duggan:

> I can't write any more & haven't really read anything for ages – wouldn't know the difference between East Lynne [a best-selling and sensational Victorian novel] & [T.S. Eliot's] East Coker though

I'd love to hear you read either. . . . [It] would be all right if only
one could write. But at my back I always hear the vacuum cleaner
hurrying near – and sometimes it is summer & that is nice – but
mostly one is just getting a year older.

The one piece of creative work that Greville seemed to have few
problems completing was, tellingly, her brutal dismemberment
of the North Shore circle: *Goodbye Forever*, a novella. Written
probably in 1946 but unpublished until 1987,[88] it is a very lightly-
fictionalised account of the aspiring and already established
artists, European exiles and self-styled bohemians she had been
living among for the last few years. It is a sardonic, sometimes
brutal portrait of people tied together less by shared sensibilities
than sheer desperation: as one of her characters observe, 'all the
intellectuals go around with refugees. In a place like Auckland
who else is there to go round with?' Locals and exiles alike, they
form a community of outcasts:

> A little group of people cast by a gale onto an island. Far away from
> the world? The rest of the world submerged. A group of people
> having nothing in common. Yes one thing. A leper colony.

The unnamed narrator is a Sargesonian writer living in a
decrepit North Shore bach. Through his eyes we observe the central
character, Lili Lehman, a glamorous but increasingly suicidal
Viennese refugee. She is at once a tragic and a comic figure – spirited,
delusional, sexually-confident, naïve, caustic, self-pitying, deeply
damaged by a past that is disclosed in fragments, careering towards
a self-destructive future whose outcome is apparent to everyone
except herself. Through Lili, Greville explores the psychic landscape
of twentieth-century exile. Yet it is not only the physically homeless
or uprooted who occupy this unhappy place, she insists; Greville's
native New Zealanders are equally displaced and desperate. Her
pitiless eye falls on the 'masochistic coffee parties with all the
intelligentsia squirming with culture, hearing what's wrong with
them in a foreign accent', the loquacious local poet John Priest 'who

kept the art of conversation alive in New Zealand', charismatic Professor Salmonson who can always be relied on to bring the beer and a retinue of desperately unconventional students 'who give one to understand that they write poetry'. Even the narrator's friend Ursula, like so many of the anguished intellectuals, wears the 'sad look of a cow gazing over a fence seeing all the juicy pastures of civilisation'. Then there is the perennially-dissatisfied Eileen Farnham, an Englishwoman stranded here by the war, who rejects the 'barbarity of New Zealanders' in favour of the 'intellectual set'. In practice, this amounts to 'drinking coffee instead of tea, eating at the Chinese, and probably sleeping with Professor Salmonson'.

There is much fun to be had in guessing the real identities behind Greville's characters – Sargeson, E.P. Dawson, Fairburn, Kavan and Hamilton are almost certainly among them. Perhaps Lili owes something to the 'incredibly handsome Jewess' from the Takapuna camping ground who occasionally visited Sargeson and whose 'chatter' he found highly entertaining.[89] Clearly, Greville is venting her frustrations with specific individuals. But *Goodbye*

An unnamed refugee Greville got to know on the North Shore: this woman was 'the real Lili', Greville said.
Photograph courtesy Cristina Patterson Texidor

Forever is not just a spiteful two-fingered salute to people she has fallen out with. It is an accumulation of all she has experienced since Spain, a product of the various leper colonies she has come to know and the many varieties of alienation and isolation with which she has become acquainted. She has spent her time in New Zealand looking hard – like Curnow, Fairburn and Sargeson – at the unaccommodating landscape and society she has been forced to call home. But where they saw an embryonic nation, she sees confirmation of human insignificance. She is essentially uninterested in the local intelligentsia's quest for an authentic cultural identity, but she is deeply interested in their struggle to live, lifelong castaways on what her compatriot Kavan called these 'weird, unearthly, resplendent islands . . . implacably blockaded by empty antarctic seas'.[90] Greville's characters come together not to build new lives or create a community but simply in fear, filled with existential dread at the knowledge that they and their 'snug little suburb . . . might blow away into the sea, and no one would ever miss [them]'.

Goodbye Forever confirms that, at least by 1946, Greville's hopes for a stimulating and purposeful literary life in New Zealand were disintegrating. Then came a development that seemed to put that life even further from her grasp.

The last ditch

In June 1947, on the shortest day of the year, Greville sat in a rocking chair on a hotel verandah, writing to Duggan. She was in Rawene, a small settlement on the shores of the Hokianga Harbour north of Auckland. The view was unexpectedly entrancing. 'Water everywhere mudflats mangroves maoris – it feels like New Zealand,' she enthused. '[F]rom the verandah . . . you can keep an eye on anything that goes on – the pictures, the restaurant, store, the coffee bar . . . . It's like an early Western – you rock on the verandah under a slew of stags heads and wait for the shooting to start.'[91]

It was not a shoot-out Greville was waiting for, however, but the birth of her second child. Seventeen years had passed since Cristina had been born in Buenos Aires, the only child of Greville and Manolo's marriage. Greville had again been pregnant at the start of the Civil War but, with Barcelona in turmoil and Werner about to depart to the front, she chose to have a termination. Now, aged 45, Greville was about to become a mother once more. Her pregnancy was almost certainly unexpected and had rather astonished the couple's friends. 'I know about Greville's, er, joy!' John Reece Cole had written to Sargeson in March of that year.[92] Sargeson himself referred to the pregnancy as 'Greville's little anxiety' and was soon reduced to weak puns, saying that if she produced a girl, 'it should be named Concepcion. She would then be known as miscon – pardon, Miss Concepcion Droescher'. Later, Greville was awaiting the birth at Rawene where she was 'under (though perhaps not) Dr Smith', Sargeson sniggered.

Greville's attending doctor was well-known to Sargeson. Dr George Marshall McCall Smith (commonly known as 'G.M.') was an unorthodox, forceful, endlessly-exasperating collaborator and friend to many in Sargeson's circle. An irascible Highland Scot, Smith's demeanour was somewhere between that of 'an Arab chieftain and an Archbishop', according to Fairburn.[93] Indeed, in both his personal and professional life, the doctor was someone for whom the word 'maverick' seemed to have been invented. For reasons he initially preferred to keep to himself, he had left a prosperous surgical practice in Perth, Scotland in 1914 to take up the position of medical superintendent at Rawene Hospital.[94] It was a grand title for what was essentially a backblocks doctor's job in an impoverished area with a soaring TB rate. At the time, the hospital served some 7,000 people scattered across the Hokianga district. More than half were Māori, and many lived in places accessible only by boat. The hospital had no water supply or X-ray facilities, and little in the way of surgical instruments. The ambulance was a horse-drawn sledge. But by 1947, Dr Smith had put Rawene on the map and become a household name. His fame extended well beyond Northland by virtue of his prolific writing (he published six books between 1938 and 1949, most of them with Sargeson's assistance) and his vehement views on everything from the economy to the treatment of venereal disease to race relations. The new hospital building he had secured for Rawene was pronounced the Hokianga's 'crowning glory . . . comparatively the best equipped and most up-to-date hospital in the Dominion'.[95] In 1941, the Government decreed the Hokianga District a 'Special Area' with its own bespoke community health scheme, devised and managed by Smith. For local residents, everything was free. Almost without realising, Smith had introduced 'truly socialised medicine', recalled one observer.[96]

Standing well over six feet tall, with a sharply-hooked nose and fierce eyebrows, Smith strode 'his' hospital wards like a shambolic demagogue. A pipe clenched between his teeth, he wore open sandals, an ill-fitting suit and a shirt open to the chest, regardless of the season. Some patients and staff feared this man they dubbed the 'King of the North'; others were in love with him. He was a folk hero who had brought the benefits of modern medicine to a neglected area and stood up to the bureaucrats in Wellington on their behalf. Conservative medical professionals, however, saw Dr Smith as a paternalistic autocrat engaged in a 'rather paranoid war against authority of any kind', an enthusiast for causes that were decidedly cranky, if not outright dangerous. Today, some of his enthusiasms certainly seem insupportable, distasteful or downright odd. He scoffed at the consumption of fruit and vegetables; 'throw the greens to the pig and eat the pig' was his regular advice to patients. He pioneered a controversial cold-water treatment for cancer, and swore by the antiseptic efficacy of cod liver oil and Vaseline, a foul brew developed in Spanish Civil War field hospitals (it was known as 'Smith's Cure' in the Hokianga, where district nurses boiled it up in old treacle tins). He opposed the Plunket Society's approach to infant feeding, believing it 'starved babies'. In the 1920s, he had raised the £20,000 needed for a new hospital by establishing a casino in Rawene – complete with beer garden, dance hall and gambling equipment imported from Paris. A decade later, he embraced the economic doctrines of Social Credit and lured its international prophet Major Douglas to New Zealand.[97] A passionate advocate for his Māori patients – whose physical, cultural and economic wellbeing he considered colonialism and assimilation policies had all but destroyed – he also maintained that Māori had no capacity for abstract thought nor for managing money.[98]

Sargeson met Smith in 1940 when he travelled to Rawene for the doctor's much-vaunted TB treatment. Doctor and patient immediately hit it off; Sargeson discovered Smith had read and admired his collection *Conversation with My Uncle*, and sensed beneath the doctor's bombastic bluster something of his own inhibitions, the 'shyness and uncertainty, doubts whether or not one might be deceived by one's own talents'.[99] They also shared a mutual appetite for political and literary conversation, although Sargeson actually preferred talking books with Smith's wife Lucy, whose 'constant reading and penetrating good sense' was clearly a strong influence on her husband. Smith was a genuine polymath, he said, a highly-trained and pragmatic scientist who knew that 'to function as a civilized man he needed as well the riches the humanities could provide'. Sargeson stayed with the Smiths (and their fourteen cats, six dogs and one outspoken parrot) for more than a week, returning home to Takapuna with sterile dressings, supplies of Smith's Cure and the encouraging assurance that Smith had 'never known a European die of [TB] up at Rawene, though of course the Maoris do.'[100] But Sargeson's admiration for Smith was tested when the doctor recruited him to copyedit his second book. Once again he had travelled to Rawene, where 'the old lunatic doctor would come and pace up and down & expect me to grapple with all his minor and major lunacies,' he complained to E.P. Dawson. 'He regards you just as an extension of himself, and you feel you have to account to him for every minute of your time . . . His crazy book will be out shortly and he thinks it's a masterpiece.' Despite his misgivings, Sargeson found himself agreeing to edit and retype Smith's next book too, a project even more anarchic than the previous one. In the new book, Smith included detailed instructions for treating boils, feeding babies and emergency midwifery alongside advice on dealing with masturbating youngsters ('leave the boy alone'), polemics on medical politics and contributions on compost gardening and healthy housing. He sent Sargeson envelopes stuffed with extracts and quotes – from sources as various as Confucius, W.H. Auden, the Bible and Oscar Wilde – demanding they be incorporated. Late in the process, Sargeson was required to drop everything to find a translator for a chapter Smith wanted to appear only in te reo Māori ('Mo Nga Taringa Maori Anake – For Maori Ears Alone'). After a particularly trying working lunch in Auckland, where Smith was 'more paranoic more bullying more fire-eating than ever', Sargeson resolved to have no more to do with him. Keeping the doctor at a distance softened his fury; just two years later, he was genuinely distressed at (false) rumours of Smith's death.

It was Dr Smith's advocacy of painless childbirth via the 'twilight sleep' method that brought Greville to his hospital in the winter of 1947. By then, Smith's remote hospital had become an unlikely Mecca for childbearing women from across New Zealand by virtue of his special brand of twilight sleep.[101] This controversial practice had been developed in Germany before the First World War. Doctors at a Freiburg clinic advanced the revolutionary view that pain was not a necessary condition of childbirth but a 'dangerous and destructive accompaniment' that could lead to injury, infection and lasting psychological distress for the mother.[102] The clinic began administering carefully-controlled doses of the drug scopolamine, in conjunction with morphine, to labouring women who would then give birth in a state of 'clouded consciousness with complete forgetfulness'. The new mother would awake from her sleep to a new baby; she had no traumatic memories and could resume normal activities with astonishing speed. Enthusiasm for twilight sleep (or *Dämmerschlaf*) spread quickly to the United States where it was heralded as 'the greatest boon the Twentieth Century could give to women', despite its concerning side-effects.[103] The drugs did not eliminate pain, but only the memory of it – labouring women sometimes needed to be restrained in straitjackets, tied to special beds or hooded to prevent injury as they thrashed about in agonies they would not later recall. Babies were regularly born semi-comatose and requiring resuscitation. Forceps deliveries and other interventions became more common, as the labouring woman was unable to change position or push the baby out. But all such drawbacks were brushed aside. As demand soared, corners began to be cut – particularly the need to carefully calibrate drug dosage to each patient and monitor them closely throughout labour.

Somewhat inevitably, the American craze for twilight sleep came to an abrupt end when, in 1915, one of its most prominent champions died giving birth under scopolamine. But a form of twilight sleep had been introduced into New Zealand in 1918 by Dr Doris Gordon, founder of the Obstetrics Society. Initially it was only for women who could afford private hospital care because it required sophisticated sterile facilities and a doctor skilled in anaesthesia. But after medical professionals and women's groups (for different reasons) campaigned for universal access, the tenets of twilight sleep – chiefly, that childbirth should be institutionalised, medically-managed and drug-dependent – took firm root in New Zealand.[104]

Dr Smith became a convert in 1933. Characteristically, he developed his own 'special method', tailored to Rawene conditions. Like the doctor himself, this method combined the casual and the regimented, the compassionate and the dictatorial, cottage-hospital informality and institutional rigidity. Women were encouraged to arrive in Rawene a week or two before the birth, stay in a nearby rest home and drop by the hospital whenever they pleased. This relaxed antenatal regime had two aims – to ensure women had a genuine holiday before giving birth, and to let them meet others who had experienced pain-free births. 'Nothing encourages them so much and allays any fear,' claimed Dr Smith of these informal encounters.[105]

Greville certainly relished the enforced rest, though perhaps not for the officially-sanctioned reasons. She stayed initially at the Rawene Hotel, whose proprietors, the O'Malleys, welcomed her warmly and gave her their own bedroom. It had 'a huge *matrimonio* bed that really means business, children and babies all over the place and virgins and flaming hearts and all the trimmings that used to set my teeth on edge in Spain', she wrote to Duggan. 'Now in my last ditch I find it very warm and agreeable, perhaps because it goes with having real drinks (rum and gin) and real log fires and real food.' As her due date drew nearer, she reluctantly left the O'Malleys and their generously dispensed drinks to stay with a Methodist landlady closer to the hospital.

She also visited the Smiths at home, where she enjoyed the doctor's animated conversation and literary readings, as well as anatomising a marital relationship she clearly found intriguing (while her husband was 'perambulating his ideas', Lucy Smith would sit with her eyes closed by the fire, finally interjecting 'in a sweet far away voice "Rubbish. All rubbish"', Greville reported). Her stay in Rawene coincided with a visit by the celebrated pianist Lili Kraus, whose public performance was wildly anticipated, although 'on what basis I hardly know as there is no piano [in Rawene] fit for her to play'. Greville was invited to a reception for Kraus at the Smiths' home but declined, telling Duggan, 'I really feel (excuse the expression) that I've had her already. Don't you? Doesn't everyone?' She was more enthusiastic about her visits to the hospital, where she joined Dr Smith and his loyal long-serving matron, Miss Bedggood, for morning tea. For Duggan's benefit, she dramatised the scene:

> Doc takes me to her sanctum that smells of dogs and cats . . .
> Mountains of mutton sandwiches and a very early settler kind of
> cake.

'Doctor you must try some of the cake.'

'For God's sake Bedggood' (Bedggood is her name). 'What about visitors? What about ladies first?'

She hands him his tea first.

'Who do you think I am, Bedggood? God Almighty?'

This requires no reply. And all going on for nearly thirty years – she is old too by now. But perhaps you wouldn't agree that this is love – only fidelity.

Greville left no account of what it was like to give birth under twilight sleep (she recalled later only that 'Dear Doctor Smith . . . was doctor and cure in one').[106] But Smith's book *More Notes from a Backblocks Hospital* outlines a typical delivery. His drug of choice was nembutal, often given in milk, which was accompanied by an injection of scopolamine. Repeat doses were administered to ensure the woman stayed asleep during even the longest labour. A birth attendant sat beside the bed, armed with a supply of peas; she would place one pea in a pot every time a major contraction occurred to measure (in the absence of the usual signs) how far labour had progressed. If the woman became highly agitated or 'troublesome', she would be buckled to the bed with a surcingle (a broad leather strap), which also prevented her from labouring unhelpfully on her hands and knees 'as so many Maori patients do'. If absolutely necessary, the woman would be forcibly restrained. During the actual delivery, forceps were used if necessary and any tears stitched. And throughout even the most difficult birth, the woman continued 'sleeping quietly on her back', completely undisturbed.[107] Within a few hours after giving birth, she would be awake and eating; in fact, some of his patients 'boast of never missing a meal, the child having been delivered between meals'.[108] At a time when women were usually kept in bed for up to a fortnight after birth, Dr Smith's patients – having avoided 'the devitalisation of a painful and brutal confinement' – were out of bed on the third day. Typically, they left hospital after nine days and sometimes much sooner. The consequently rapid patient turnover helped ensure Smith's method was not only safe and painless, but cheap. But the best advertisements for Smith's methods were his patients. 'Oh-hh, it's just lovely,' remembered Maud Tito, who had 'about ten' babies under Dr Smith. 'You wouldn't think you're having a baby at all. You don't feel a thing. You just wake up and it's all over.'[109]

Few women would deny the appeal of pain-free childbirth. For Greville, the attractions would have been even stronger. Although certainly no stranger to physical hardship, she was having a second child in her mid-forties, meaning she was (in obstetric parlance) very much an 'elderly multigravida' with all the risks that implied. But Dr Smith's belligerent non-conformity and animus towards the establishment also appealed to Greville, always irresistibly drawn to people and causes outside the mainstream – including alternative health practices. Kate Kurzke described Greville's 'great faith in Dr Smith' as a natural extension of her sister's lifelong enthusiasm for 'cranky' treatments and therapies.[110] Moreover, as she had shown in 'Anyone Home?', Greville had a keen interest in anaesthesia and the unique sensations and insights it gave access to – sensations not dissimilar to the chemically-induced oblivion she had earlier found in recreational drugs. Perhaps, in seeking out Dr Smith and twilight birth, Greville was not so much running *away* from the prospect of physical pain as running towards 'the rubber darkness' of anaesthesia, the familiar release into nothingness – perhaps too, she may have hoped, towards an unblocking of the creative impulses that were increasingly eluding her.

Greville and Werner's daughter was born at Rawene on 30 July 1947. They named her Rosamund, apparently after Greville's friend, the author Rosamond Lehmann who was the sister and publishing partner of John Lehmann in London.[111] They returned to the North Shore and for a time Greville seemed almost at peace. She rather enjoyed babies, although her daughters have commented that she enjoyed them less once they grew into children. Everything at 'Chez Droescher' was going well, she reported to Duggan who was holidaying in Northland:

Cristina is a box of birds, Werner a well-tempered clavichord, Mrs F. peering over the edge of her tomb trying to find out what's going on around her, Rosie peeping over the edge of the pram and muy contenta because everything she finds out is simply delightful.[112]

Greville's equilibrium was shaken, though, by the polio epidemic that began in Auckland in November 1947 and spread quickly across the country. Within days, schools and other public places were closed, afflicted children quarantined and travel restrictions imposed as the authorities sought to arrest the paralysing and sometimes fatal disease. Greville feared the worst. According to Sargeson, 'Nobody is allowed to approach the child, and nobody who has been over to town is allowed to approach *her*. Nevertheless everybody is accused of trying to murder her baby in spite of all precautions – it will be just too tragic if the infant becomes a victim after all this.'[113]

Mrs Foster in Auckland with two of her grand-daughters – Cristina Texidor and (right) Charlotte Kurzke
State Library of New South Wales, ref. PXA 1210

Rosa thrived, but Greville remained restless and fitfully unhappy. Her writing habits had never been well-disciplined, but now there were formidable practical obstacles that made writing virtually impossible. She told Duggan that her only contact with books came when she was washing nappies and Cristina read aloud to her 'about choristers & cypresses & horrible maxims out of the Primer of Love. Very improving – but owing to the peculiarities of our plumbing most of it goes down the drain'.[114] Under the customary caustic humour, Greville could not disguise her growing discontent. It was not just the practical constraints of motherhood that were holding her back; Greville knew she was faltering as a writer. As the sustaining literary relationship she had enjoyed with Sargeson and Duggan cooled, her output dwindled, and with it her confidence.

As ever, the juicier pastures of somewhere else – anywhere else – promised a fresh start. Previously, she and Werner had talked of returning to Europe to work with refugees, but he was now lukewarm about leaving. He was enjoying his teaching position at Takapuna Grammar School; a new school curriculum had been introduced after the war that was more compatible with his own educational philosophies, he had gained additional qualifications as a sports instructor, and had begun an MA. Werner liked the New Zealand lifestyle and now had a daughter who was 'a real New Zealander by birth'. But Greville was determined to leave, telling Duggan she needed to get away from 'the narrowness of New Zealand' and would 'crack up' if she remained.[115] She told Werner she would go to Brisbane with Rosa at the end of March 1948, a destination she chose seemingly for no better reason than that they had German refugee friends living there, the Schiessels.[116]

And suddenly she was off, without farewell – 'Never coming back, so it is said!' exclaimed Sargeson to Dawson.[117] Many of the Droeschers' acquaintances found out only after the event and were in the dark as to whether Greville would return, or why she had gone. Sargeson, who was left to manage the long-delayed publication of

These Dark Glasses, had his own theories. He told a Literary Fund
official in September 1948 that Greville had experienced 'signs
of rather serious change of life troubles, and quite impulsively
went off to Brisbane to consult a doctor she felt she could trust.
Apparently his report wasn't too good as Droescher . . . went off
after her quite recently.'[118] Greville may well have been suffering
menopausal problems, but that was clearly not the only reason for
her abrupt departure. Perhaps it was easier to let Sargeson believe
her departure was due to a 'delicate' medical reason than risk him
thinking she was simply running away from creative and personal
difficulties; he was, after all, an avowed 'puritanical anti-puritan'[119]
who believed dogged persistence was among a writer's greatest
assets. Perhaps she also felt guilty for abandoning her manuscript
to him.

As Sargeson indicated, after a few months Greville was
indeed joined in Brisbane by Werner. For the time being, Mrs
Foster remained in Auckland with Cristina, now working as a
typist and soon a librarian at the university's fledgling School of
Architecture. But before long Greville once again required her
mother's support as she set about making another new beginning,
this time in rural New South Wales.

Greville in 1953

Photograph by Bill Mansill. Copyright and reproduced with permission of the Bill Mansill
Photographic Archive

4. Australia and after

'Here we are, living together on the outer fringe of the world . . . offshoots of the same stock, guardians of a common heritage,' A.R.D. Fairburn wrote in 1947 of New Zealand's cultural relationship with Australia. 'Yet what do we know of each other? Practically nothing.' Even so, most New Zealanders suspected the cultural life of their trans-Tasman neighbours was much superior to their own 'state of semi-stagnation', Fairburn suggested.[1] His theme was soon picked up by the Australian editor and writer Max Harris, who said the ignorance was mutual. 'How many Australians have heard of Frank Sargeson, Greville Texidor, Allan [sic] Curnow, Dennis [sic] Glover, or A.R.D. Fairburn for that matter?' Amid many references to pots and kettles, Harris concluded that New Zealand was not alone in its insular cultural conservatism; 'apathy, smugness, and a village pump attitude towards cultures other than its own' were rife in Australia too.

Nonetheless, the belief that Australian cultural life was livelier and more progressive than New Zealand's was pernicious, and seems to have taken root in Greville's mind. She left Auckland because she was bored with its 'limited intellectual life', wrote Werner, knowing little about Australia except that it was 'more vigorous, socially and intellectually'.[2] When Werner joined Greville and Rosa in Australia later in 1948, he too judged it 'a land of great prospects'.

But after a few weeks in Brisbane, those prospects did not look so rosy. After their initial stay with the Schiessels, they rented a shabby flat that had no running water and then a shed in Moreton Bay. Finally they moved to a garage in the seaside suburb of Redcliffe, where they lived what Greville gaily called a life of 'picaresque vagabondage'. Of course they had nothing, she told Duggan, 'but there is a nice tap in the yard'.[3] Werner pursued all kinds of job opportunities, however improbable. He had stints as a groundskeeper at a bowling club and a sideshow attendant at Luna Park; he nearly became a warden at a koala sanctuary. He hoped to find a teaching position eventually, though Queensland's rigid and unimaginative education system dismayed him. Meanwhile, Greville wrote witty letters to her Auckland contacts about the pleasures of Queensland life: the hot climate, the greater availability of wine, the abundance of tropical fruit. She was curious about Australian politics, the impact of post-war European migrants on the Anglo-Celtic mainstream, the energetic and apparently hazardous outdoor lifestyle of the locals ('Lots of fun over the holidays,' she reported ghoulishly, '11 drowned surfing and one eaten by a shark'). But she was forced to admit that Brisbane's social and intellectual life was not noticeably more vigorous than Auckland's. Although Australians were refreshingly friendly and more nonchalant than New Zealanders – 'they don't give a damn about anything as far as I can see, except keeping their own vast continent white and British,' she told Cole – Brisbane was even more 'prim and wowserish' than Auckland. 'Culture is absolutely nil, vitality a great deal lower than Sydney, and it's full of notices saying you mustn't. . . . I can smell Methodism pretty close'.[4]

Greville's depiction of Brisbane as a cultural desert was not entirely fair. Soon after arriving, she was invited to address the Queensland Authors and Artists' Association and shared the platform with a visiting English writer – a rather excruciating occasion which she restaged for Sargeson's benefit:

> [The host] got in a terrible tangle with my names but mentioned that
> I was a noted short story writer and that the N.Z. Gov. was backing

Picaresque vagabondage: the garage in Redcliffe
State Library of New South Wales, ref. ON 400

'Mrs Treasure' with Rosa (left) and friend at the migrant camp at Bathurst
State Library of New South Wales, ref. ON 400

my latest novel about N.Z. life and customs and then there was some
mention of Conrad and it was a great achievement for a young writer
not writing in her own language. Then I was asked to rise and of
course I knew exactly what to say – how it was such a pity that the
bonds between N.Z. and Australian writers were not closer – and
writers with international reputation – such as Frank Sargeson –
but you know how awkward I am in public. In private too for that
matter. And the other distinguished guest of the evening (from
England) who was planted next to me, and who probably was really
a writer being so like the pictures you see of them . . . a sensitive
little sip in a pinstripe suit, a hat that was not quite a beret nor yet a
hat and a mole tippit, did even less. She did not even rise but sat all
through it knitting her well-groomed hands and after the address by
Mr Sholl (head of the A.B.C.) [about] Writers and the Radio, after
she'd sat there all the evening not exchanging a single idea with me
she said she was sure it must be very late so I said I was sure it was
and tiptoed out just as we were going to be introduced to Mr Sholl
again.[5]

They hoped to exit discreetly, but the lights and lift were out of
service. Greville and the sensitive English writer were escorted
down the stairwell by an elderly poet bearing matches.

However farcical, events like this were good for Greville's
morale. They affirmed the continuing existence of the writing life
she had established in New Zealand with Sargeson's support. She
may have been washing nappies in a rented Brisbane garage but, in
some people's eyes at least, she was still a bona fide writer whose
promise, projects and ambitions remained merely suspended.

But Greville was not in fact writing. She thought of beginning
a story about some of the 'very interesting characters' Werner
worked with at the amusement park but could not find or make
the time to write it (as both Rosa and the landlady went to bed at
six, she was unable to use her typewriter in the evening). From a
distance, she sent apologetic and encouraging messages to Sargeson
as he wrestled *These Dark Glasses* into print, without offering
to assist. Werner also tried to help Sargeson in various practical
ways but could not do much from afar. They would both be 'very

thrilled' to see the finished product, he wrote rather guiltily, and
urged Sargeson not to spend too much time on it. [6]

DPs and Dark Glasses

In 1949, the family made a second new start in the so-called lucky
country, this time in New South Wales. Werner was appointed
to teach English at a government reception centre for migrants at
Bathurst, a job whose scope 'for social-pedagogic involvement' he
found attractive. He and Greville decided his new role required
a new family name, stripped of any awkward national or ethnic
associations: a German surname would always be problematic in
the immediate post-war period, they reasoned, and even more so
in the charged atmosphere of a refugee camp. Thus the Droeschers
became the Treasure family – Vernon, Greville and little Rosa
Treasure. The anodyne English name was a safe if rather peculiar
choice. It had especially positive connotations in New South
Wales, Werner assured Sargeson, thanks to a popular boxer, Roy
Treasure.

Migrant reception centres like Bathurst had been opening
across Australia since 1947 when the government agreed to help
resettle Europe's vast post-war population of displaced persons
(DPs).[7] Millions left homeless by either the war itself or the Soviet
Union's subsequent territorial expansions had been stranded in
refugee camps since 1945. According to one historian, Australia's
decision to open its doors was not primarily a humanitarian act
but a recognition of the country's need to 'populate or perish' in
the face of a serious post-war labour shortage. With fewer than
expected new settlers from Britain, accepting DPs was largely a
politically-expedient way to swell the working population with
'assimilable "white" migrants'. By 1952, more than 170,000 had
arrived.

The reception centre at Bathurst was a former army camp capable
of housing up to 7,000 people, sometimes more. It was situated near
the Blue Mountains in countryside familiar to Greville from D.H.

Lawrence's *Kangaroo*.[8] Temperatures could plunge below zero in winter, forcing camp residents to plunder the surrounding area for firewood; at such times, they were uncomfortably reminded of the countryside around the concentration camps of eastern Europe. But when Greville first saw the camp, the setting was extraordinarily lovely: 'Our side of the camp is bounded by "un mar de trigo", a sea of wheat,' she wrote to E.P. Dawson. 'Trees are growing amongst the wheat and make patterns of purple shadow on the gold. Behind is the bush and then the Blue Mountains. The mountains are peacock green – covered with bush but in the winter they are very blue.'

The camp's residents came from all corners of central and eastern Europe. Curiously, all were referred to locally as 'Balts' – proof of the success of an official publicity campaign depicting the DPs as desirably blond middle-class Baltic migrants, the next best thing to Britons. The reality was somewhat different, as Greville discovered: 'Ex-nazis and Jews from Belsen rub shoulders. Latterly we have been getting Americanised Russians from China but today we are having Albanians.'[9] The camp's goal was to prepare the DPs for employment. They were given clothing, medical care and work opportunities, and introduced to the Australian way of life. Teachers like Werner were employed to drill them in the basic English they would need for basic jobs: the government did not want immigrant ghettoes in Australian cities, and was determined the new arrivals would assimilate fast.

Greville's role at the Bathurst camp was less defined. She taught some English language classes but it is unclear whether she was ever formally on the staff. She certainly spent much of her time with residents – especially women, like her, with young children. Indeed, she could hardly have avoided such interaction even had she wanted to. She, Werner and Rosa, now a toddler, occupied a single room at the end of a camp hut, one of a row of identical huts. They ate the same institutional food as the DPs ('mostly grease and parsley and porridge'),[10] they were deafened by the same incessant clamour from loudspeakers broadcasting in four or five languages, they were subject to the same unwelcome routine of hut inspections and power cuts. The flow of DPs in and out of the camp – 'displaced, misplaced, pleased, diseased, good bad and worse' – was constant as new transports arrived and longer-term residents moved on. Conflict and disruption were common. Many DPs were psychologically damaged, families had been split up, some resented being forced into menial jobs. There was constant dissatisfaction with the accommodation and food. Sometimes Greville would hear the small children in the hut next door, left alone for the day while their mother went to work, 'screaming and banging their heads against the wall'.

The sheer diversity of the camp population created unique tensions. In an effort to weed out communists and Nazis, prospective DPs were nominally screened before entering Australia. Even so, some camp residents had worked (or even fought) for the Nazis while others had suffered terribly at Nazi hands; anti-Semitic persecution of Jewish DPs occurred at several camps, including Bathurst.[11] According to Werner, the volatile mix of residents at Bathurst included 'fanatically nationalistic Ukrainians, Czechoslovaks, Hungarians, and the very sad Balts – who seemed to be very much affected by the loss of their homeland'. Nonetheless, the camp was a community of sorts, and within it Greville and Werner found it possible to construct another makeshift home. Perhaps the regular gatherings round the hut stove in the evenings reminded them of the camaraderie of the anarchist militias; they certainly reminded Greville of the North Shore. '[W]hen the curtains (army blankets) are drawn and the coffee brewed,' she told Sargeson, 'it is just like Milford because the same sort of people come to sit round in the evenings.' There were the same grog parties, where Greville once again had a receptive audience: '[After] I've washed up the cups and glasses and emptied the ashtrays I feel very good because it was such a nice party and the people hadn't heard all my stories.'[12] Among this new group of hopeful, disappointed, traumatised castaways, she even found a degree of equanimity that had eluded her in Auckland. Here,

The Bathurst camp and its residents – 'displaced, misplaced, pleased, diseased, good bad and worse' – stimulated Greville's writing, at least for a while
State Library of New South Wales, ref. ON 400

Rosa and friend
State Library of New South Wales, ref. ON 400

she could reclaim and express the European sensibility that had so often seemed a conspicuous and rather shameful aberration in New Zealand. 'Being with these migrants and yet a little out of it (being at least in their eyes not a D.P.) [has] helped to knot together some of the loose threads in my European self,' she wrote to Duggan.[13]

Greville was also hopeful that the environment of the camp, despite its privations and distractions, might reinvigorate her stalled writing life. It may not have been the ideal place to raise a child, she admitted, but it certainly offered abundant raw material for fiction. 'It is like those cultures in laboratories – everything happens as in the world outside [but] at a much increased tempo,' she told Cole.[14] Working late into the night by candlelight, she began writing a novel about camp life provisionally titled *Days of Hope*. The narrator was Oscar, a left-wing European activist recently arrived in an Australian refugee camp; the novel would loop back into his European past, including his involvement in the Spanish Civil War and its reverberations as he sought to build a new life in Australia. Greville drafted several chapters at Bathurst and returned to the novel sporadically for some years afterwards, filling notebooks with sketches, snatches of dialogue, even an uncharacteristically purposeful chapter plan. At one point, her notes suggest the novel was becoming a play, while some passages seem to rehearse or perhaps rework parts of her (also unfinished) Spanish novel, *Diary of a Militia Woman*. But no 'camp novel' ever emerged.

However, in 1949 Greville did complete an essay about camp life, which was later published under the title 'Bogomil – Kaffka – Timoshenko'. Narrative non-fiction was new territory for Greville, and writing it opened up new creative possibilities. Pleased with the result, she told Sargeson she would like to try more reportage, finding the genre less daunting than long-form fiction. Writing for radio also appealed, mostly for its ephemeral nature: 'I feel like I should like to do some writing that wasn't expected to keep for years'.[15] But even as she glimpsed the opportunity, it seemed to diminish. She did not know how to go about such writing, she confided, nor how to find outlets. Something else was missing, too: Sargeson himself. Having distanced herself from his practical support – not to mention the bracing 'suggestions, proddings, scornings, and even downright condemnings' he claimed had been so crucial to her achievements – Greville found she needed him more than ever. His absence left a void, and into it flooded the same inhibiting anxieties and habits that had started to intrude in Auckland. Her letters reveal a return of the familiar defensive lassitude that allowed writing to remain undone or unfinished because of the expectation of failure, the certainty that whatever she wrote would never amount to anything worthwhile. 'The sad truth is that since you gave up being responsible for it I have never written another thing,' she wrote to Sargeson. 'Rather I have but I'm never satisfied with them – write several drafts and then chuck in the sponge.'

'Bogomil – Kaffka – Timoshenko'[16] is evocatively written, full of sharp, telling detail – the stolidly sleeping Ukrainian babies swaddled in rabbit-skin capes; the handsome blonde who 'crushes out her cigarette on the table and plunges the ladle into the fatty soup'; the singing of the refugees late at night, which sounds 'like Palestrina, infinitely old and strange, in the wild loneliness of the Australian bush. They sang so well it was almost unbearable.' The essay is flecked with sardonic political comment, too, for those who choose to notice. It registers not only the political and historical conditions that have made the camp necessary but also the combative climate of Australian domestic politics, bitterly divided over issues such as labour relations, immigration and the latent communist 'threat'. Perhaps the most striking feature is Greville's tone and attitude to her material, which is curiously and consciously inconstant throughout. At times, she treats the DPs with intimate tenderness, elsewhere with savage satire. They are by turns pitiable victims, waiting outside the huts in the cold night air to be transported to new lives, and devious brutes who can be readily imagined wearing SS uniforms. 'I think they will be a headache and a heartache, these fanatical uprooted peasants,' she writes, refusing to fix her sympathies – or direct those of her readers – towards or against the camp's residents and the communities they are soon to join. The essay ends with a group of Polish DPs being sent away to salvage abandoned war materiel in the Pacific. Presaging a future chapter in Australia's immigration story, their destination is Manus Island.

Despite having contacts of her own in Australia, Greville asked Sargeson to help get the essay published. She may have feared the consequences of publishing it locally, less for its portrayal of the DPs than for its depiction of the camp administrators and their virulent anti-communism. Sensing that Greville's confidence was waning, Sargeson responded enthusiastically. But privately he bemoaned the atrocious spelling and punctuation, as well as the essay's unsatisfactory structure. It needed a lot of remedial work before he could send it out, and he was loath to be distracted from his own work (at the time, he was dealing with the generally disappointing critical response to his 1949 novel *I Saw in My Dream* and making painstaking progress on his new project, the short diary novel *I For One . . .*). He confided to Dawson that Greville's chaotic and unfinished draft proved his theory that 'those who can organise themselves can't write; and those who can, can't organise themselves.'[17] But he gritted his teeth, tidied up the essay and submitted it to both *Landfall* and *Penguin New Writing* in London. When both turned it down, Greville claimed to be unsurprised – it was clearly 'too dull even for *Landfall*'.[18] But she felt Sargeson's job was not yet done. Overlooking his already generous efforts on her behalf, her tone was both peevish and despondent: 'Couldn't you get someone to have it before it's *quite cold*? If not, [it] better be scrapped.'[19] Eventually, the essay was accepted by the New Zealand journal *Here & Now*, appearing in the March 1951 issue.

Greville's most significant literary accomplishment also dates from her time in Bathurst, and it too owed much to Sargeson's patient ministrations: the long-awaited publication of *These*

Dark Glasses by the Caxton Press in 1949. This slender novella is
many things – a controversial roman à clef, an elegy for Europe's
vanished pre-war bohemia, perhaps 'the oddest book ever to have
been supported by a New Zealand Government'.[20] Contemporary
critics variously described it as 'the product of a sick mind' and
a 'masterpiece'. Werner called it Greville's 'abandoned baby', and
its gestation was certainly prolonged and problematic.[21] She had
completed it in New Zealand around 1944 and sent it to John
Lehmann, then a partner in Leonard and Virginia Woolf's firm,
the Hogarth Press. He rejected it. Sargeson's London contacts
reported that Lehmann had read the manuscript 'with great
interest and admired it in many ways' but judged it 'too short for
publication under present conditions'; in wartime, it was simply
uneconomical to publish a book of only 100 pages.[22] The scholar
Marcia Allentuck offers a different account, quoting a draft of
Lehmann's rejection letter praising the novel as 'full of feeling and
subtle observation' and noting how well Greville had captured 'the
atmosphere of that particular moment in history'. However, he
writes:

> I do not feel it is altogether a success, partly, I think, because the
> current of bitterness which controls the style is too strong and too
> unvarying. I feel it would be much more alive artistically if it had
> more emotional relief.[23]

Greville thanked Lehmann for his helpful criticism – in New
Zealand, she observed, 'we all admire each other so extravagantly
that we are in danger of stifling in a fog of appreciation' – but
reported that the novel had since been accepted for publication
in Australia. However, the publisher in question was Reed and
Harris. When the firm collapsed (see chapter 3), *These Dark Glasses*
was stranded. Sargeson stepped in, arranging for the Caxton Press
to take over production and persuading the newly-formed New
Zealand Literary Fund to pay for it.[24] He also wrote a jacket blurb
praising the powerful 'visionary writing' and asked the young poet
and artist Kendrick Smithyman to design the cover. Writing to

Greville as the first copies were about to be dispatched, Sargeson described Smithyman's cover as 'really wizard – 3 sub-human creatures with their sunburn raw round the edges from excessive copulation'. The printer had done a beautiful job, and the book was 'quite up to the standard of the best English [novels]'.[25]

In the middle of 1949, Greville finally received her advance copies and an encouraging note from Sargeson. But she was almost instantly dissatisfied. She found some typos (albeit 'in a dream bit so no-one would notice probably') and judged Smithyman's cover merely satisfactory, asking pointedly if the artist was 'the same K.S. who used to write that awful poetry?' However, she conceded that Sargeson's blurb was superb: 'It makes me feel very good. I believe every word of it.'[26] In what was by now a familiar pattern, sardonic self-criticism became a protective shield against the expectation of failure.

These Dark Glasses is a curious work of fiction, written at a considerable distance – temporal and geographic – from the historical moment it depicts, and from the literary techniques and traditions it draws on. Set in the summer of 1938, it is narrated by a young English communist, Ruth Brown, who has arrived from Spain at the fictional Riviera resort of Calanques. Surrounded by unforgiving sunshine, glittering sea and self-absorbed artists, she seeks respite from the recent horrors of the Civil War where her friend (and perhaps lover) Victor has been killed.[27] In a series of diary-like entries, Ruth records nine days spent wandering between Calanques's cafes, shuttered pensions and the 'mercilessly lighted cabaret of the beach'. Not much happens; she meets old friends, acts as a secretary to an aspiring young novelist, visits Marseille, has a meaningless affair with a local hairdresser and contemplates suicide. The novella ends with the enigmatic image of a boat disappearing into the hazy horizon, leaving the reader uncertain if Ruth has in fact taken her life.

When *These Dark Glasses* appeared in 1949, some New Zealand readers were doubtless struck by its affinity with the contemporary European existentialist literature that was just

starting to reach them.[28] They might already have encountered
Camus's *L'Étranger* and his essay *Le Mythe de Sisyphe* (both
published in 1942), as well as Sartre's *La Nausée* (1938) – Greville,
Sargeson and many of their North Shore friends certainly knew
these works and others in the growing canon of existentialism.[29]
One of the most arresting visual images in *These Dark Glasses* is
pure Camus: a ruined American drunk, dead on the beach in
the midday sun like the murdered Arab in *L'Étranger*. However,
the novella's debt to existentialism goes beyond such obvious
narrative flourishes. Like Camus, Greville puts the Sisyphus myth
to work, but to different ends. She prefers its more traditional
interpretation (a chronicle of despair and futile human struggle
in a godless world) to Camus's re-telling (in which the king's
endless task of pushing a boulder uphill is an exercise in freedom
and human agency). Once Ruth has been robbed of both the
ironically-named Victor and her political dreams, her struggle to
find purpose in life is manifestly meaningless; death is its only
possible conclusion. Greville repeatedly signals the inevitability
of this outcome through images of uphill struggle, the sickening
fall, the welcome descent into oblivion. Noting the absence of gas
ovens in Calanques, Ruth flirts briefly with drowning, allowing
herself to sink down into the ocean, observing herself in the third
person as she descends – 'She said to herself, Mad'moiselle you are
drowning. How near it is how very easy it is.' Finally, she decides
to throw herself from the high rock daubed with the slogan *Vive le
Parti Communiste*, a local landmark – a fitting point of departure
for a failed political activist whose valiant efforts in Spain now
seem simply a rehearsal for this inevitable end. 'It always seems
too late to do any good. It's like slipping down a hill. Everything
goes so fast,' observes Ruth of her political convictions.

But as much as *These Dark Glasses* draws on the mood and
materials of existentialist writing, it is also clearly and intentionally
informed by modernist fiction of the 1920s and 30s. Greville's
sunglass-wearing, anis-drinking, apaché-dancing bohemians
might well have migrated from Cyril Connolly's fictional Trou-

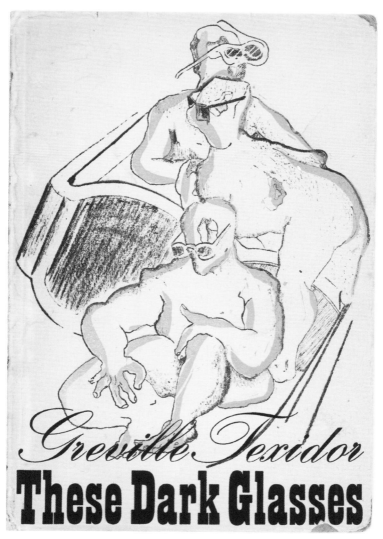

Greville Texidor

These Dark Glasses

The oddest book ever to receive New Zealand Government funding?

sur-Mer (*The Rock Pool*, 1936) or the terrace cafés of Bayonne in Hemingway's *The Sun Also Rises* (1927) or the Left Bank bars haunted by Jean Rhys's fragile Sasha Jensen (*Good Morning, Midnight*, 1939). Stylistically, there are obvious affinities with even 'higher' modernists such as Joyce and Woolf. Both the material world and the sensations of individual consciousness are rendered in suitably disjointed, oblique prose. The tonal indicators, authorial exposition and linear structure found in traditional narrative realism are conspicuously absent. Instead, the reader is required to pick their way between splinters of narrative, jolts and juxtapositions, apparently contingent episodes in which characters drift without purpose or plan from beach to nightclub to one another's beds. Sometimes the narrative pace is as unsettled and febrile as the ever-present mistral that 'sickle[s] the shallows', sometimes as turbulent as the jazz that plays in the outdoor nightclub above the bay. Elsewhere, the prose becomes dreamily becalmed, as when Ruth nearly drowns in the 'dense folds' of the warm, heavy sea. Chronology, place and voice are constantly destabilised. Here is Ruth arriving at a café, where she reluctantly joins her friends' table:

> My usual place. I have found a place on the edge of the lighted circle. Kate has made them move up a little for me. Poor Ruth! Losing poor Victor like that. And the way she throws herself into that party work. I know it does make a person rather dreary. . . . My friends, my good friends.

A roving microphone seems to control this fragment of narrative, retrieving slivers of conversation and unarticulated thought, picking up whatever voices are in range – Kate's, a note of calculated malice always audible beneath the sympathetic surface; Ruth's with its overlay of protective irony.

And in true modernist fashion, the narrative is self-consciously preoccupied with the artistic process itself. 'Why are they in my story?', Ruth puzzles of the characters who appear unannounced on the page, displacing the elusive words she senses waiting 'to unfold like a Japanese waterflower'. Elsewhere, she describes the political slogans slung about by her fashionably-politicised friends as '[c]annibal words that eat their own meaning', poor substitutes for 'the real words and the sound of thoughts' that she and Victor thought they would find in Spain. Ultimately, the act of writing fails Ruth; in her final diary entry, she acknowledges that words are insufficient to express or transform 'the debris of [her] Spanish dream'. Symbol, dream and myth are used to suggest latent desires and fears that lie beyond the characters' rational apprehension; the strange sea plant Ruth keeps after a fishing trip, a 'pale fleshy thing with a blind face', remains an enigmatic symbol (of sex, fate, death, or cosmic indifference?) that finally expires on the day her diary ends.

But despite such recognisably-modernist attributes, the novella was not of course a product of the high modernist period (traditionally said to have ended in the years before the Second World War). Nor was it written in the metropolitan centres in which 'modernism' purportedly happened – England, America, the garrets and cafés of continental Europe – but in Paparoa and suburban Auckland. Because of these incongruities, *These Dark Glasses* struck some readers as anachronistic, a novel that had missed its moment. It used outmoded techniques to illuminate a world that, by 1949, seemed 'tremendously unimportant', said one reviewer. Others found it heavily derivative: its similarities to *The Rock Pool* – in which a young Englishman of literary aspirations documents the dissolute bohemian life of a fictional Riviera resort town – were particularly conspicuous.[30] Greville had certainly read Connolly's novel, either in Europe at the time of its publication (1936), after she came to New Zealand (Sargeson owned a copy which she may have borrowed), or in 1947, when *The Rock Pool* was republished with a revealing new author's note. Connolly's title had become a common catchphrase among her friends and fellow-writers, who regularly applied it to the narcissistic world of the North Shore intelligentsia – after Greville's departure, Duggan wrote scornfully that 'the [local] Rock Pool is become a

chromium electrically heated tank lighted . . . by the weak beams
of Art and Appreciation'.[31] But while Greville's familiarity with
Connolly's work is clear, *These Dark Glasses* is written from a
vantage point that was unavailable to Connolly in 1936. He had
to rely on extra-textual means to signal the fate of Trou-sur-Mer's
inhabitants, adding a postscript to the 1947 edition that itemises
what happened to the real people on whom he based his characters:
one succumbed to consumption, another was murdered in a Nazi
concentration camp, a third died 'in the black winter night above
Germany'.[32] In *These Dark Glasses*, by contrast, 'what is to come'
is already embedded in the 'now' of Greville's story. It is a story
heavy with the knowledge of its own ending, every sentence
proleptic. The certainty that the world of the novel is about to
be swept away – regardless of its inhabitants' modish politics,
their faith in the artist-as-revolutionary-hero, and slogans such
as 'solidarity' and 'revolution' – is central to it. That most of the
characters remain oblivious to a future known to the author, her
readers and her protagonist is one source of the novel's painful and
characteristically-modernist irony.

While *These Dark Glasses* draws explicitly on modernist and
existentialist traditions, it also has obvious autobiographical
sources. In August 1938, Greville holidayed in Cassis on the
Riviera after fighting in Spain where, like Ruth, she had written
propaganda for the Republican cause. In Cassis, as her protagonist
does in Calanques, Greville became immersed in a demi-monde
of self-absorbed artists, bohemian drifters and lost souls. They
included several long-time friends and associates from London,
some of whom appear in the novella. Mark Gertler becomes the
neurotic artist Julian; his wife Marjorie figures as the put-upon and
snobbish Jane; Kate Foster appears ('brown and business-like in
dark glasses') with her lover Jan Kurzke whom Greville recasts as
the radical political refugee Otto, 'a dream of an Aryan'; the painter
and art writer Richard Carline becomes the doctrinaire Howard.
Werner clearly considered the work strongly autobiographical,
and not only because of the real people it referenced. It was a

'melancholy novel' that depicted Greville's state of mind after 'the Spanish debacle' that had so deeply affected her, he said.

But Sargeson – although endlessly fascinated by Greville's pre-war life in Europe – was not chiefly interested in *These Dark Glasses* as autobiography. His jacket blurb praised it as 'a powerful moral fable' for its times. Elsewhere, he called it 'a comedy with tragic undertones, a memorable illumination of one small corner of the vast European psychosis before the large-scale catastrophe which closed the thirties'.[33] The novella confirmed Greville's extraordinary accomplishment as a prose stylist and was, he wrote years later, 'one of the most beautiful prose pieces ever achieved in this country'. And Sargeson insisted that, despite its wholly European frame of reference, *These Dark Glasses* had both sprung from and left its mark on the New Zealand scene. It made a significant impression in this country, he said, 'especially with women readers and writers' (they included Janet Frame). Sargeson perhaps rather overstates the book's impact on domestic readers – the print run was only 300 – but his comments show he valued it as something other than confessional autobiography. Certainly, Ruth Brown should not be read as an unconditional proxy for Greville, despite the clear biographical parallels. Their politics differ for a start (although, arguably, disillusioned communists and anarchists had much in common after their shared betrayal by the foreign powers working in the background of the Spanish Civil War). But Greville also keeps a determined authorial distance from Ruth, subjecting her to the same ironic gaze she turns on the other characters. As Kendrick Smithyman comments in his introduction to Greville's collected fiction (in which *These Dark Glasses* appeared in 1987): 'Whatever Ruth owes to Greville's experience, she is not so much a projection as a target. Greville is not sorry for Ruth.'

The New Zealand critical reaction to *These Dark Glasses* ranged from bafflement to distaste and outright hostility. Many reviewers seemed disconcerted by the same 'current of bitterness' Lehmann had noted when he read the manuscript. Writing in the *Arts Year Book* for 1950, Patrick Macaskill opined that any work of art, 'however morbid its subject matter', should offer readers some glimmer of hope and inspiration: he found 'nothing redeeming in this novel except its form, which is a considerable intellectual achievement'.[34] In the *New Zealand Listener*, Phillip Wilson called it 'the product of a sick mind' but admired the skill and sophistication of the writing. The author's pessimistic world view, preoccupation with 'free love and sexual abnormality' and technical accomplishment all seem to have come as something of a surprise to Wilson, even though he had probably met Greville through Sargeson: 'One or two short stories with a local background had revealed a considerable ability, but they had not prepared us for anything quite like this'.[35] But the most considered, and damning, response was a three-page review in *Landfall*. The author was J.C. Reid, lecturer (later professor) in the University of Auckland's English Department and a prominent Catholic layman whose conservative religious convictions were well known. From Greville's perspective, Reid's values and literary tastes made him an unfortunate choice as reviewer. Few in Sargeson's circle regarded him as a supporter of New Zealand literature, even though he would later help introduce it to the university curriculum. He had recently accused Sargeson of a 'predilection for the sordid' and an all-consuming 'cynicism from which health is absent'.[36] In Sargeson's letters to Greville and others, Reid crops up occasionally as a butt of malice and mockery: 'stinker' was one of Sargeson's kinder epithets.[37]

Reid attacked *These Dark Glasses* on multiple fronts. It was an 'attempt at cleverness' that unsuccessfully aped Anglo-American writers and movements of the twenties and thirties. In addition to Cyril Connolly, Reid also saw the unmistakeable influence of sources ranging, rather dizzyingly, from Evelyn Waugh, Gertrude Stein, Ernest Hemingway and Bloomsbury to John O'Hara, Camus and Sartre.[38] He condemned the author's refusal to censure the shabby and hedonistic lives of her protagonists; she lacked 'the healthy anger of a satirist who finds lives meaningless because he knows they should have a meaning or the urbane judgement of one whose own vision of life rests on positive values'. As for the prose style, Reid could not decide if it was strained, banal or merely monotonous (although he did acknowledge some well-wrought dialogue and a 'consistency of atmosphere'). *These Dark Glasses* was not only a derivative work, he concluded, but also a curiously muddled and anachronistic one; the novella's wearied existentialist tone, laden with post-war disillusion, seemed ill-matched to the pre-war period and 'types' it depicted. But despite its manifest failings, it did deliver on one unexpected count:

> It is interesting to find a piece of fiction written in New Zealand which deals convincingly with a foreign setting, which is not concerned with the fantasy-world of a child, 'dumb oxen', adolescent sex repressions, life on a backblocks farm or men who drop cats into hot stoves, and which at the same time has a local application, for this country has its Calanques, too.

The comparison between *These Dark Glasses* and Sargeson's story 'Sale Day' (1939) – in which another Victor memorably drops a randy tomcat into an open stove – is puzzling. To Reid, that act of sado-sexual attention-seeking exemplifies the sordid impulses he insists have no place in the national literature. Why, then, did he not censure Greville's novella – in which married Englishwomen have 'rather Lawrencian' sex with fishermen behind rocks, and clever and amusing 'fairies' dance together in the cafés – on the same grounds? The answer, perhaps, was that Reid did not consider Greville a bona fide New Zealand writer. Her marginal claim on New Zealandness – quite apart from the insuperable problem of her gender – exempted her forever from the serious mission of building a national literature. Her novel is a failure in Reid's eyes, but it fails on grounds other than its ill-suitedness to the project of moral regeneration he wants local writers to embrace. Reid's review of *These Dark Glasses* – which repeatedly emphasises its irrelevance to the local post-war scene – helped confirm Greville's exclusion from the New Zealand canon.

Landfall later printed Greville's spirited riposte to Reid's 'book-eating' review. If her novel is indeed the kind that might not unfairly be described as clever, she wishes it had warranted a review of the kind 'that might not unfairly be described as criticism'.[39] She accuses Reid of using a disproportionately large sledgehammer to demolish what is no more than 'a small light-weight novel' and professes astonishment at the literary pantheon he calls on to demonstrate its inadequacies: 'everyone is here but James Joyce who is probably being held in reserve for a National Emergency like Sargeson'. Reid deliberately rolls out the big names only to damn *These Dark Glasses* by comparison, she claims: 'It is Sartrian [sic] Existentialism without Sartre, Hemingway without passion, Connolly without malice . . . clever but only in inverted commas. Does this mean not clever?'

Sargeson thoroughly approved of Greville's letter, praising her for 'tick[ing] off that Reid swine very nicely'.[40] And he again took the opportunity to encourage her to return to her typewriter, perhaps to experiment with new genres beyond fiction: 'The letter couldn't have been better – not a wrong or superfluous word, and every point so beautifully turned. Clever woman – see what you can do when you try. I mean with that particular kind of writing.'

But the damning *Landfall* review was not the only problem created by the publication of *These Dark Glasses*. When copies reached England, Mark Gertler's widow Marjorie was distraught at the novella's thinly-veiled characterisations. She and other long-standing friends reportedly 'rejected [Greville] strongly'.[41] Years later, Kate Kurzke told Sargeson she too was 'mildly annoyed' that Greville had given her name to one of the characters 'as that summer, 1938, Jan and I were never in Cassis but [visited] for one day from another resort, and after G[reville] had left'. According to Kate, Marjorie 'rounded up all the copies . . . and destroyed them. . . . Thus the book was wiped from the face of London. The people referred to in *These Dark Glasses* were happy to assist in its elimination because they did not like the sharp and "nasty" references in the book to personal details.' Maurice Duggan recalled Greville 'sending out a sort of letter of justification to all the people who might be hurt' and it seems that the rift was eventually mended or at least papered over: Marjorie Gertler (or Kostenz, as she later became) remained close to Greville's daughters until her death.

A failing follower of the muse

In Australia, the novella made no impact whatsoever. Greville did not distribute copies at the camp, claiming to know no one who would be interested; she also feared the possible reaction of the camp authorities, presumably on account of Ruth's politics. Later, when she showed *These Dark Glasses* to a few friends elsewhere, they 'returned it in absolute silence. Except for [novelist] Kylie Tennant who is such a good sort and couldn't hurt a fly, let alone a failing fellow follower of the muse', she reported to Sargeson glumly.[42]

The response to *These Dark Glasses* revived uncomfortable questions Greville had been asking herself – or perhaps avoiding asking herself – since her final months in New Zealand. Some were primarily literary. What sort of writer did she really want to be, and by whom did she want to be read? On the one hand, she was irresistibly attracted to the accoutrements of high modernist fiction – the glittering shards of narrative, the dream language, the symbols, the psychological landscapes. But she also wanted to anchor her fiction in the world 'out there', to engage with the materials of history and politics and social relationships. Moreover, she wanted to be published and to reach an audience beyond a literary elite. When E.P. Dawson sent her a glowing critique of *These Dark Glasses*, Greville said Dawson had over-estimated her ambitions. But she also hinted at the ambiguity of those aims:

> The truth is that I am so fascinated by life as it is or as it appears particularly that part of it known as nature – simply by the physical aspect of things – just the way they look and feel and taste and haven't any particular anxiety about the outcome.[43]

Her interests, she suggests, lie more in the faithful rendering of sensation, the subjective experience of the world, than in using those impressions in the service of narrative ('the outcome'). But in the very next sentence, she avows a different goal:

> My ambition has always been to write a sincere but best selling book with a good set of characters who stick to their roles and are firmly wedged between good solid hunks of scenery.

Sargeson had earlier expressed unease at Greville's seemingly unresolved intent as a writer when he told Duggan of the 'two Grevilles'. One was evident in the 'private soul searching' and personal symbolic language of 'Anyone Home?'. The other had produced the leaner, less introspective work he admired more, such as 'An Annual Affair' and even 'Santa Cristina'.[44] Now Greville herself seemed increasingly troubled by these conflicting impulses. Should she strive for the rarefied aesthetics of literary fiction or the readability of the popular novel? Was she writing to excavate and relive intense personal experience, or to communicate and universalise it? If it had still been possible for her to readily exchange drafts and confidences with Duggan or Sargeson, to resume the intimate literary conversation of a few years earlier, Greville might have found answers to these questions. But she had distanced herself from the sources that had enabled and then nourished her writing life; without them, she lacked the resilience or resources to sustain it.

Her unresolved literary dilemmas blurred with familiar personal anxieties, particularly the enduring terror of ageing and irrelevance. Despite her crisp demolition of J.C. Reid's review, she could not help but agree that the novella was dated. Worse was her suspicion that it was *she* who was dated – a woman whose moment had been and gone, whose life would never again hum with the vitality and sense of purpose she had once found on the stage or, like Ruth, in Spain. Young friends had recently described her friend and fellow-writer Kylie Tennant, ten years younger than Greville, as having gone to seed. Thoughtlessly cruel, maybe, but perhaps there was a grain of truth in their judgement. Did they say the same of her? The prospect seemed all too likely. Her spirits were briefly raised when she saw the photo that accompanied the *Listener*'s review of *These Dark Glasses* (it had 'a certain faded charm' she told Sargeson; 'I mean you can think the photo is faded') and she immediately resolved to get another taken soon 'in case I write another book and further pictures are needed. Anyway it might be as well to have it done while I'm still recognisable'.[45]

The family's departure from the Bathurst camp in 1950 thwarted Greville's resolve to resume regular writing habits. Werner's position at the camp had become increasingly untenable due to escalating conflict with the camp bureaucracy over the bitter coalminers' strike of June 1949. The strike ended only when the Labor Government imprisoned the miners' leaders and sent in troops to cut coal. When the camp director publicly endorsed the government's vigorous anti-miner stance, Werner objected; he thought camp staff should take a neutral position since the new migrants would end up working alongside Australians with a wide range of views. Immediately tarred as a supporter of the striking miners (and 'all strikers were Communists in the eyes of the authorities'), Werner became a marked man. With few prospects of promotion or transfer, he decided to return to secondary school teaching. Thus began 'five black years' in a succession of schools where, all too often, Werner found himself forcing a dull, stale curriculum onto troubled pupils who did not wish to learn. The style of teaching was comparable to lion-taming, he wrote: 'one stood in the middle of the arena and brandished the whip – with the constant danger that the beasts would devour the trainer if he did not at all times keep on top of the situation. In my case the beasts were often on top.'

Greville and Rosa now followed Werner as he moved unhappily from school to school across rural New South Wales, each post more unsatisfactory than the last. He taught in Macksville, at Sawtell and at a private Anglican boys' school in Wentworth Falls where the family lived on the grounds and Greville was conscripted

Werner and Rosa

to play the hymns at Assembly. When she was not pounding out 'Jerusalem' on the school piano, she exchanged occasional letters with Duggan, now ensconced with Barbara in London. He sent her caustic vignettes of her old companions, haunts and relatives – they included Kate, in whose Steeles Road house the Duggans stayed for a while, and Manolo Texidor, who employed the Duggans briefly in his cork business. 'How odd,' Greville wrote. 'Now you will be going to Kenwood . . . instead of me and meeting my old friends, who perhaps are not my old friends, instead of me.'[46] Duggan was far from enamoured with expatriate life in London and agreed with Greville that England's chief merit was its proximity to continental Europe; 'of course no one would want to live [here], only until one gets the fare to somewhere else', he wrote from Cambridge where he had been invited to tea with E.M. Forster.[47] But his letters stirred in Greville an uncharacteristically sentimental longing. She envied his meeting with Forster and wistfully recalled visiting Cambridge as a teenager, when she had stayed with L.P. Hartley and his family. 'Do write and send something for my nostalgia which is very bad at this time of the year,' she ended. Already, Greville was growing disenchanted with Australia and its meagre attractions, just as she had with New Zealand a decade earlier. Some things were looking up, it was true. She was once again living close to the entrancing Blue Mountains, with their Lawrencian associations. Greville's mother, always a stabilising presence, had finally joined them from Auckland and was staying nearby in a small hotel run by European migrants. Compared with the DP camp, the family was 'simply smothered in scenic splendour' and day-to-day life was decidedly more comfortable. But it was also colourless and strangely enervating, Greville complained. She was unable to apply herself to writing, in any form. Even the relatively undemanding task of book reviewing was beyond her, she claimed; it might be a way 'to escape from engrossment in the family' she told Sargeson from Sawtell, 'but don't suppose I shall ever get round to it'. A more settled existence was proving as inimical to serious literary activity as an unsettled one, perhaps even more so. 'We are so settled down that we hardly know we exist,' she wrote to Duggan in November 1950. 'For anyone who would be contented with nature there is nothing wrong with this place. I expect to turn into a nature lover. Look out for "Leaves From My Garden".'

Despite the camouflaging self-mockery, her evident despondency troubled Duggan: '[I] had a note from Greville asking for something for her nostalgia,' he wrote to Sargeson. 'But everything refined, almost out of existence, so that one has to search for the slight overtones before one can tell that it is Greville at all.'[48]

It was not just the stultifying effects of the scenery that was frustrating Greville, but also the social isolation of the small communities in which she found herself. The DP camp, for all its challenges, had brought her into contact with like-minded people, both Australian and European, who shared similar politics and artistic interests. Through Werner, she had got to know Kylie Tennant, whose empathetic portrayals of the poor and unemployed – informed by direct experience of the Sydney slums and even a stint in jail – had earned her unwelcome comparisons with John Steinbeck in the 1940s.[49] Tennant became not just a friend but a generous and sympathetic reader. It was perhaps through her that Greville also got to know the New Zealand-born writer Ruth Park, whose prolific output (of both babies and prizewinning novels) she respected. But this potentially supportive network was now out of reach as Greville followed Werner from town to town, no longer a working author but merely a supportive wife and schoolmaster's helpmeet. Her other literary contacts – including publishers Max Harris and John Reed, and the poet and literary editor Barrett Reid – were in Melbourne and Adelaide, for all practical purposes as far away as they had been when she was in New Zealand. The family joined a 'hellishly dear' lending library in Sydney that posted out books and, at one point, Greville was working her way through André Gide's *Journals*. But she claimed to know no one else who read books.[50] As Werner recalled, probably with considerable understatement: 'My wife found the intellectual isolation rather depressing and asked me to try to get back to the neighbourhood of Sydney, where she had made friends with literary people.'

And so they came to Hazelbrook, a small town ninety kilometres west of Sydney in the Blue Mountains. There they bought Mount View, a dilapidated homestead on sixteen hectares of sloping bush-clad land. This was to be not just another relocation, but the start of a new kind of living. They began building a new house on another corner of the property; Greville would have a purpose-built hut for writing, Werner would teach at nearby schools or in the city, Rosa would go to the local primary school. At the weekends, their Sydney friends would visit or they would travel into the city. Mount View was to be the realisation of the semi-rural, semi-communal existence – materially simple, but socially and intellectually rich – that they had often talked about.

Out in front of the new house, Werner constructed an outdoor fireplace where the family and their guests could sit and talk into the evenings, enjoying good food, wine, poetry readings and political discussion – a veritable salon in the bush. Some of their Sydney friends built their own huts on the property and became regular guests. Others came to Mount View for occasional breaks from the hard-drinking, hard-partying bohemian scene that made inner-city Sydney a magnet for young writers, students, free-thinkers and fellow-travellers from the late 1940s onwards. There was the young film-maker Richard (Dick) Preston, soon to depart for New York; Jack Rolley, a nomadic Englishman who later pioneered aviation in Tahiti; and his partner Miriam, a Māori woman from the Bay of Islands whose serene spirituality greatly impressed Greville.[51] Photographer Bill Mansill and his wife Val, friends of Cristina's, had recently left Auckland and were inching towards London; they too became part of the circle. Connecting strands ran in all directions and at Mount View, they converged.

Some of Greville and Werner's visitors were associated with the Sydney Push, the post-war counter-culture that borrowed its name from the swaggering gangs of street toughs whose crimes had scandalised nineteenth-century Sydney. Less a movement

Greville and Rosa, 1953
Photograph by Bill Mansill. Copyright and reproduced with permission of the Bill Mansill Photographic Archive

The house that Werner built at Mount View, photographed in 2014
Photograph by author

than 'a blowtorch to the belly' of conservative post-war Australia,[52] the Push's origins lay in the free-thinking and libertarian groups formed at the University of Sydney in the late 1940s. Influenced particularly by Challis Professor of Philosophy John Anderson, students and a few like-minded academics had fomented an idiosyncratic creed of 'anarchism, pessimism, sexual freedom and anti-careerism', coupling it to less esoteric enthusiasms including beer-drinking, horse-racing and general larrikinism. By the early 1950s, the Push's centre of gravity was shifting from the university to the watering holes of the inner city and Kings Cross. In pubs and coffee shops, its followers drank, talked, swapped sexual partners and loudly showed their disdain for middle-class morality and the small-mindedness of those they termed the 'Alfs and Daphs'.[53] A considerable number of Push followers were young European migrants, relieved to finally feel at home in a milieu 'where differences went unnoticed, where foreignness was not an issue, where the suffocating values of this weird new country were laughed at and dismissed'. Although subsequent myth-making has elevated the role of a handful of cultural celebrities – Germaine Greer, Clive James, Robert Hughes, even the more reactionary Barry Humphries – the real spirit of the early Push was embodied by less-remembered figures. Among them were Harry Hooton, self-styled anarchist poet and street philosopher; the preposterously handsome failed vet student Darcy Waters, founder of the Society for the Promotion of a Fantastic Way of Life; horse-racing aficionado, recidivist squatter and champion bridge player Roelof Smilde; and music journalist Lillian Roxon.[54] While left-leaning, they were seldom politically committed – the early Push disdained all forms of organised political authority or activity, including the Communist and Labor parties. Some Push people dedicated themselves to preserving the intellectual libertarian tradition, while others believed in 'permanent protest', an attitude of open-ended dissent 'that did not attempt to institute change but merely protested against particular circumstances'. Still others simply relished the excitement of escaping parental expectations and a dreary suburban future. The women of the Push sought the liberty to speak and behave as they wished, to play roles beyond the handful of sanctioned possibilities: working spinster, girlfriend, housewife, mother. They did indeed find unprecedented freedoms; they drank at public bars, paid their own way, and slept with whom they liked. But such freedoms often came at considerable cost to their emotional, intellectual and sexual health. Many women discovered beneath the Push's free-and-easy ways a vein of exploitation, condescension and hypocrisy all too reminiscent of the establishment values they were fleeing. One prominent figure observed that, even in the twenty-first century, 'people remember Push men for what they believed, and Push women for who they were "on with".'[55]

To Greville, a habitué of other earlier and equally rackety bohemias, the Push felt endearingly familiar. It was not just the ostentatious iconoclasm of those involved, their provocative tastes in art and music, their earnest conviction that they were the first generation to truly reject the stifling norms of their society. The Push's philosophical base (even if some followers seldom got beyond the slogans) was also familiar to Greville. The early twentieth-century Spanish anarchists whose ideas had helped stir her to arms in 1937 were important influences on the Sydney libertarians, too. They shared the same vision of a stateless society, although the Push's anarchism had its own distinctive complexion. Push people largely shunned organised programmes, agendas and specific objectives – if they ever actually achieved anything, they reasoned, it would show they had sold out. Physical violence was generally disdained, despite the apparent conviction of the Australian security agencies that some in the Push 'wouldn't hesitate to drop a bomb on the Sydney Harbour Bridge or de-rail a train' and therefore warranted surveillance.[56]

Greville never became part of the Push. She did not publish in its magazines and broadsheets; she does not figure in memoirs of the period, nor in more recent scholarly studies of the Push's intellectual roots and social impact. The only work she published while living in Australia appeared in journals shunned by the Push, notably *Ern Malley's Journal*.[57] However, she undoubtedly came into contact with Push culture and was energised by it, especially on her visits to the city where she regularly stayed with friends in Kings Cross. She knew Push people like George Munster, the Austrian refugee who founded the influential journal *Nation*, and the historian and teacher Grahame Harrison, at that time a university dropout with a deep interest in Spanish anarchism. But the Push was primarily a cultural space for a young generation in revolt – and Greville was, as she regularly reminded herself and others, no longer young. She remained firmly on its fringes. She was interested, sympathetic and stimulated, but her distance from the Push paralleled that of Hazelbrook to Sydney.

Living at Mount View not only reintroduced Greville to bohemia but also to the Quakers, with whom she had worked in Spain and who had helped secure her release from Holloway. Sometimes she was an 'attender' at the silent outdoor Quaker meetings hosted by the Wolhwills, a Sydney family of German refugee origin who had bought the adjoining land. She became interested in Buddhism, too, through her friendship with another adventurous Englishwoman, Lucy Mustard – a tall, striking woman who had travelled to India in the 1920s and married the independence activist Dr N.R. Deobhankar, later imprisoned with Gandhi. Their only child, David Mustard, had come to Sydney for his schooling in 1947 and Lucy later joined him from India, eventually making her way to Hazelbrook.[58] When Greville left Australia, Lucy stayed on at Mount View as tenant and caretaker, saying she would leave only when she was dead. Greville remarked that the only reason for her to return would be to die.

But in the early 1950s, she still had cause for optimism. She may have been on the margins of Sydney's avant-garde scene but there was also a Hazelbrook scene of sorts and she was at its vanguard. According to Rosamunda, Mount View was remembered 'by quite a few of that generation . . . It was a sort of a country fringe of Sydney's "bohemia".'[59] A lot of people were visiting, Greville wrote to Ian Hamilton in the early 1950s: 'Most of them are young and beautiful and fairly interesting', and their presence made life 'rather exciting'.[60] At one point, Greville and Werner bought a printing press and experimented with printing small runs of 'terrible poetry' (whether their own work or others' is unclear).[61] And importantly, Greville started writing again – fitfully, often despairing of publication, but writing nonetheless. Her most successful work was for radio, with two pieces broadcast in 1952–53. The ABC promoted her play *The Laughing Spirit* as a 'poignant love story' about a Pākehā minister's son and a Māori girl torn between commitment to her husband and her own culture.[62] Greville based it on an admittedly sketchy knowledge of various Māori myths, overlaid with a strong autobiographical element. 'It's about a batty old Maori woman (no more a maori than I am, in fact it is me)', she confessed to Duggan, from whom she sought advice about suitable Māori songs to incorporate.[63] In Paparoa, she had been uneasily aware of the tangata whenua's near-invisible presence; now, Greville regretted 'that I wasn't interested in maoris while I lived in N.Z.' But if *The Laughing Spirit* lacked accuracy or authenticity, listeners did not seem to mind. The Adelaide *Mail* called it a rarity; a radio play that made you think, even if overladen with 'side issues' that detracted from its powerful message. It was a 'tragedy of misunderstanding' that left the listener 'with a feeling of unutterable weariness at the unnecessary misunderstandings that separate race from race'.[64]

Greville also came to regret not knowing more about gypsy culture when she wrote her second radio feature, *Death of a Gypsy*, based on Lorca's *Diálogo del Amargo*. After it was broadcast by the ABC, Sargeson tried (unsuccessfully) to interest the New Zealand Broadcasting Corporation in airing it. Greville was especially enamoured with the Spanish music recorded for the broadcast, and even more with the guitarist who performed it. Juan was a self-described gypsy who dazzled her with his instinctive feeling for Lorca's verse; 'Juan is not spoilt by being acquainted with any kind of culture so he doesn't get worried about Lorca being ART . . . he is invaluable in having the right feelings and picking up clues', she told Duggan.[65] She and Juan embarked on an affair about which nothing is known except that it ended unhappily. Werner seems to have been sanguine about the relationship itself, but less so about Juan, whom he considered distinctly 'flakey'. At one point, Greville's gypsy lover drew a knife on him.

Meanwhile, Greville applied herself to translating Lorca. Some years earlier, perhaps in lieu of payment, the editors of *Angry Penguins* had given Greville a full set of Lorca's verse, which she now put to good use. She was producing some 'excellent translations', she told Duggan in buoyant mood; she hoped to place them in selected 'small mags' and ultimately publish a collection.[66] In early 1953, she was in discussions with a Sydney theatre company keen to perform her version of Lorca's *Así Pasan Cinco Años* ('Five Years Go By'), said to be its first English translation. Although it does not seem to have made it to the stage, an extract appeared in the second issue of *Ern Malley's Journal*. Greville's skills as a translator, now largely forgotten, received some prestigious endorsements at the time. Lorca's literary executor, Arturo Barea, who was exiled in London during the Second World War, is said to have declared her translations 'by far the best ever made into English'.[67] Her rendering of Lorca's 'He Died at Dawn' was chosen by New York publisher New Directions for the definitive *Selected Poems of Federico Garcia Lorca* (1955), having won the approval of Lorca's brother Francisco. 'I feel as if someone had said: "As Jesus Christ is dead St John will have a look at your translations",' wrote Greville nervously to Sargeson when she heard Francisco would be vetting the collection. This was work she relished and considered important – 'I really think what I am doing now is worthwhile and you know what I always have been about Lorca,' she told Duggan. It also displaced the more problematic task of writing her own fiction.

Greville's Lorca translations undoubtedly attracted some interest in Australia – years later, Rosamunda was told that 'the familiarity of Sydney writers with Lorca . . . in the early 50s' was due in large measure to her work.[68] But her passionate attachment to the Spanish poet was in other ways awkwardly out of sync with her times and place. She was unable to get most of her many translations published; in the post-Ern Malley era, Australian magazine editors, publishers and readers were largely unreceptive to Lorca's romantic poetics. Sunday Reed – literary patron, muse, champion of modernism and wife to Greville's erstwhile publisher John Reed – was shocked when a poet friend described Greville's renderings of Lorca as merely 'pretty'; it seemed 'all the young ones are turning up their noses', Sunday commented.[69] Such indifference was not uncommon. When Greville's film-maker friend Dick Preston shifted to New York, he tried to interest the publisher Evergreen in her translation of *Así Pasan Cinco Años*. They returned the playscript saying 'it was very good but . . . it was "slight" Lorca', Preston reported in 1960, promising to show it to an off-Broadway director 'who does off beat stuff'.[70] Nothing more was heard.

And so the bulk of Greville's fifty-odd Lorca translations remain in the archives, unpublished. They sit there alongside poetry, playscripts and various non-fiction pieces also written at Mount View and later – including a satirical essay titled 'A Collector's Rejection Piece'. In it, Greville claims her speciality field 'is the rejection letter and I can fairly claim to be an expert in it. Other writers, I am aware, have amassed larger collections, but mine is, I believe, unsurpassed for variety and originality.'[71] Spiky self-mockery masks genuine dismay at her dwindling literary output, which she elsewhere summarised for Sargeson as 'half a dozen abortions of short stories, the makings of a migrant novel and apart from that only translations and a radio play which is designed to be popular'.[72] Even published work that had once brought her satisfaction now disappointed her. When 'An Annual Affair' was reprinted in Dan Davin's *New Zealand Short Stories* (1953) – the first New Zealand volume in the World's Classics series from Oxford University Press – Greville judged it one of the only two duds in the collection; 'Now that I look at it again [it] seems far too long and tedious'.

Curiously, Greville's list of non-achievements does not include the writing project that in fact consumed much of her time at Hazelbrook: redrafting her autobiographical Spanish Civil War novel, *Diary of a Militia Woman*. She had begun the novel soon after arriving in New Zealand and had probably completed a first draft before she left. Typescripts held in the State Library of New South Wales support this theory; some are typed on the back of Sargeson's discarded drafts of *When the Wind Blows* (1945), drafts of Greville's own stories and even Cristina's student typing exercises. But the novel seems to have stalled on the North Shore. When she returned to it at Hazelbrook, it was with more ambitious aims. What had begun ten years earlier as a lightly-disguised record of her Civil War experiences was now to be a richer, more nuanced and more equivocal work of imaginative fiction.

Reflecting its protracted gestation, *Diary* is an uneven and frustratingly-disjointed manuscript. It lacks the coherence or sustained artistic vision of a work produced over a concentrated period. Yet it deserves attention, both for its own sake and as an aggregation of the manifold anxieties and fears Greville's wartime experiences had produced, and which erupted repeatedly into her life and her fiction – displacement, disenchantment, guilt, the twin desires to obliterate the past and memorialise it. She had already tentatively explored this painful territory in her short stories: in fact, some of the same characters, incidents and images recur in *Diary*.[73] In early work like 'Home Front', Greville had been content to frame wartime Spain as an exotic elsewhere, romantic and passionate – a limited, somewhat sanitised representation, perhaps intended to satisfy a sympathetic but uniformed New Zealand readership, including Sargeson. But in other stories – including 'Maaree', 'At Home and Alone', 'Jesús Jiménez' and the uncollected 'San Toni' – she had offered a darker, more politically and aesthetically nuanced account of the Spanish war. She had deployed a range of registers (colloquial, lyrical, satirical) and styles (symbolism, surrealism, realism); she had positioned herself at varying distances from her subject matter, sometimes intimately immersed in it, sometimes detachedly observant. These stories affirmed that, for those caught up in the Civil War, suffering and failure were not its only legacies; it had also provided a fleeting sense of community, purpose, even exhilaration. Here, Greville could be seen making the same disconcerting 'double-edged and subtle slippage[s] between tragedy and joy' as other war writers like Rosamond Lehmann, whose work has been said to simultaneously register the 'equivocal sense of life's excitement and its corollary, suffering'.[74] In Greville's account of a wartime funeral in Barcelona (in 'Maaree'), for example, the narrator's eye takes in not only the crowds of weeping women but also the absurd grandiloquence of the anarcho-syndicalist slogans: 'The procession moved like a black river, bearing banners like boats. Conquer Or Die (Carpenters Union) was swept along on the flood. They Shall Not Pass (United Hairdressers) faltered and came to a halt before me.' In the space of a single sentence, political reportage gives way to a private joke, and the mood tips disconcertingly from gravity to the absurdly comic.

Yet the short story form was necessarily limited. A novel not only offered Greville a larger canvas on which to work, but also a different kind of creative experience – the chance to revisit experiences that had both exhilarated and nearly broken her, to submit them to more searching and painful examination.[75]

Diary opens in the winter of 1936. Its protagonist Magda[76] and her English husband Martin are living in the artists' colony of Turissa (the original Roman name for Tossa de Mar) on the Costa Brava. Of mixed English and Argentinian descent, Magda is determinedly non-political, more interested in renovating the couple's old farmhouse than in rumours of the Republican Government's impending collapse. But when the nationalist rebellion begins, her idealistic husband resolves to help defend the Republic and enlists with the small Partido Obrero de Unificación Marxista (POUM). At the same time, a land dispute unfolds that affects the couple's occupancy of their house, and Magda follows Martin to Barcelona. There she works as a translator and gets to know Republican supporters of all complexions – the anarcho-syndicalists who now control the city, doctrinaire communists from Spain and abroad, ardent foreign volunteers, middle-class locals who fear the anarchists' rumoured ferocity and godlessness. But Magda is increasingly drawn into the anarchist community, largely through the Cruz family whose sons are prominent in the movement. She travels to the Aragón front where Martin has been posted, persuades him to leave the POUM in favour of an anarchist militia, gets rid of the young German volunteer he has taken as his lover, and enlists alongside her husband (commandeering her rival's sought-after rifle in the process). She is soon in battle, including at Almudévar where Martin is killed. After a brief and unhappy stay in England, Magda returns to Barcelona and rekindles her connections with the Cruz family, becoming Pedro's lover. But by this time, the Republican cause is in chaos: Moscow-aligned communists control the government, other leftist factions are suppressed, the anarchists are increasingly marginalised. Internecine street fighting breaks out and Pedro is killed in suspicious circumstances. Soon Barcelona is under bombardment by the nationalists and their fascist allies. Magda keeps working as a translator, has a desperate affair with Pedro's brother Liberto, and is eventually evacuated by warship back to Britain. She is later shown working there in an orphanage, exhausted, unstable, distraught with guilt: 'A traitor. She lost the war. It was she who lost the war', Magda tells herself.

Although Greville seems to have conceptualised and held fast to this basic plot from the outset, at Hazelbrook she repeatedly reworked the novel's structure and style, and experimented with various narrative frames. Both between and within drafts, she can be seen recasting register and tone, refashioning scenes to different artistic ends. What reads as anodyne exposition in one draft – '[she] had been nearly two years at the Fonda Lopez. Without having planned it she had just stayed on after a perfect holiday there with Martin. At the week ends they tramped the country looking for a house' – becomes oblique, disjointed or more politically-charged narrative in another. A conventionally descriptive passage –

The ground floor housed a wretched peasant and his wife and a flock of goats and children. The chimney had fallen in and the house was always filled with smoke which covered the walls with a heavy coating of soot. There was little to distinguish the living room from the stable.

– is recast more impressionistically in another version:

The upstairs room rotten floored, uninhabitable, below the wretched peasants, the children, the goats, the chimney fallen in, the place full of smoke, the walls coated with soot, the moving carpet of fleas on the floor, little to distinguish the living room from the stable.

Characters not only change names between versions but are effectively reimagined. In some, Magda, who can be reliably read as Greville's alter-ego, speaks with the breezy inflections of the English upper-middle-class: 'Good God, look at that . . . The Fascists have ever so much more of Spain than we have,' she exclaims brightly, inspecting a map. Over successive drafts, though, Magda transforms from formulaic construction – an accumulation of familiar attitudes and tropes – into a more singular and surprising presence. Such recalibrations suggest that Greville was constantly reimagining her characters and the fundamentals of the story she was telling. Was this an insider's story or an outsider's? Was it a barely-fictionalised account of historical events, or an unfettered work of fiction that nonetheless bore the weight of imaginative truth? Then there was her usual stylistic ambivalence: did the novel's political content demand documentary realism? Or could she write a politically-engaged novel that was also aesthetically inventive? The novel's prolonged gestation did not help her resolve these questions; if anything, as her many unfinished drafts demonstrate, it served to complicate them. Lengthy expositions about anarchist theory and the progress of the war impede the plot and swamp the characters. And the more Greville worked and reworked the draft, the more the novel started to falter under the weight of the multiple literary, confessional and therapeutic burdens she required it to bear.

Greville abandoned *Diary* around 1954. Exactly what kind of novel it might have become is a matter of speculation; different versions seem to be veering towards different genres. In places, it reads as a classic bildungsroman charting the personal and political growth of a young woman against the background of war; consistent with bildungsroman convention, our heroine achieves maturity and self-knowledge but at considerable cost. Then again, *Diary* is also unmistakably a roman à clef. Magda and Martin are recognisable versions of Greville and Werner (albeit with some distinct differences) and many of their wartime experiences are identical. Thinly-disguised friends and acquaintances figure as minor characters. Numerous real political figures and activists also populate the novel, though some are camouflaged – the Cruz brothers are modelled on the anarchist Conejero brothers,[77] and Martin's associate Tom Mann on the English poet and international brigadist Tom Wintringham. The anarcho-syndicalist leader Juan García Oliver approves Magda's request to travel to the front; John Dos Passos and Ernest Hemingway make offstage appearances.

As the work of a former combatant, *Diary* is a distinctive addition to the canon of twentieth-century war fiction; that it is written by a female combatant, and one deeply immersed in the subtleties of Catalan anarchism, makes it more unusual yet. It is also unusually equivocal in its politics. Much of the iconic Civil War literature in English is animated by a fervent and single-minded belief that art can propagate political and social change.[78] Thus Auden's poets explode 'like bombs' as they embrace 'to-day the struggle'; John Cornford beseeches his countrymen to ensure Spain's 'agony was not in vain'; committed communists, such as Greville and Werner's erstwhile houseguest Ralph Bates, faithfully harness their fiction to the cause. But those works were written in the heat of the conflict, when it still seemed possible that an educated, mobilised international movement could help the Spanish Left defeat fascism. To these writers and others, literature had the power of a recruiting poster. Greville's *Diary*, by contrast, was written at an ever-increasing distance from that moment, its

author all too aware that the cause had been comprehensively
defeated, by forces of the Left as much as the Right. Every moment
in the novel resonates with the inevitable failure of the characters'
intentions; their words cannot be read without the taint of
hindsight.

Greville's real interest lies not in agitprop but in particularising
and humanising a conflict that had already been mythologised
into near-abstraction. She does so most effectively when she
allows her prose to slew between registers and styles, producing
the same jagged texture found in her best short stories. Perhaps
the strongest passages in the entire book are those set at the
front, where moments of violence are suffused with a dream-like
unreality and detachment, even comedy. Magda watches as an
armoured car advances down a nearby road – 'the strange creature
. . . blindly nosed its way along the open stretch of road between
the quiet trees' – and is blown up. Her response is not horror or
distress, but utter disengagement. Even she seems mildly surprised
at finding the scene '[i]ntensely interesting to watch but not having
any connection with anything'. Elsewhere, abrupt tonal slippages
disrupt the expected conventions of war writing. Within a single
paragraph, Greville treats war as a quotidian social activity (combat
as a job like any other), as a surreal act of physical and psychic
violence, and even as farce. Berated by an officer for running too
slowly under fire, Magda readily admits her failings:

– I can't run fast enough.
– Why did you come then?
– I didn't know. I won the mile race at school.

Later, waiting to advance on the enemy lines, Magda has an
incongruous drawing-room exchange with another officer:

– You are not afraid, mademoiselle?
– Not just at the moment, thank you.
– You speak excellent French.
– Thank you.

– But you are English?
– Yes I lived in Paris. You speak excellent French also.
– I too lived in Paris. It is a wonderful city.
– Truly.
– We can move now. Au revoir, mademoiselle, and good luck.
– Good luck.

Sargeson, had he been asked to critique the manuscript, might well have advised Greville to strip it of its polemics and trust instead the capabilities she demonstrates in passages like these: an instinct for absurdity, a powerful visual imagination, an acute ear for the evasions and dissimulation of political discourse. But it is doubtful that Sargeson ever saw the novel in its more developed form, although he may have read some early material. Perhaps it was at his suggestion that Greville raided it for short stories such as 'Jesús Jiménez'. If so, he may have considered Greville's material and talents more suited to the shorter form, a view she herself periodically expressed and which contributed to her eventually giving up on the novel. Like the American writer William Styron – who spent a decade writing and rewriting a novel based on his experiences in the Korean War, before finally abandoning it – Greville found herself losing control of a narrative which, despite her closeness to it, had never quite come into focus.[79] 'It may be that I can't write a full length novel. I wasted a lot of time on that Spanish one', she wrote from Hazelbrook.[80]

However, her abandonment of *Diary* points to more than technical difficulties. Writing it was an act of exhumation both painful and revelatory. It laid bare a past that remained both horrifyingly proximate and completely beyond palliation – the experience of combat, the collapse of the revolution's ideals, the bombing of Barcelona, imprisonment in Holloway. In *Diary*, the doctor who encounters the traumatised Magda after the war sees: 'an excited English woman [whose] ... large unguarded movements contradicted the slightly shrill English voice. The woman was definitely not normal.' Standing behind this image of damage and obsession, it is possible to make out Greville herself, chain-smoking as she types in her hut at Mount View, reworking her war and prison experiences over and over, torn between wanting to remember and needing to forget. She had chosen to take up arms; whether or not she ever killed anyone (and that is unknown), had she done wrong? Her own country had abandoned and incarcerated her; was this the punishment she deserved? At the time *These Dark Glasses* was published, Sargeson had urged Greville to keep writing about her past, not just as a source of material but as a way to live with it: 'that's your solution old dear – just write another [novel], and remember the past only in what you write. For the rest – forget about it'.[81] But it seems the act of writing *Diary* made it even *less* possible for her to forget or come to terms with this part of her history. And so she wrote on and on with sometimes ferocious intensity, unearthing layers of culpability and guilt that, once brought into the light, could not easily be reinterred or reckoned with.

In this sense, Greville's unfinished novel belongs to yet another literary genre – 'trauma writing', a quintessentially modern response to the singularly brutal and barbarous nature of twentieth-century warfare. In trauma writing, the boundaries between literature and therapy blur, as the writer wrestles with 'what it really means for the mind to be possessed by an experience it cannot represent to itself' and to be 'inhabited by a lost past'.[82] Like one of the authors most often associated with trauma writing, the American poet H.D., Greville, too, 'wrote and wrote again the narrative of life-shattering events' that obsessed and came to define her.[83] Yet, for her, writing *Diary* was neither a salve nor a refuge from trauma; it was like repeatedly touching an open wound. With every iteration, she seemed less and less able to reach a satisfactory resolution, either to the narrative itself or to what Freud called the 'traumatic neurosis' activated by revisiting a painful past.[84] What remains is less a finished work of fiction than an increasingly disturbed and ultimately inconclusive conversation with herself. She had written herself into silence.

* * *

By the mid-1950s, Greville's sense of literary failure was near-complete. She physicalised it, describing a writing self in terminal decline. The words had dried to an 'anaemic flow', she wrote,[85] and with them had gone the sensations and powers of observation that once animated her fiction: 'As far as I am concerned there are only 2 states – one in which you can see and feel . . . the other in which the current is cut off and you're lucky to be keeping alive on pinpricks', she told Duggan. She was convinced that whatever she had managed to accomplish on the North Shore would not now be repeated; New Zealand had 'eaten' her words.

Greville's declining output was not only a sign of creative paralysis; it was also the consequence of unfortunate timing. Steeped in the European modernist tradition, keen to put that tradition to new literary purposes in the post-war antipodean world, Greville could not have chosen a worse time to be a writer in Australia – Sydney in particular. By the early 1950s, as Barrett Reid concluded glumly, a 'hostile philistinism had attacked and demoralised modernism's project' in Australia.[86] Things had been different a decade or so earlier; indeed, surrealism and modernism had erupted more forcefully into Australian cultural life than they had in New Zealand. In particular, the literary journal *Angry Penguins*, in which Greville had published in the 1940s, had helped bring together socialist and modernist interests, integrating international influences and national forms to create a uniquely Australian modernism.[87] But then came the Ern Malley hoax of 1944, when *Angry Penguins*' editors Reed and Harris were duped into publishing the work of a purportedly undiscovered Australian literary genius. In fact, 'Ern Malley' and his haphazard outpourings were the invention of two young poets intent on ridiculing what they saw as pretentious and meritless modernist verse. The hoax took an unforeseen turn when parts of the Malley poems were judged to be obscene. Harris was convicted and fined for publishing them, forcing *Angry Penguins* to close. The whole business unleashed a popular backlash against modernist experimentation of the kind *Angry Penguins* had championed, and the retreat into literary conservatism observed by Barrett Reid. Greville's work fell victim to this shift in cultural politics and taste. When her fractured, unsettling post-war story 'Time of Departure' appeared in the 1945 issue of *Angry Penguins*, it was stingingly dismissed by the *Sydney Morning Herald*. While some contributions showed artistic merit, in '[this piece of] what appears to be automatic writing by Greville Texidor . . . it is hard to see anything.'[88] Among other things, this response indicates the cultural battle-lines dividing Australia's major cities. Indeed, the poets of the Sydney Push were among the most vocal critics of all that *Angry Penguins* represented. In 1948, Harry Hooton described the work of 'the three best poets of our generation', all Sydney-based, as 'realistic, classical, intellectual, in contradistinction to the surreal worthless poetry which was issuing from Adelaide, Melbourne . . . during the war years.' Two of Hooton's chosen poets were James McAuley and Harold Stewart, the same young men who had together invented and written as the infamous Ern Malley.[89] Just as when *These Dark Glasses* was published, in 1950s Sydney, Greville was once again a writer whose work was out of step with its time and place.

As always, Greville's dissatisfaction with her writing bled into discontent with her external circumstances, and vice versa. It became impossible for her to disentangle one from the other, source from result, cause from effect. Everywhere she looked, she seemed to see confirmation of her own decline. The young visitors who made their way to Mount View were delightful, but their presence painfully reminded Greville, now fifty, that she herself was ageing. Only half-jokingly, she imagined some kind of Faustian trade-off between literary talent and youth, claiming she would happily give away all hope of writing again simply 'to wake up tomorrow, say – a barmaid – say – under forty'.[90]

She was also increasingly incapacitated by depression and anxiety, and the medications she used to treat them. Family members and friends remember her as frequently jumpy, tense, withdrawn. When Barrett Reid met Greville for the first time at a dinner party, he was struck not only by her beauty but by her 'surprisingly brittle manner' that made it difficult to 'get below the deliberately constructed surface'.[91] Her daughter Rosamunda suggests that, during the years at Mount View, Greville was in fact exhibiting classic symptoms of what would now be considered post-traumatic stress disorder (PTSD) stemming from her experiences of war and imprisonment. A retrospective diagnosis is clearly impossible, but Greville's own comments on her state of mind do strikingly echo the language clinicians use when diagnosing this complex condition in the present day.[92] They refer to a sense of emotional numbness ('the current is cut off', Greville wrote), unpredictable outbursts (the 'spiteful yelps' that could disrupt the harmonious domestic atmosphere so valued by Werner), difficulty concentrating, and what the American Psychiatric Association calls 'a sense of a foreshortened future' (when Greville thinks of returning to Europe, she concludes that 'it seems at least for me, rather too late').[93] Anxiety and depression commonly occur alongside PTSD, 'suicidal ideation' is not infrequent, excessive alcohol and drug use is known to further complicate PTSD symptoms, and clinicians agree many sufferers are disabled by a sense of guilt. In Greville's case, Rosamunda believes she did not feel guilty for abandoning the cause like some foreign fighters who quit Spain before the final defeat. Rather, Greville judged herself guilty of betraying her humanity by taking up arms – a crime made even worse when committed in the service of a failed cause.

If Greville's mental distress was indeed symptomatic of PTSD, it was never diagnosed as such (in any event, the condition would more likely have been termed 'traumatic neurosis' or 'war trauma' at the time). Even had it been, there was little likelihood of finding effective treatment in 1950s Australia. At Werner's insistence, Greville occasionally visited a psychiatrist during their visits to Kings Cross, although past encounters with dubious practitioners in Spain had left her suspicious of the profession. She may also have been influenced by fashionable anti-psychiatry sentiment; some members of the Sydney Push, for example, regarded psychiatry as a form of social control and claimed 'neuroses were what helped you to live'.[94] Greville was especially wary of the profession's over-eagerness for electroconvulsive treatment. Determined to avoid it, Greville probably saw medication as a lesser evil. She combined a steady regime of tranquillisers with her customary heavy drinking; she wrote better letters when she was drunk, she confessed to Duggan around this time, 'which is nearly always'.[95] If this was a response to the combined effects of war trauma and the painful sense that the war had been her finest moment, it was certainly not an unusual one. Medical researchers have long recognised the strong association between PTSD and alcohol or drug abuse,[96] while the difficult, drunk or druggy PTSD victim has become a commonplace of contemporary fiction, film and drama. All too often, those who love them become victims too, as the son of the surrealist and war photographer Lee Miller attests. Well into adulthood, Tony Penrose regarded his mother – who, as a war correspondent, had recorded the liberation of Dachau and was photographed contemptuously naked in Hitler's bathtub – as 'a useless drunk . . . [a] hysterical person who couldn't do a blooming thing . . . most of the time she was demanding and feckless and throwing dramas at every possible thing.' It was only after Miller died that he discovered how profoundly her war experiences had scarred her, as well as a vast treasure trove of previously unknown work. Penrose said both discoveries finally gave him a more compassionate understanding of who his mother had been.[97]

For Greville, things reached breaking point in 1953, when the end of the messy affair with Juan coincided with the death of her mother, now aged eighty-seven. Greville had remained extraordinarily close to Editha all her life. Wherever her erratic impulses had led her, Editha had followed – uncritical, practical, loyal, a still centre in an often chaotic existence. She had provided her granddaughter Cristina with the constancy and unconditional affection that Greville did not. And through it all, Editha had serenely pursued her own independent course, establishing new circles of friends and projects wherever she had ended up. Greville recalled her in wartime Auckland, 'as well-balanced as ever, buy[ing] new hats in the spring and trip[ping] off briskly to the Red Cross.'[98] She had continued to read voraciously, paint and write verse in the most unpropitious circumstances and, only a few months before she died, insisted Greville send Sargeson a copy of her latest poem – 'she said you always liked her poetry'. With Editha gone, Greville was bereft. She tried to summon up her mother in fiction – the face 'that extreme age had made perfectly innocent', the blue eyes that 'blazed with the blazing sightless blue of blue flowers' – and her inability to do so satisfactorily simply compounded the loss.[99] Soon after Editha's death, Greville made an unsuccessful suicide attempt and was hospitalised.

At some point in the miserable weeks that followed, she decided to leave Australia; indeed, her recovery became contingent on doing so. When Greville had quit New Zealand so abruptly in 1948, Sargeson had commented pointedly on her manifest belief 'that to be in some other place other than where you are is going to make you happy'.[100] Greville now convinced herself she could be happy only by being somewhere other than Australia, which had proved to be 'just as far away as N.Z.' from those things she truly valued and which made her 'see and feel'. She wanted culture, ancient landscapes, sophisticated conversation, intellectual stimulation, she said; in short, she wanted Europe.[101] Although she claimed to be finished as a writer, perhaps at some level she also hoped that returning to Europe might – in some miraculous alchemical process – reignite the current that had sparked her writing into life for a few short years.

Greville's restlessness fed off that of others. 'Everyone nice we know or knew is going or gone to Europe', she complained – the Mansills were about to leave, Cristina and her New Zealand artist husband Keith 'Spud' Patterson were already in Mallorca, Grahame Harrison had gone to Granada where he would spend the next ten years experiencing the Franco regime first-hand (documented in his 2002 book, *Night Train to Granada*). A vague possibility of a job for Werner in Spain arose, prompting Greville to tell Duggan: 'You know we would go back [to Europe] at a minute's

Top: Cristina and Keith Patterson, 1956. Left: Mrs Foster at Mount View.

Photographs by Bill Mansill. Copyright and reproduced with permission of the Bill Mansill Photographic Archive

notice if there would be a chance of a job outside of England'.[102]
That particular chance vanished, but her resolve remained. She
announced she would be returning to Spain in December with six-
year-old Rosa. Werner would join them eventually but would first
visit France and perhaps England.

Life at Mount View was chaotic as they prepared for departure,
'booking, unbooking, not believing much in going to England,
France, Germany, Spain, and not caring much'.[103] The house was to
be leased, there was building work to complete, her mother's seven-
volume set of George Eliot to ship across to Sargeson, unwanted
possessions and papers to dispose of. Greville assured Duggan
she would always keep their correspondence safely among her
tablecloths. But, in a place regularly swept by bushfires, all other
letters, diaries and manuscripts were now to be burned in a fire of
her own making. Gone were 'all the fruits of a lifetime of literacy,'
she reported when the job was done, 'dead leaves, I should say'.

A ghost returns

By 1955, Greville was back in Barcelona, the city she had left under
bombardment more than fifteen years before. Returning to it now
under the Franco regime was like a disturbing dream of a childhood
home; everything apparently in its right place, yet grotesquely
altered. The ebullient city where the anarchist revolution had
erupted in 1936 was now a place of austerity and repression. Its
inhabitants seemed to have succumbed to a kind of state-sponsored
amnesia. Werner compared their willed oblivion to the condition
of 'inner emigration' many Germans had adopted in order to live
under the Nazis; most Catalans dealt with the new regime simply
by 'completely disregarding it', he said. 'One did not talk about
it, took no part in the official party life. People had withdrawn
into their private spheres, were putting up with the system in the
same manner as one who suffers bad weather or any other natural
catastrophe.' While official commemorations noisily honoured
the nationalist dead, the remains of 1,700 executed Barcelona

Republicans – men, women and children; civilians and soldiers alike – lay under quicklime in an unmarked pit on Montjuïc, the hill overlooking the central city. Republican supporters were still being executed and thousands remained in prison. In schools and in public life, the regime energetically promulgated its own Civil War history, one in which Franco and his supporters had 'stepped in to save old Catholic Spain from the alien, hostile forces of atheism and communism'.[104]

The family rented a top-floor flat overlooking the church of Santa Ana in the heart of Barcelona's old quarter – a temporary home only, Greville hoped, until she found a farmhouse to rent. Leaving Rosa with Cristina and Keith, she explored the countryside, looking for the perfect place. She did not find it, though; what she really wanted was to return to her beloved house outside Tossa de Mar, abandoned at the start of the Civil War and now reoccupied by the previous peasant lessee. It was, of course, impossible.

Greville also hoped, without much conviction, to return to writing. Here she was, back at the source of so much of her fiction; perhaps mere proximity would bring it to life again? But if Barcelona was an echo of the revolutionary city it had been in 1936, Greville too was diminished: damaged by imprisonment and subsequent banishment as an alien, depressed by the waning of her writing life so soon after its brief efflorescence, still recovering from her suicide attempt and the loss of her mother. 'One had the very sad spectacle of a person still vital and attractive but who had lost the power of concentration for the creative work which she inwardly needed to do – frittering away all this energy and talent, restless, frustrated,' remembered Kate. Coming back to a place where she had once been happy and energetically engaged with life was a grave mistake, her sister considered. 'When she returned to Europe she had changed very much. . . . [She] had been away so long she was like a ghost'.[105]

Notebooks from this period suggest some faltering attempts at fiction – there are handwritten drafts of a story called 'The Attic'

and another titled 'A Golden Glow', both incomplete. Greville
also tried, for the first time, to make regular money from writing.
An Australian publication commissioned her to write a piece on
Spanish life soon after she arrived, but nothing seems to have
come of it. It was the same when some (unnamed) Beat poets
she met in Barcelona expressed interest in using her translation
of Lorca's *Así Pasan Cinco Años* for a forthcoming theatrical
production.[106] But she did manage to secure some translation
work for a pharmaceutical company, possibly with the help of her
former brother-in-law Sherry Mangan, who once again became
a regular correspondent and reliable counsellor. He was then in
Málaga – all but broke, in poor health and hopelessly overworked.
But he managed to eke out a living through strikingly diverse
contract work. Alongside translating jobs, he accepted freelance
assignments for American publications such as *Time* and *Life* (he
told Greville of recently covering a 'cavemen' party on the Costa
Brava, where 'ladies in leopard-skin bras and bikinis danced
innocently with gentlemen in wild-rabbit-skin jockstraps') while
producing an impressive body of poetry, novels and opera libretti.
At the same time, Mangan toiled tirelessly and largely unpaid for
the Trotskyist cause, including almost single-handedly producing
the journal *Fourth International*.[107] Pleased to have met up with
his former sister-in-law again – he told Manolo Texidor that
Greville had been 'so knocked about by life that the Fosterism has
been practically all knocked out of her and she makes delightful
and intelligent . . . company' – he took it upon himself to get her
back to her typewriter. 'Mark my words, honeychile: if you get 500
to 1000 words on paper every day, neither weather nor anything
else can get you too far down,' he urged Greville. If nothing
else, working was 'a great stabilizer' wrote Mangan, who himself
suffered regular bouts of deep depression. Freelance writing and
translating work was the answer: not only would it pay the bills,
but it would 'get [her] warmed up again' for 'real' writing.

And occasionally, Greville did have bursts of literary activity.
In early 1956, she was writing what she called 'a nasty little piece'

about the work of a friend, John Lodwick, a British writer who allegedly 'has to live out his novels before he can write them which lands him and his dependents in a lot of trouble.'[108] Her unpublished essay 'A Collector's Rejection Piece' also dates from this period. Mangan found it 'very funny indeed' – although, like Sargeson, he thought 'the contrast between the brilliance of the style and the rather unbelievable illiteracy are a bit on the hair-raising side'. Just as Sargeson had done with her essay on the Bathurst camp, Mangan offered to 'tidy' it up for publication, but Greville seems to have lost interest in it – likewise the Lodwick piece. But she reciprocated Mangan's attentions by sending a sharp critique of a story he had shown her in draft, 'For Keeps'. Her comments on language, plot and, above all, the reader's experience were as perspicacious as ever. Mangan claimed to be 'shattered' that a story he had intended 'in the light of Tchechov tradition of pity and satire' had reminded Greville of the American naturalist author Theodore Dreiser ('however powerful, [Dreiser] was one of the world's heaviest-footed writers' Mangan protested).

But when it came to fiction – ultimately, the only kind of writing that mattered to her – Greville claimed she was finished. In one of her increasingly rare letters to Sargeson, she declared with finality, 'Alas I never write any more'.[109] 'Not writing' was no longer a secret dread or a temporary lapse; it was bleak, accomplished fact. To Mangan, she was a little more forthcoming about abandoning fiction. 'It takes it all out of me', she wrote, although her difficulties with *Diary* suggested precisely the opposite. Writing the Spanish novel had not in fact emptied her of painful memories; it had intensified them. But the net effect was same: she was done with fiction – 'for me there will be no more breezes from heaven', she told Mangan after hearing one of his poems had been accepted for publication.

In 1956, Greville was back in Tossa de Mar. After protracted negotiations, she managed to purchase Can Kars, the former home of the Jewish-Czech painter Georges Kars whom she had known in the 1930s. Kars's widow was a hard bargainer and, in purely business terms, the house was not a good buy. But as Mangan reassured Greville, Tossa was somewhere she had been happy and felt instinctively she would be happy again; this alone justified the purchase.

Greville and Werner were at first disconcerted at how much Tossa had been changed, less by the Franco regime than by the beginnings of cheap mass tourism. But many things remained as they remembered. The Delgado family still ran the *pensión* where Greville had stayed in 1936 and left Cristina during the war; Angeleta was among a group of old Catalan friends waiting tearfully at the cold dark bus-stop to welcome her return. It was at the Pensión Delgado that Werner was finally reunited with the lost manuscript of his novel. The couple was relieved to find there had been no reprisals against the Delgados or other Republicans in Tossa after the war. Although 'many in the village knew that I and Greville had fought on the Republican side,' wrote Werner, 'we realized there was a lot of sympathy for us among the people.' In fact, there was little evidence of the Franco regime in Tossa at all. Locals told them that the local headquarters of the Falange (Franco's party) was closed 'due to lack of interest'.

Returning to Tossa temporarily energised Greville. She did not lack for plans – indeed, she told Sargeson, 'there is altogether too much "plan" in Tossa'.[110] But those plans did not include writing. Instead, she decided to open an English teashop offering the comforts of home to English tourists venturing to the Costa Brava for their first, alarming taste of 'abroad'. Recognising her own lack of business skills, Greville enticed her old friend and fellow dancer Dorothy Dickson to come to Tossa and run it; since retiring from the stage, Dorrie had built a second career running a swanky London teashop, making her the ideal business partner. Soon, renovations were in full swing as Can Kars was readied for the summer tourist season, Greville 'holding my own with wild hordes of lampistas, paletas and electricistas [plumbers, builders and electricians]'. She was in a buoyant mood now, tearing around the countryside in a battered Citroën, confident that returning to

The English Tea Room

TOSSA

═ MENU ═

Pot of Tea per person	7 Ptas.
Bread & Butter, white or brown. . .	6 »
Buttered Toast	9 »
Jam, per portion	3 »
Biscuits per portion . . .	5 »
Pastries	7 to 8 »

Sandwiches

Egg & Cress, Tomato, Cucumber, Cheese .	10 »
Ham & Lettuce	15 »

Eggs

Boiled . . .	one egg, 7 ptas.	two	14 »
Scrambled on Toast .	» » 12 »	»	19 »
Fried with Tomato .	» » 15 »	»	22 »
» » Ham. . .	» » 20 »	»	27 »

Omelettes

Plain   12 ptas.   Cheese   15 ptas.   Ham   20 »

Plate of Cold Ham & Mixed Salad . .	25 »
Large Cup of White Coffee . . .	8 »
Orange Juice	8 »
Coca Cola	6 »

Picnic Lunches or Sandwiches Packed

Comfort food for British tourists at Can Kars

Tossa had been no mistake. And just as she had done so many times before, she effected another striking personal transformation. In a letter to Sargeson, she described her new life as business-owner and sometime tourist agent: she was 'letting rooms, all sorts of lurks and being so helpful. This year I represent Wayfarers. You know the agency with the *friendly* atmosphere. [Tourists] step from the train right into my bosom. Dependable, well balanced, well groomed, coppery hair tints, call me Margaret'. Lest Sargeson fail to recognise in this cheerfully efficient figure the sardonic Greville of old, she concluded with a barb: 'the nice people from Wigan are so *rewarding*'.

During the high season, Werner too was inveigled into the tourism business to escort busloads of 'docile Britishers' around Gerona and Barcelona. He and Greville became adept at predicting how the new arrivals would spend their Spanish holidays – 'the young girls would get sunburnt the first morning and go out in the evening to make a desperate attempt to get hold of a Spanish boy . . . The middle-aged tourists and the older ones would drink too much and would moan about the food'. Depressingly, their predictions were nearly always correct. Tossa in the summer, as Sherry Mangan observed on a visit, had become indistinguishable from Blackpool.[111]

They heard occasional echoes of North Shore literary life, from Sargeson and Duggan or through Cristina and Keith, whose home in Mallorca was a popular port of call for travellers. In early 1957, an actual envoy from New Zealand reached Tossa in the form of novelist Janet Frame. Greville had left Auckland before Frame moved there, and so they had never met. But she had heard a great deal from Sargeson about the so-called 'mad girl' he had taken under his wing and who was now writing in the old army hut on his section. Greville was cautiously impressed by what she had seen of Frame's fiction. 'She is very lyrical,' she said of Frame's story 'The Day of the Sheep' (1952), adding, however, that 'the writer who lilts . . . must keep a watch on herself else she goes lilting lilting tilting into sentimentality.'[112] When Frame decided to sail alone

to London in 1956, with plans to continue on to Spain, Sargeson
flew into a frenzy of anxiety on behalf of his one-time lodger,
whom he regarded not only as a mad genius but as vulnerable as
a child. He covertly contacted everyone he could think of who
might help smooth Frame's passage through Europe – including
Cristina, whom he charged with making sure Frame boarded the
ferry to Ibiza.[113] While passing through Barcelona, Frame briefly
met Greville too. She recalled sitting in the Droeschers' Santa Ana
apartment, 'smiling, empty headed and shy' while her host passed
sardonic judgement on New Zealand: 'Greville says the only
worthwhile things in New Zealand are Frank and the scenery.'[114]
As for Greville, she found it hard to reconcile her reserved but
pleasant visitor with the helpless young woman Sargeson had
described, and took evident pleasure in telling him that Frame had
travelled on to Ibiza without incident. In fact, 'Janet seemed quite
hep to everything and had got herself the cheapest lodging on the
island,' Greville wrote pointedly.[115] When Frame subsequently
arrived on the doorstep of Can Kars, she seemed at ease there, too.
The only anxious moment came when Frame confided she had a
heavy manuscript with her. As she intended to hitchhike over the
Pyrenées after leaving Tossa, Greville and Werner suggested she
leave it with them for safe-keeping. But Frame became agitated,
fearing that 'someone might look at it' and would agree to leave
it behind only if it remained in a sealed package. Unfortunately,
when she came to deliver it the next day, the electricity was off at
Can Kars so no one heard the doorbell; it probably 'looked as if we
were all against her', Greville surmised, perhaps warming a little
now to Sargeson's theories about Frame's fragility. Janet had simply
left a note of thanks, said Greville, and headed off.

But behind the competent performances Greville gave when
hosting itinerant New Zealanders or serving tea to red-faced
English tourists, her life in Tossa was steadily unravelling. She
was trying to drink less and had temporarily stopped smoking.
But, according to Kate, she was 'heavily hooked on drugs' (over-
the-counter tranquillisers) and becoming 'less and less anchored

to reality'. At one point, Greville told Mangan she had retired behind dark glasses after what she described as 'an acute emotional disturbance', perhaps another failed love affair.[116] Her physical health was poor, too – various letters from this period refer to hypertension and unspecified kidney and liver troubles that required medical investigation in London. Her doctors advised her she should not live alone.

But for much of the time, she did. Werner was spending more time away from Tossa, visiting friends in England and France and, on one occasion, his family in Germany. He spent the winters in Barcelona teaching at the British Institute and the university, until the uncertainty of his untenured position prompted him to look for academic posts elsewhere. Increasingly, he and Greville were leading separate lives. Werner described it as a 'mutual alienation . . . [We] no longer felt dependent on each other and found it easy – at least for the time being – to go our own ways.' But Greville did not find the estrangement 'easy' at all. She had always tolerated Werner pursuing new relationships, or what Mangan called 'amatory novelty', and she had reciprocated in kind.[117] But this was different. It felt like abandonment. Kate recalled her sister's panic and grief at the thought of losing Werner entirely: 'Greville said to me "But I *must have a husband*. I have always had one". . . . [She] went to pieces when she had not a man in the background. Not at all independent. Very odd.'[118]

In 1960, Werner – by now feeling he was 'wasting the best years of [his] life' in Barcelona[119] – was appointed to a lectureship at the University of Auckland's newly-established German Department. Whatever Greville may have thought about returning to New Zealand, it seemed she would not have the opportunity; Werner made it clear that he did not wish her to accompany him. 'Oh what have I done? What must I do now?' she wrote in despair to Mangan.[120] He tried to mediate, offering considered and scrupulously neutral advice to both Greville and Werner. Minimising the impact of the separation on Rosa and allowing her to complete her education – whether in Spain,

England or New Zealand – were paramount, he insisted. Mangan urged Greville to suspend emotion, evaluate all practical options, and commit 'to a treaty of friendship and alliance' for the next few years. On that basis, he assured her after a long conversation with Werner, her husband might after all 'be willing to have you and Rosa join him in New Zealand'. Greville was heartbroken by so qualified an invitation. She was 'old and sick and defenceless', she told Werner. How could she possibly remain detached and unemotional when 'this, for me, is the end of something', she asked Mangan, before firing off another letter to Werner, urging him to reconsider. Such naked desperation was symptomatic of the underlying problem, Mangan pointed out. Werner had become frustrated with Greville's neediness, which had grown since she had abandoned writing; '[he] would in general enjoy your company at all times if you were a little more independent, doing your work when he is doing his, etc . . . and would not keep *at* him about things.'

'Do your work' had been a constant refrain in Mangan's recent exchanges with Greville. In 1957, he had extravagantly praised her powers of description in a letter she had sent him about a journey from Caldas. Her astonishing sentence – 'The usually green too pretty hill slopes were sad and splendid with burning vines and blood-red trees from forgotten orchards' – was charged with poetry, he wrote. 'Why anyone who can write like that does not write more than you do I simply cannot imagine. . . . Jaysus Christ, woman, get to work.'[121] Now, with her marriage in collapse, Mangan made one last attempt to persuade Greville to return to her writing – not just because it might bring some serenity to her domestic life with Werner, but because her talent demanded it: '[My] only real regret,' he wrote in March 1960, 'is that I have failed in my effort, sometimes direct and nagging, sometimes indirect and stimulating, to get you back on to that typewriter. But I cling to the hope that my so far fruitless efforts may prove fruitful à retardement, like time bombs, and that, once you are settled somehow for the summer, you will begin once more to be productive.' And in one of his final letters to Greville, he reminded her of the possible literary returns from even the deepest unhappiness:

> if, whatever you do, the result is what seems to you emotionally disaster, write down the disaster. Who are you, anyway, just a wife and mother, or also a writer? . . . As we aging beauties and geniuses steer our way through deaths and illnesses and separations and poverties and incompetences and misunderstandings and lonelinesses, we should learn, if we have guts, that it is all material.[122]

But by this time, Werner was back in New Zealand and Greville – following his advice 'to pick up the broken pieces of [her] life' – had sold Can Kars and moved back to Barcelona. 'I'm in hell,' she wrote to Werner.[123] For the time being Rosa remained with her mother; as English schools were too expensive, it was decided they would eventually return together to Australia so she could complete her schooling.

At this point, Greville becomes even more of a ghost in her own story. The few surviving letters from this time show her moving listlessly between England and Spain. In Barcelona she formed a new relationship with a married man she met on a tram, Alonso. A tall, handsome Andalusian, Alonso was younger than Greville, a car-painter by trade and an amateur flamenco singer. He was 'just the consolation' Greville needed, said Kate, who believed they would have married were either of them free to do so. The couple travelled to London where they stayed with the Fosters' old family friend, Richard Carline, while Greville tried to arrange for Alonso and his family (including his estranged wife) to emigrate with her to Australia or New Zealand. She also sought to repair her relationship with her younger daughter, which had suffered since Alonso appeared on the scene; the teenage Rosa was now living in New Zealand with Werner. From London, Greville wrote to her from the very same hotel they had stayed in together two years before when 'we were so unhappy . . . Everything is just the same. The Nescafe out of the tap. The ashtray we used as a plate.'

Once again, going somewhere else seemed the only palliative for her misery: 'Such hell over the past 3 years now. Such insecurity. I miss you so and miss having a place and something to do can't even write any more. . . . I want to go to Australia. . . . This can't go on.' She wrote encouragingly of the life they could share in Australia, even with Alonso in the background. With Mount View and a flat in Sydney, it would surely be possible 'to have some sort of life without anyone being hurt'.[124]

By 1962, Greville was indeed back in Sydney with Alonso. Her younger daughter remained with Werner. The 'hell' of the past few years, Greville found, had simply travelled with her. She was not writing and she knew she had been wrong: it was not possible to have this sort of life without damage, not least to her own already-damaged self. And, after a lifetime of arrivals and departures, Greville had run out of places to go. As Sargeson wrote later, now 'there remained only the one thing for her to do, and that was what she did'.[125]

Rosa with Frank Sargeson and John Reece Cole at a book launch in Auckland in the 1960s
State Library of New South Wales, ref. PXA 1210

On the night of 20 August 1964, she caught the train to Hazelbrook. She wore a long black cape. At the bottom of the hill below Mount View, she remembered a stand of bush, a place sacred to local Aboriginal women. Like the grove of lime trees in long-ago Sedgley and the woods surrounding Kenwood House, like the forested rise on which Can Sans had sat and the Bathurst landscape where trees cast purple shadows on the golden wheat, it was a place Greville felt powerfully drawn to. As she once wrote of Kenwood, it was the kind of place where 'something of eternal moment is going to happen'.[126] She lay down. With a fistful of barbiturates and a bottle of Tío Pepe, the many lives she had occupied and then erased – Margaret Foster, Margot Greville, Margarita Texidor, Mrs Treasure, dependable well-balanced Margaret Droescher – were extinguished. Only Greville Texidor, writer, would remain.

> Night of four moons
> and one lone tree,
> with one lone shadow
> and one lone bird.

(Lorca 'He Died at Dawn', transl. Greville Texidor)

Photograph by Bill Mansill. Copyright and reproduced with permission of the Bill Mansill Photographic Archive

5. The secret of her unsuccess?

'I am envious as hell and my heart runs cold when I think of how possible it was for either of us to be good', wrote Greville to Maurice Duggan from her attic apartment in Barcelona.[1] It was 1956 and she had just received a copy of Duggan's first short story collection, *Immanuel's Land*, recently published to critical acclaim.

With depressing clarity, she recognised the gulf that now separated them. Duggan – variously her respectful admirer, infatuated lover and fellow apprentice – was on an upward trajectory. *Immanuel's Land* had cemented his place as a distinctive voice in New Zealand fiction, although admittedly no longer a young one. He would always be a slow, painstaking writer – compounded, from the 1960s, by his pursuit of a parallel career in advertising – and his output was far from prodigious. The significant novel he hoped to write never eventuated. But Duggan's short fiction would continue to earn him critical praise, awards and honours over the next two decades, admired for its elegant inventiveness, uncompromising demands and refreshing rejection of the straitjacket of social realism.

Meanwhile, she knew the arc of her own writing life was in decline. The last fiction she had published, the much-postponed *These Dark Glasses*, had appeared in 1949. Since then, she had started and failed to finish multiple projects. She could not find

242 ALL THE JUICY PASTURES

publishers for the little work she had managed to complete and had now largely given up trying. Numerous typescripts, drafts and notes had been destroyed when she left Australia – but not everything. Back at Mount View, in the care of Lucy Mustard, a battered blue suitcase contained at least eighteen short stories, translations, poems and three novels at varying stages of completeness. Rejected or simply abandoned, they remained accusatory intimations of what Greville called 'the secret of my unsuccess'.

Literary biographies often conclude with an estimation of their subject's achievements, usually predicated on absolutes – success or failure, boundless possibility or stagnation, acclaim or obscurity, significance or inconsequence. It becomes a kind of accounting process, whereby an input (talent) is offset against an output (the body of published work). The latter is the logical consequence of the former; a sizeable output confirms the existence of a sizeable talent. The writer who has published little has clearly squandered their talent, or perhaps had little to speak of in the first place.

The problem with this reductive approach is that it makes no allowance for the writing life that is inconstant, delayed, derailed or slow-burning. Inevitably, too, it is rife with unacknowledged value judgements; literary achievement becomes a measure of personal virtue. We are invited to shake our heads at writers who have wasted their allotted quota of talent, lacked application, allowed themselves to become diverted or overwhelmed by self-doubt. We consider a solid body of published work evidence of a writing life – indeed, a life in general – that has been well spent.

By all such calculations, Greville Texidor's literary achievement looks decidedly slender. In her lifetime, she published just seven short stories, a novella with a very limited print run, some poetry translations and a handful of other pieces. Two stories appeared in significant anthologies in her lifetime. A collection of her fiction was published long after her death, and a few stories were later anthologised or republished elsewhere.

Other forms of estimation and categorisation – particularly those concerned with stylistic, national and temporal classification

– are also problematic in Greville's case, as they often are for writers whose affiliations and origins are ambivalent. Does her work belong in the canon of New Zealand literature, for example? If this country's literary histories or surveys mention her at all, it is largely to highlight her exoticism, her transience or the allegedly alien gaze she turned on the local scene while here. One describes her connection with New Zealand literature as a kind of 'historical accident', while another states firmly that she was 'not identified with the New Zealand scene'.[2] Even Sargeson characterised Greville as a talented literary tourist in the manner of Lady Barker, Charles Darwin or Samuel Butler.[3] Little surprise, then, that in his introduction to her collected stories, Kendrick Smithyman is at pains to establish Greville's credentials as a *New Zealand* writer – as if this were a necessary condition of our continuing attention. Perhaps all that needs to be said on this count is that Greville Texidor was a New Zealand writer more than she was a writer of any other nation. She had never properly ventured into fiction before coming to New Zealand, and all her published fiction was written here. It was this seemingly uncongenial place alone, and the author who more than any other has been conflated with its national fable, that together enabled Greville's emergence as a writer. Tellingly, once removed from these influences, her writing dwindled and finally ceased completely. It is difficult, in fact, to think of any other mid-century writer who was so comprehensively 'made' in New Zealand (and at the very time, coincidentally, that a new, self-conscious literary culture was in the act of making itself). Nor one who was so utterly unmade without it.

In fact, it's tricky to find any satisfactory slot for Greville's work. She declared herself uninterested in New Zealand's project of cultural nationalism. Yet her work registers responses to the 'beautiful but dumb' landscape[4] and its purportedly stunted inhabitants that strikingly echo those we associate with the local project. So too with the life that informs the fiction; the personal experiences Greville mines in her stories, especially the Paparoa stories, seem to enact and authenticate everything the *Phoenix*–

Caxton writers had claimed as 'the' local reality. Meanwhile the refusal of her prose to settle, tonally and thematically, hinders stylistic categorisation. The work is restless but never placeless, always acutely responsive to location and atmosphere. She regularly utilised the toolkit of European modernism but was doing so in a time and place well removed from the modernist high noon and its centres of production. Greville aspired to aesthetic innovation, obliqueness and interiority; she revelled in symbol, myth and her beloved 'hiatus lagoons lacuna'. But she also wanted to engage with the material world she had lived in so intensely – the places, people and politics that had stirred and changed her – and to reach a popular audience. Reconciling this ambition with the more avant-garde literary practices that also attracted her was one of the constant preoccupations of her literary project.

If it must be made to fit somewhere, Greville's work perhaps sits best on the messy, haphazardly-stacked shelf sometimes labelled 'intermodernist' fiction – or, more tendentiously, the literature of 'the back bedroom'.[5] Here can be found the work of authors like Storm Jameson, Rebecca West, Jean Rhys and Rosamond Lehmann. They are (predominantly women) writers whose delayed or interrupted or stalled careers – and sometimes their excursions into non-literary or populist genres – conspired to set them outside the heroic project of twentieth-century modernism. Like Greville, many sought to express personal and social disruptions wrought by political activism, war and displacement. And like Greville, they often did so not only by means of social realism or political exposition, but through the oblique, unsettling idiom of high modernism. They deployed its aesthetics even as they were excluded from the modernist moment by virtue of their times, their gender, their class and sometimes their distance from the metropolitan centres where modernism had ostensibly happened.

But it's ultimately more fruitful to consider Greville's literary achievement solely on its own singular terms – as an incomplete and variable thing, a mix of astonishing accomplishment and unrealised promise, a brief efflorescence followed by a sad, slow unravelling. What might have happened if she had stayed in New Zealand? Despite the sure-footedness of *These Dark Glasses* and other work, she was still very much an apprentice writer when she left this country, still – with the support of Sargeson and Duggan, but also through her own efforts – learning how to harness sensation and impression to an underlying narrative framework, to integrate image and story. She had discovered that descriptive economy and disciplined revision could lend greater potency to her instinctively lyrical prose. She was finding new ways to approach her material – inhabiting characters who were not extensions of herself, trying out different forms and idioms for the things she alone wanted to say. Increasingly, she was moving away from the Sargesonian model, despite her proven ability to use it. In her capacity as Sargeson's ideal reader, her sharp and unapologetic critique contributed to his reinvention as the writer he wanted to be in the post-war world. But had she stayed in New Zealand, I suspect her own fiction – unlike many of Sargeson's other protégés, apart from Duggan – would have sounded less and less like her mentor's, certainly his 'classic' stories.

And then, right in the midst of this process, she chose to separate herself from the environment that had enabled it. Without recourse to Sargeson and Duggan and the supportive scaffolding they offered, neither innate talent nor powerful feelings were enough to keep Greville writing. What she lacked most was application: the discipline, perseverance and confidence that's needed to keep going as a writer, regardless of the outcome. The activity we blithely call 'writing' is in fact a complex machine of many moving parts. The moment when the writer's mind strikes against the world 'out there' and sets something in motion that demands to be arrested on the page is just one component. 'Writing' is also the disciplined craft needed to deliver that moment to the reader – turning a sentence, getting characters from A to B, wrangling plot and point-of-view and narrative structure. 'Writing' encompasses the pedestrian but necessary tasks of self-critical reading, self-editing, engaging with publishers. And at times, 'writing' is nothing more than dogged perseverance – simply keeping at it. It is clear that Greville liked being a writer; I'm not so sure that she liked *writing*, in this more workmanlike sense. But for much of the time she was in New Zealand, Sargeson in particular ensured she overcame that deficit. She took from him what she needed: discipline and application most of all. And without him, she faltered.

But Greville also faltered because the material she mostly worked with after leaving New Zealand – her experiences in the Spanish Civil War and subsequent imprisonment – came to paralyse her. The more she wrote and rewrote her Civil War novel, the less likely she was to ever complete it, or anything else. Here, Greville's ambition was too big and too destructive. The novel was to be her conclusive reckoning with the pivotal experiences of her life. But those experiences had damaged Greville so deeply that they had hardened around her like a carapace; they could not now be easily retrieved and refashioned into fiction. Once, when Sherry Mangan sent her a story for critique, she commented that it was 'too long and somehow blurred'; the blurriness came from him being 'too close to the source of [his] material', she said.[6] And as she repeatedly tried and failed to realise her Spanish novel – first in Australia and finally in Spain, where she ceased to write altogether – a lack of distance became Greville's problem too. Perhaps this partly suggests why New Zealand proved such fertile ground for her; the further she was from the source of her material, psychologically and geographically, the freer she was to write about it – and to find new sources. By the time she got to Australia, depression and disappointment was already putting paid to that liberating sense of distance. The past was no longer usable material but a malignancy. It could not be excised and it blocked her from responding creatively to the present. Ultimately, it silenced her.

From Australia, Greville once wrote of being in a state where 'the current is cut off', kept alive only by 'pin-pricks' that were faint reminders of the powerful feelings and creative energies that had once compelled her into print. Brittle and damaged, that was the Greville other people recalled knowing in the 1950s. By the time she returned to Europe, said her sister, she was not just 'more negative & retiring who had always been so sociable'; she was a ghost. 'I am sorry you did not know [her] when she was full of vitality and enthusiasm,' Kate wrote regretfully to Sargeson, 'though it was a bit exhausting for the rest of us.'[7] Greville's diminishment is, I think, the most affecting part of her story – more so than simply the drying-up of a promising literary career or her limited output. If her story is indeed one of 'unsuccess', this is at its heart – the withdrawal into unhappiness, reticence and finally silence of a woman who had set out to find all the juicy pastures the world could offer. Yet she managed, for a few brief years, to turn a deeply-felt and intensely-lived life into fiction that continues to reward attention. Sometimes, unsuccess can look a lot like its opposite.

Greville in Barcelona, 1936
State Library of New South Wales, ref. PXA 1210

Acknowledgements

Thanks to:

- Cristina Patterson Texidor and Rosamunda Droescher for sharing family information, reviewing drafts, responding to numerous questions and providing hospitality and kindness during my visits to Spain and Australia. Special thanks to Cristina for showing me Barcelona and Cantonigròs, and to Rosa for taking me to the Blue Mountains and Tossa de Mar; also for guiding me (passportless) through the small towns and former battlefields of Aragón.
- In Spain: Roger Suriol, Ana Patterson, Fernando Latorre, Alexis Rossell, Carlos Velilla and James Horth for generous help with transport, translations, photography and more.
- In Australia: Sue Mansill and Graham Moss for photographs by the late Bill Mansill.
- Creative New Zealand for funding support.
- The Frank Sargeson Trust for permission to consult the Sargeson Papers held at the Alexander Turnbull Library.
- Librarians, archivists and curators at the Alexander Turnbull Library and National Library in Wellington, Auckland University Library, the Hocken Collections in Dunedin, the State Library of New South Wales, Wolverhampton Archives, the UCL Slade School of Fine Art, Cheltenham Ladies' College (Rachel Roberts), the City of Westminster Archives Centre (Georgina Colbeck), Harvard University's Houghton Library, the New York Public Library, the National Museum of Wales, and the Victoria and Albert Museum.

- Professors Harry Ricketts and Mark Williams of the English Programme in the School of English, Film, Theatre, and Media Studies at Victoria University of Wellington, who supervised the doctoral thesis from which this book grew. Thank you also to Victoria University for the scholarship that enabled me to work fulltime on my thesis, and to the Research Committee of the Faculty of Humanities and Social Sciences for grants to undertake research in Spain and New Zealand.
- Nick Duggan, Ian Richards, Graeme Lay and Leonard Bell for help sourcing and identifying photographs.
- Fergus Barrowman, Mark Derby and Farrell Cleary for sharing their knowledge of Greville Texidor, Werner Droescher and the Spanish Civil War, and putting me in touch with other helpful sources.
- Katherine McIndoe for taking the time to do research on my behalf in London.
- My friend, colleague and fellow 'writing lady' Jane Westaway – critic par excellence and provider of good company.
- My family – Graeme, Andrew and Katherine McIndoe, and my father Alex Schwass (1927–2016) – for unflagging interest and encouragement.

A note on sources

Greville Texidor's published work: Unless stated otherwise, all quotations are from *In Fifteen Minutes You Can Say a Lot: Selected Fiction*, ed. Kendrick Smithyman (Wellington: Victoria University Press, 1987).

Unpublished Texidor material: Throughout, I quote from unpublished and unfinished typescripts, notes, workbooks and letters held at the State Library of New South Wales (SLNSW: Greville Texidor Papers, ML-MSS 5235) and the University of Auckland Library (UAkld: Greville Texidor Papers, MSS & Archives A-198). See endnotes for more details.

Werner Droescher's memoir *Towards an Alternative Society*, 1978, is another key source held at the University of Auckland Library (UAkld: MSS & Archives 90/6). The original German version of the memoir, *Odyssee eines Lehrers*, was published by F. Hirthammer, München in 1976. A portion of the English text has since appeared, with an introduction by Farrell Cleary, as *Free Society: A German Exile in Revolutionary Spain* (London: Kate Sharpley Library, 2012). Other material relating to Werner's life is held with Greville's papers at the State Library of New South Wales.

I also quote from correspondence by, to or about Greville in the following collections:

Alexander Turnbull Library, Wellington (ATL)
- *Frank Sargeson Papers*: (accessed and quoted from with permission of the Frank Sargeson Trust) MS-Papers-0432-102,

0432-149, 0432-171, 0432-177, 0432-182, 0432-186, 0432-191, 0432-198, 4261-044, 4261-097
- *Maurice Duggan Papers*: MS-Papers-1760-08, 1760-09, 1760-10
- *John Reece Cole Papers*: MS-Papers-4648-16, 4648-17
- *(Walter) Ian Hamilton Papers*: MS-Papers-5597-03
- *Dr Michael King Papers*: MS-Group-0667, series 13, research papers for *Frank Sargeson; A Life*, 97-042-20/12

Hocken Collections, Dunedin (Hocken)
- *Dawson, E.P.: Letters from Frank Sargeson*: MS-2404/001 (1939–42), MS-2404/002 (1943–45), MS-2404/003 (1946–54).

Houghton Library, Harvard College Library, Cambridge, Mass. (Houghton)
- *Sherry Mangan Papers*: MS Am 1816

Where correspondence is undated, or only partly dated, the likely year it was written is shown in square brackets, followed by a question mark.

Interviews with Greville Texidor's daughters: Unless stated otherwise, all direct quotations from Cristina Patterson Texidor and Rosamunda Droescher are from interviews I recorded with them in Spain and Australia: Cristina – 22, 23, 24 and 30 April, 1 May 2015 (Spain). Rosamunda – 17 March 2014 (Australia, via Skype); 3 and 4 December 2014 (Australia); 25, 27, 28 and 29 April 2015 (Spain); 23 November 2017 (Canada, via Skype); 7 July 2018 (Australia, via Skype).

Margot Schwass and Rosamunda Droescher, Tossa de Mar, 2015
Photograph by Roger Suriol

Cristina Patterson Texidor at the hostel in Cantonigròs, c. 2010
Photograph by John Patterson

Select Bibliography

Allentuck, Marcia, 'Greville Texidor's *These Dark Glasses*: Bloomsbury in New Zealand', *World Literature Written in English*, 19.2 (1980), 227–232

Barnes, Felicity, *New Zealand's London: A Colony and Its Metropolis* (Auckland: Auckland University Press, 2012)

Barrowman, Rachel, *A Popular Vision: The Arts and the Left in New Zealand, 1930–1950* (Wellington: Victoria University Press, 1991)

Beaglehole, Ann, *A Small Price to Pay: Refugees from Hitler in New Zealand, 1936–46* (Wellington: Allen & Unwin/Historical Branch, 1988)

Bell, Leonard and Diana Morrow, eds, *Jewish Lives in New Zealand: A History* (Auckland: Godwit, 2012)

Bell, Leonard, 'Border Crossings: The Visual Arts', in Bell and Morrow, eds, pp. 50–104

——, *In Transit: Questions of Home & Belonging in New Zealand Art* (Wellington: School of Art History, Classics and Religious Studies, Victoria University of Wellington, 2007), p. 18

——, *Strangers Arrive* (Auckland: Auckland University Press, 2017)

Benson, Dale. 'A World Like This: Existentialism in New Zealand Literature' (University of Otago, 2000). Unpublished PhD thesis.

Binswanger, Otti, *'And How Do You Like This Country?' Stories of New Zealand* (Christchurch: Brookes, 1945)

Bluemel, Kristin, *Intermodernism: Literary culture in mid-twentieth-century Britain* (Edinburgh: Edinburgh University Press, 2011)

Borkenau, Franz, *The Spanish Cockpit* (London: Faber and Faber, 1937)

Burke, Janine, *The Heart Garden: Sunday Reed and Heide* (Sydney: Vintage, 2004)

Calder, Alex, 'Defiance and Melodrama: Fiction in the Period of National "Invention", 1920–1950' in Williams, pp. 98–111

——, 'Unsettling Settlement: Poetry and Nationalism in Aotearoa/New Zealand', in *REAL: Yearbook of Research in English and American Literature 14, Literature and the Nation*, ed. by Brook Thomas (Tübingen: Gunter Narr Verlag, 1998), pp. 165–181

Chapman, Robert, 'Fiction and the Social Pattern', in *Essays on New Zealand Literature*, ed. by Wystan Curnow (Auckland: Heinemann Educational Books, 1973)

Cleary, Farrell, introduction to Droescher, pp. 1–5

Cohen, Lisa, *All We Know: Three Lives* (New York: Farrar, Straus and Giroux, 2012)

Connolly, Cyril, *The Rock Pool* (London: Hamish Hamilton, 1947)

Curnow, Allen, *Look Back Harder: Critical Writings 1935–1984*, ed. by Peter Simpson (Auckland: Auckland University Press, 1987)

Davison, Sarah, *Modernist Literatures* (London: Palgrave Macmillan, 2015)

Derby, Mark, ed., *Kiwi Compañeros: New Zealand and the Spanish Civil War* (Christchurch: Canterbury University Press, with the Labour History Project NZ, 2009)

Droescher, Werner, *Free Society: A German Exile in Revolutionary Spain* (London: Kate Sharpley Library, 2012)

Dudding, Robin, ed., 'In Celebration, for Frank Sargeson at 75', *Islands*, 6.3, Special issue (Auckland: Dudding, 1978)

Duggan, Maurice, *Collected Stories* (Auckland: Auckland University Press/Oxford University Press, 1981)

Dyer, Geoff, *Out of Sheer Rage: In the Shadow of D.H. Lawrence* (London: Canongate 2015, first publ. 1997)

Evans, Patrick, *Gifted* (Wellington: Victoria University Press, 2010)

——, *The Penguin History of New Zealand Literature* (Auckland: Penguin Books, 1990)

Frame, Janet, *An Autobiography* (Auckland: Vintage, 1989)

Fundació Caixa Girona, *Berlín, Londres, París, Tossa: La Tranquil·litat Perduda* (Girona: Centre Cultural de Caixa Girona, 2007)

Hilliard, Christopher, '"Rough Architects": New Zealand Literature and its Institutions', in Williams, pp. 138–149

Holroyd, Michael, *Augustus John* (New York: Farrar, Straus and Giroux, 1996)

Horrocks, Roger, 'The Invention of New Zealand', *And* 1 (October 1983): 9–30

Hoskins, Katherine Bail, *Today the Struggle: Literature and Politics in England during the Spanish Civil War* (Austin and London: University of Texas Press, 1969)

Jackson, Angela, *British Women and the Spanish Civil War*, Routledge/Canada Blanch Studies on Contemporary Spain (London, USA and Canada: Routledge, 2002)

Jones, Lawrence, 'Frank Sargeson [Norris Frank Davey], 1903–1982', *Kōtare* 7.2 (2008), 157–211

——, *Picking Up the Traces: The Making of a New Zealand Literary Culture 1932–1945* (Wellington: Victoria University Press, 2003)

——, 'The Wrong Bus: The "Sons of Sargeson", Dan Davin and the Search for the Great New Zealand Novel, 1943–56', in Shieff, ed., *Speaking Frankly*, pp. 27–48

King, Michael, *Frank Sargeson. A Life* (Auckland: Viking, 1995)

Lay, Graeme and Stephen Stratford, eds, *An Affair of the Heart: A Celebration of Frank Sargeson's Centenary* (Auckland: Cape Catley, 2003)

Leggott, Michele, 'Opening the Archive: Robin Hyde, Eileen Duggan and the Persistence of Record' in *Opening the Book: New Essays on New Zealand Writing*, ed. by Mark Williams and Michele Leggott (Auckland: Auckland University Press, 1995), pp. 266–293

Lorca, Federico, *The Selected Poems of Federico Garcia Lorca*, ed. by Francisco Garcia Lorca and Donald M. Allen (New York: New Directions, 2005, first publ. 1955)

Macia, Xavier, 'Hotel in Spain: The Johnstones of Tossa de Mar', *Footnotes: A collection of occasional thoughts and recollections*, (8 August 2012, web), accessed 15 May 2015, <http://footnotes-catalan.blogspot.co.nz/2012/08/hotel-in-spain-johnstones-of-tossa-de.html>

Mackay, Marina and Lyndsey Stonebridge, eds, *British Fiction After Modernism: The Novel at Mid-Century* (New York: Palgrave Macmillan, 2007)

Mannin, Ethel, *All Experience* (London: Jarrolds, 1932)

——, *Young in the Twenties* (London: Hutchinson & Co, 1971)

MacDougall, Sarah, *Mark Gertler* (London: John Murray, 2002)

Murray, Stuart, *Never a Soul at Home: New Zealand Literary Nationalism and the 1930s* (Wellington: Victoria University Press, 1998)

New, W.H., *Dreams of Speech and Violence – The Art of the Short Story in Canada and New Zealand* (Toronto: University of Toronto Press, 1987)

Newton, John, 'Allen Curnow at Joachim Kahn's', *Landfall* 220 (2010), 16–20

——, 'The Death-Throes of Nationalism', *Landfall* 205 (2003), 90–101

——, *Hard Frost: Structures of Feeling in New Zealand Literature, 1908–1945* (Wellington: Victoria University Press, 2017)

——, 'Homophobia and the Social Pattern: Sargeson's Queer Nation', *Landfall* 199 (2000), 91–107

——, 'Surviving the War', *Journal of New Zealand Literature*, 2013, 84–106

Nicholson, Virginia, *Among the Bohemians* (New York: Perennial, 2005)

Orwell, George, *Homage to Catalonia* (London: Penguin Books, 1989, first publ. 1938)

Pound, Francis, *The Invention of New Zealand: Art & National Identity, 1930–1970* (Auckland: Auckland University Press, 2009)

Rhys, Jean, *Quartet* (London: Penguin Books, 2000, first publ. 1928)

Richards, Ian, *To Bed at Noon. The Life and Art of Maurice Duggan* (Auckland: Auckland University Press, 1997)

Roberts, Hugh, 'The Same People Living in Different Places: Allen Curnow's Anthology and New Zealand Literary History', *Modern Language Quarterly*, 64.2 (2003), 219–237

Said, Edward, 'Reflections on Exile', in *Reflections on Exile and Other Literary and Cultural Essays* (London: Granta, 2000), pp. 173–86

Sargeson, Frank, *Conversation in a Train and Other Critical Writing*, ed. by Kevin Cunningham (Auckland: Auckland University Press/Oxford University Press, 1983)

——, 'Greville Texidor 1902–1964', *Landfall* 19.2 (1965), 135–138

——, *More than Enough: A Memoir* (Wellington: Reed, 1975)

——, *Never Enough: Places and People Mainly* (Wellington: Reed, 1977)

——, *Once is Enough: A Memoir* (Wellington: Reed, 1973)

——, ed., *Speaking for Ourselves: Fifteen Stories* (Christchurch: Caxton Press, 1945)

Sedley, Steven, 'Reflecting on the World: Jewish Writers', in Bell and Morrow, eds., pp. 106–131.

Shieff, Sarah, ed., *Letters of Frank Sargeson* (Auckland: Vintage, 2012)

——, ed., *Speaking Frankly: The Frank Sargeson Memorial Lectures, 2003–2010* (Auckland: Cape Catley, 2011)

Shiach, Morag, 'Periodizing Modernism', in *The Oxford Handbook of Modernisms*, ed. by P. Brooker et al. (Oxford and New York: Oxford University Press, 2010), pp. 17–30

Simpson, Peter, *Bloomsbury South: The Arts in Christchurch 1933–53* (Auckland: Auckland University Press, 2016)

Smith, G.M., *More Notes from a Backblocks Hospital* (Christchurch: Caxton Press, 1941)

Smithyman, Kendrick, 'Introduction', in Texidor, pp. 7–22

Sturm, Jennifer, *Anna Kavan's New Zealand* (Auckland: Random House, 2009)

Taylor, N. M., *The New Zealand People at War: The Home Front*, Official History of New Zealand in the Second World War 1939–1945, Volume II (Wellington: Historical Publications Branch, Dept of Internal Affairs, 1986)

Texidor, Greville, *In Fifteen Minutes You Can Say a Lot: Selected Fiction* (Wellington: Victoria University Press, 1987)

Trussell, Denys, *Fairburn* (Auckland: Auckland University Press/Oxford University Press, 1984)

Voit, Friedrich, 'Poet in Exile – Karl Wolfskehl in New Zealand', in *Exile, Identity, Language: Proceedings of the IV Jewish Heritage and Culture Seminar*, ed. by Monica Tempian and Hal B. Levine (Wellington: Victoria University of Wellington in association with the Goethe-Institut, 2009), pp. 38–53

Wald, Alan, 'The Pilgrimage of Sherry Mangan: From Aesthete to Revolutionary Socialist', *Pembroke Magazine*, 8 (1977), 85–98

Weintraub, Stanley, *The Last Great Cause* (London: W.H. Allen, 1968)

Williams, Mark, ed., *A History of New Zealand Literature* (New York: Cambridge University Press, 2016)

Wittmann, Livia Käthe, 'Living Without Regrets', in Otti Binswanger, *'And How Do You Like This Country?' Stories of New Zealand*, ed. by Friedrich Voit (Frankfurt am Main: Lang, 2010), pp. 77–118

Wolfskehl, Karl, *Poetry and Exile: Letters from New Zealand 1938–48*, edited and translated by Nelson Wattie (Lyttelton: Cold Hub Press, 2017)

Notes

Foreword

1   Sargeson to E.P. Dawson, 12 August 1942. Hocken, Dawson: Letters from Frank Sargeson, MS-2404/001.

2   Frank Sargeson, 'Greville Texidor 1902–1964', *Landfall*, 19.2 (1965), pp. 135–38 (p. 135).

3   Janet Frame, *An Autobiography* (Auckland: Vintage, 1989), p. 269.

4   The publisher in question was Reed and Harris, who also published the journal *Angry Penguins*. Texidor to M. Duggan, undated [April 1945?]. ATL, Duggan Papers, MS-Papers-1760-09.

5   This was 'San Toni', probably written in 1944, according to Evelyn M. Hulse who prepared it for its 2006 publication in the online journal *Brief*, 34, pp. 85–119.

6   Texidor, 'A Collector's Rejection Piece' (unpubl.) SLNSW, Greville Texidor Papers, ML-MSS 5235, Box 2, Folder 17.

7   Steve Braunias, 'Snouts in Troughs: Who Got What to Write Things Few People Will Read', *The Spinoff*, 2017, https://thespinoff.co.nz/books/22-05-2017/snouts-in-troughs-who-got-what-to-write-things-few-people-will-read/ [accessed 30 May 2017].

8   Texidor to Duggan, 26 January [1953?]. ATL, MS-Papers-1760-09.

9   'Those we knew when we were young, / None of them have stayed together, / All their marriages battered down like trees / By the winds of a terrible century'. 'He Waiata mo Te Kare', *Collected Poems*, pp. 537–40.

10 Ethel Mannin, 'Audition', in *All Experience* (London: Jarrolds, 1932), pp. 93–95.

11 Virginia Nicholson, *Among the Bohemians* (New York: Perennial, 2005), p. 257.

12 Nicholson, p. 276.

13 Ethel Mannin, *Young in the Twenties* (London: Hutchinson & Co, 1971), pp. 20–21.

14 Kurzke to Sargeson, undated [1977?]. Wellington, ATL, Frank Sargeson Papers, MS-Papers-4261-097.

15 Ian Wedde, quoted in Hugh Roberts, 'Nationalism', in *The Oxford Companion to New Zealand Literature*, ed. by Roger Robinson and Nelson Wattie (Oxford: Oxford University Press, 1998), pp. 391–93 (p. 393).

16 Patrick Evans, *The Penguin History of New Zealand Literature* (Auckland: Penguin, 1990), p. 7.

17 *The Phoenix* (Auckland: Auckland University College, 1932), 1.1, n.p.

18 E.K. Cook, 'The Phoenix', *Canta*, 1932, p. 2.

19 Elleke Boehmer, *Colonial and Postcolonial Literature: Migrant Metaphors*, 2nd ed. (Oxford: Oxford University Press, 2005), p. 204.

20 Charles Brasch, *Indirections: A Memoir, 1909–1947* (Wellington: Oxford University Press, 1980), p. 25.

21 'Colonial literaturishness' was Curnow's disdainful judgement on earlier New Zealand writing; see 'New Zealand Literature: The Case for a Working Definition', in *Look Back Harder: Critical Writings 1935–1984*, ed. by Peter Simpson (Auckland: Auckland University Press, 1987), pp. 191–208 (p. 200). Poet, short-story writer and playwright Isobel Andrews (b. 1905) coined the evocative term 'tui and treacle', which Lawrence Jones quotes in *Picking Up the Traces: The Making of a New Zealand Literary Culture 1932–1945* (Wellington: Victoria University Press, 2003), p. 222.

22 Denis Glover, *Hot Water Sailor* (Wellington: Reed, 1962), p. 99.

23 Allen Curnow, 'Author's Note', in *Collected Poems 1933–1973* (Wellington: A.H. & A.W. Reed, 1974), p. xiii.

24 M.H. Holcroft, *The Waiting Hills* (Wellington: Progressive Publishing Society, 1943), p. 42.

25 Quoted in Francis Pound, *The Invention of New Zealand: Art & National Identity, 1930–1970* (Auckland: Auckland University Press, 2009), p. 84.

26 John Newton, 'Surviving the War', *Journal of New Zealand Literature*, 2013, pp. 84–106 (p. 94).

27 Sargeson to Dawson, 26 July 1942. Hocken, MS-2404/001.

28 Michele Leggott, 'Opening the Archive: Robin Hyde, Eileen Duggan and the Persistence of Record', in *Opening the Book: New Essays on New Zealand Writing*, ed. by Mark Williams and Michele Leggott (Auckland: Auckland University Press, 1995), p. 266.

29 A.R.D. Fairburn, 'Notes by the Way', *Tomorrow*, 1936, p. 15.

30 Timothy Brennan, 'The National Longing for Form', in *Nation and Narration*, ed. by Homi K. Bhabha (London; New York: Routledge, 1990), pp. 44–70 (pp. 60–61).

31 Edward Said, 'Reflections on Exile', in *Reflections on Exile and Other Literary and Cultural Essays* (London: Granta, 2000), pp. 173–86 (p. 176).

32 *Jewish Lives in New Zealand: A History*, ed. by Leonard Bell and Diana Morrow (Auckland: Godwit, 2012), p. 18.

33 Michael Dunn, 'Theo Schoon: Outsider Artist', *Art New Zealand*, 102 (2002), pp. 69–74 (p. 69).

34 Sarah Shieff, 'Nathan's Kin: Jews and Music in New Zealand', in Bell and Morrow, pp. 27–49 (p. 45).

35 Jennifer Sturm, *Anna Kavan's New Zealand* (Auckland: Random House, 2009), pp. 18–43.

36   Sargeson to Dawson, 16 July 1941. Hocken, MS-2404/001. By the end of the
      1930s, Sargeson knew several Europeans of diverse backgrounds who had
      found refuge in New Zealand. It was during this period that he wrote 'The
      Making of a New Zealander' (1940), tracing a fleeting encounter between an
      alienated European exile and a 'colonial' narrator.

37   George Steiner, 'A Kind of Survivor' (1965), in *George Steiner: A Reader*
      (United States: Oxford University Press, 1984), p. 226. Quoted in Ann
      Beaglehole, *A Small Price to Pay: Refugees from Hitler in New Zealand,
      1936–46* (Wellington: Allen & Unwin / Historical Branch, 1988), p. 143.
      My account of wartime exilic life draws heavily on Beaglehole's text, especially
      chapter 3.

38   R.A. Lochore, *From Europe to New Zealand: An Account of Our Continental
      European Settlers* (Wellington: A.H. & A.W. Reed, in conjunction with the
      New Zealand Institute of International Affairs, 1951), p. 89.

39   Lochore, p. 87. When Lochore wrote this in *From Europe to New Zealand*,
      he was no longer a government official. However, his book received official
      endorsement in the form of an introduction by the Secretary for Internal
      Affairs, welcoming Lochore's contribution to the post-war immigration
      debate. Lochore has since been condemned for views and rhetoric that can
      only be called racist and anti-Semitic by contemporary standards. In his
      1990 autobiography, businessman and former refugee Fred Turnovsky noted
      Lochore's previously unknown links with pre-war Nazi Germany (*Fifty Years
      in New Zealand*, pp. 89–95). Michael King, though, considered Lochore's
      opinions 'more silly than sinister' (quoted in Bell and Morrow, p. 231). Lochore
      later helped establish the Security Intelligence Service and was New Zealand
      ambassador to Germany.

40   Initially, internment was restricted to people known to actively support nazism
      or fascism, but the policy was later widened to include aliens whose loyalty or
      character was considered questionable. N.M. Taylor, *The New Zealand People
      at War: The Home Front*, Official History of New Zealand in the Second
      World War 1939–1945, Volume II (Wellington: Historical Publications
      Branch, Dept. of Internal Affairs, 1986), pp. 853–54.

41   See, for example, Leonard Bell, 'Border Crossings: The Visual Arts', in *Jewish
      Lives*, Bell and Morrow, eds, pp. 50–104.

42   Porsolt died in 2005 and is buried in Auckland, where his gravestone describes
      him as a 'Messenger of Modernism'. Leonard Bell, *Strangers Arrive* (Auckland:
      Auckland University Press, 2017), pp. 173, 150.

43   Wolfskehl was almost seventy by the time he arrived in New Zealand as a
      refugee from Hitler – impoverished, nearly blind, but receptive to whatever
      opportunities his new home might offer. Somewhat astonishingly, he
      experienced a late-career renaissance; by the time he died in Auckland in 1948,
      he had written three major cycles of poems, all published posthumously in
      Europe. Until recently, his impact on the New Zealand literary landscape was
      limited by the fact that he wrote in German. Apart from his fellow refugees,

few locals could read his work until it appeared in translation; a selection, *Three Worlds / Drei Welten* (translated and edited by Andrew Paul Wood and Friedrich Voit) was published in 2016.

44   Stead, in Sturm, pp. 9–10.

45   Anna Kavan, 'New Zealand: Answer to an Inquiry', *Horizon: A Review of Literature and Art*, 8.45 (1943), pp. 153–62 (pp. 156, 161).

46   Stead, in Sturm, p. 9.

47   Said, p. 176.

48   Bell and Morrow, p. 340. See also Peter Simpson, *Bloomsbury South: The Arts in Christchurch 1933–53* (Auckland: Auckland University Press, 2016).

49   Leonard Bell, *In Transit: Questions of Home & Belonging in New Zealand Art*, Gordon H. Brown Lecture, 05 (Wellington: School of Art History, Classics and Religious Studies, Victoria University of Wellington, 2007), p. 18.

50   Strewe met Sargeson on an Auckland beach soon after arriving in New Zealand in 1938. The left-leaning Strewe had already been ostracised by his 'xenophobic' North Shore neighbours and would be interned on Somes Island during the war. Later, he abandoned his literary ambitions to become a landscape gardener; he and Sargeson remained lifelong friends. Strewe's experiences inspired Maurice Gee's 1998 novel *Live Bodies*. See Odo Strewe, 'Do You Remember', in *In Celebration, for Frank Sargeson at 75*, ed. by Robin Dudding, *Islands*, 3 (Auckland: Dudding, 1978).

51   Ian Richards, *To Bed at Noon. The Life and Art of Maurice Duggan* (Auckland: Auckland University Press, 1997), p. 92.

52   Said, p. 186.

53   Nelson Wattie, 'Frank Sargeson's Encounter with Karl Wolfskehl', *Two Essays, Stout Centre Occasional Papers*, 1 (1991), pp. 35–48 (pp. 48, 41).

54   Peter Vere-Jones, 'Maria Dronke', in *Out of the Shadow of War: The German Connection with New Zealand in the Twentieth Century*, ed. by James N. Bade (Melbourne; Auckland: Oxford University Press, 1998), pp. 113–17 (p. 116).

1. And now Greville has turned up . . .

1   Except where stated otherwise, information in this chapter is sourced from my interviews with Cristina Patterson Texidor and Rosamunda Droescher (2014–18), Kate Kurzke's (mostly undated) letters to Frank Sargeson in the 1970s (ATL, Sargeson Papers, MS-Papers-4261-097) and Rosamunda's comments on the draft introduction to VUP's Texidor collection (Droescher to F. Barrowman, 7 July 1987. SLNSW, ML-MSS 5235, Box 5, Folder 12).

2   Here I draw on the research of Christine Buckley, who wrote text for an interpretation board about The Limes that the Sedgley Local History Society erected in 2014. Ms Buckley passed on information she had unearthed about the house and the Foster/Prideaux families to Charlotte Kurzke (Greville's niece), who in turn shared it with Cristina Patterson Texidor. I am grateful to Cristina for allowing me access to Ms Buckley's letters.

3   Una Platts, *Nineteenth Century New Zealand Artists: A Guide & Handbook* (Christchurch: Avon Fine Prints, 1980), p. 199.

4   Michael Holroyd, *Augustus John* (New York: Farrar, Straus and Giroux, 1996), p. 47. However, the course of study for women differed slightly from that for men; their life-drawing models were partially draped, and they worked under the eye of a female attendant. See Philip Attwood, '"The Slade Girls"', *British Numismatic Journal*, 56 (1986), pp. 148–77; Charlotte Weeks, 'Women at Work: The Slade Girls', *The Magazine of Art*, 6 (1883), pp. 324–29.

5   Claire Brock, *British Women Surgeons and their Patients, 1860–1918* (Cambridge: Cambridge University Press, 2017), p. 14.

6   Email to author from Cheltenham Ladies' College archivist Rachel Roberts, 'Margaret Greville Foster', 18 October 2013.

7   Texidor to Mangan, April 1956. Houghton, MS Am 1816, Folder 94 (3). See also Kendrick Smithyman, introduction to *In Fifteen Minutes You Can Say A Lot* (Wellington: Victoria University Press, 1987), p. 8.

8   It appears Hickman received information that Labour's candidate Dr Kynaston had seduced another man's wife, married her, had an illegitimate child and maltreated his wife's daughter. William Foster was asked to investigate and verify these allegations. Hickman went on to repeat them at an election meeting and also distributed an inflammatory leaflet entitled 'Dr Kynaston's Credentials'. See 'An Election Libel Action', *The Times* (London, 5 November 1919), p. 6.

9   'The Election Libel Action: Disagreement of the Jury', *The Times*, (London, 6 November 1919), p. 5.

10   'Mr W.A. Foster Meets with Terrible Death on Railway', *Express and Star* (Wolverhampton, 9 January 1919), p. 4.

11   Holroyd, *Augustus John*, p. 444.

12   Sargeson, 'Greville Texidor 1902–1964', p. 135.

13   Platts, p. 199.

14   Nicholson, *Among the Bohemians*, p. 269.

15   Elizabeth Cowling, Carline family, *Oxford Dictionary of National Biography (online)* (Oxford: Oxford University Press, 2004), https://doi.org/10.1093/ref:odnb/64713. The portrait is in the possession of Cristina Patterson Texidor.

16   Quoted in John Woodeson, *Mark Gertler: Biography of a Painter, 1891–1939* (London: Sidgwick & Jackson, 1972), p. 136.

17   Douglas Goldring, *The Nineteen Twenties* (London: Nicholson & Watson, 1945), p. 187.

18   Quentin Bell, *Bloomsbury* (London: Weidenfeld & Nicolson Ltd, 1968), pp. 83, 102.

19   Frances Partridge, *Memories* (London: Victor Gollancz, 1981), p. 90.

20   Evelyn Waugh, *Vile Bodies* (London: Penguin, 1996), p. 78.

21   Waugh, p. 44.

22 Michael Holroyd, 'John, Augustus Edwin', *Oxford Dictionary of National Biography (online)* (Oxford: Oxford University Press, 2004, article revised 2006), https://doi.org/10.1093/ref:odnb/34196.

23 Michael Holroyd, *Augustus John* (New York: Farrar, Straus and Giroux, 1996), p. 120.

24 John produced several portraits and drawings of T.E. Lawrence from 1919 onwards.

25 Christopher Wood, quoted in Holroyd, *Augustus John*, pp. 446–47.

26 Unpublished workbook, undated (Australia). UAkld, Texidor Papers, MSS & Archives A-198, Box 1, Folder 6.

27 Richards, *To Bed at Noon*, p. 62.

28 Holroyd, *Augustus John*, p. 113.

29 As told to Una Platts, in Smithyman, p. 9.

30 M. Gertler to R. Droescher, 1975. SLNSW, Texidor Papers, ML-MSS 5235, Box 5, Folder 21. All subsequent quotes from Marjorie Gertler are from this source.

31 J.P. Wearing, *The London Stage 1920–29* (Metuchen, N.J., and London: The Scarecrow Press, 1984), 1: 1920–1924, pp. 160, 302, 403.

32 Holland House was largely obliterated in an air raid in 1940, although Stavvy's extraordinary library was mostly saved. Holland Park now occupies the site, and a small plaque to Lord Ilchester can be found outside the park walls. Simon Nowell-Smith, 'Strangways, Giles Stephen Holland-Fox, Sixth Earl of Ilchester (1874–1959)', *Oxford Dictionary of National Biography (online)* (Oxford: Oxford University Press, 2004), https://doi.org/10.1093/ref:odnb/33237.

33 S. Mangan to Texidor, 9 November 1959, Houghton, MS Am 1816, Folder 94 (3).

34 Richard Davenport-Hines, *The Pursuit of Oblivion: A Social History of Drugs* (London: Phoenix Press, 2002), p. 149.

35 The novel was *Dope, A Story of Chinatown and the Drug Traffic* by Arthur Sarsfield Ward (writing as Sax Rohmer). It was based on the cocaine-related death of the rising young West End star Billie Carleton in 1918. Her death helped bring about the passing of the Dangerous Drugs Act (1920) in Britain which restricted the manufacture, sale, possession and distribution of opiates and cocaine to authorised people (Davenport-Hines, pp. 169, 171–72, 175).

36 Davenport-Hines, pp. 189–90.

37 See, for example, 'Most Beautiful Blonde and Brunette in All England', *The Buffalo Enquirer* (New York, 15 August 1921), p. 2.

38 Sarah Street, *Colour Films in Britain: The Negotiation of Innovation 1900–53* (London: Palgrave Macmillan / British Film Institute, 2012), pp. 22–32.

39 Another cast member was Dodie Smith, who had recently graduated from drama school and would go on to write *I Capture the Castle* (1949) and eight other novels, plus a dozen plays and screenplays.

40 Review in *Pictures and Picturegoer*, March 1924, p. 38. Quoted in Street, p. 36; see also pp. 32–36.

41   Texidor to Duggan, undated [1951?]. ATL, MS-Papers-1760-09.
42   The Thomson score, 'Ten Easy Pieces and a Coda', remains a family treasure.
     In her commentary on Smithyman's draft introduction, Rosamunda Droescher
     said her mother 'talked about [Gershwin] a fair bit and seems to have greatly liked
     him (a sentimental liaison with him has been suggested but not confirmed)'.
43   Texidor to Editha and Kate Foster (Kurzke), undated postcards, SLNSW,
     ML-MSS 5235, Box 5, Folder 21.
44   At the time, heroin addiction was often treated in the United States by
     what was known as the 'withdrawal cure'; in Europe, treatments included
     maintenance prescriptions of other narcotics. Davenport-Hines, p. 290.
45   Ethel Mannin, 'Barcelona', in *All Experience* (London: Jarrolds, 1932),
     pp. 154–59 (pp. 154, 158).
46   The architect was Manuel Joaquín Raspall (1877–1937).
47   Texidor to Duggan, undated. ATL, MS-Papers-1760-09.
48   Alan Wald, 'The Pilgrimage of Sherry Mangan: From Aesthete to
     Revolutionary Socialist', *Pembroke Magazine*, 8 (1977), pp. 85–98 (p. 85).
49   M. Texidor to Mangan, 1 October 1954, Houghton, MS AM 1816, Folder 372.
50   Mangan to M. Texidor, 29 September 1954. Houghton, MS Am 1816, Folder
     794.
51   Goldring, p. 225.
52   The municipal register of residents records the presence of Marguerida Foster
     and her daughter Cristina from at least 1932; it seems that Editha also lived
     with them for some of this period. Fundació Caixa Girona, *Berlin, Londres,
     Paris, Tossa: La Tranquil – Litat Perduda* (Girona: Centre Cultural de Caixa
     Girona, 2007), p. 226. The descriptions of Tossa in this paragraph draw on this
     source too; see especially pp. 221–27.
53   Catalan poet Joan Maragall recorded these impressions in the early years of the
     twentieth century. In Fundació Caixa Girona, p. 219.
54   'Lorca and His People', unpublished and undated typescript. UAkld, MSS &
     Archives A-198, Box 2, Folder 8.
55   In Greville's unfinished and unpublished Civil War novel, *Diary of a Militia
     Woman*, the ardent young protagonist is berated by an anarchist compañero for
     her misguided affection for the 'old Spain of the tourists' that Lorca allegedly
     celebrated. SLNSW, ML-MSS 5235, Box 1, Folder 5.
56   Nicholson, *Among the Bohemians*, pp. 234, 232.
57   Gertler to Thomas Balston, 11 August 1938. Mark Gertler, *Selected Letters*, ed.
     by Noel Carrington (London: R. Hart-Davis, 1965), p. 245. Their encounter
     took place in Cassis during the summer of 1938, Gertler's last: he committed
     suicide in June 1939. See Sarah MacDougall, *Mark Gertler* (London: John
     Murray, 2002), pp. 326–27.
58   Mannin, *Young in the Twenties*, pp. 34, 45.
59   Unless stated otherwise, all comments and views attributed to Werner in this
     chapter are from his memoir *Towards an Alternative Society* (1978). UAkld,
     MSS & Archives 90/6.

60   Texidor, 'Lorca and His People'.

61   Quotations in this paragraph and next are from Texidor's unpublished memoir of Frances Hodgkins, 2 December 1951. SLNSW, ML-MSS 5235, Box 2, Folder 17.

62   The differences between these factions were nuanced and not easily grasped by outsiders. As Franz Borkenau describes, the CNT had been established as an anarchist trade union centre after the 1909 general strike and, in its insistence that 'the state of war between employers and wage-earners must be continual', was strongly influenced by French syndicalism. The FAI was formed in 1925 to bring together 'all those elements who are not simply CNT trade unionists but convinced and active anarchists'. It opposed any reformist tendencies within the Spanish anarchist movement and sought 'to keep it close to its original rebel faith'. *The Spanish Cockpit* (London: Faber and Faber, 1937), pp. 34, 37.

63   Texidor, unpublished memoir of Frances Hodgkins.

64   This description of Barcelona draws on both Werner's memoir and Franz Borkenau's *The Spanish Cockpit*, pp. 69–70. Greville greatly admired Borkenau's first-hand account of the Civil War, published soon after it ended.

65   POUM was formed in 1935 by communists who rejected the policies and strategies of Stalin's Soviet Union. George Orwell also fought with the POUM militia in 1937, recounting his experiences in *Homage to Catalonia* (1938).

66   Although women fighters were originally welcome to join anarchist militias, they were banned not long after the war began. This was at least partly 'because of the unforeseen enlistment of prostitutes, or those who had recently been prostitutes, in the first militias to go to the Aragón front, with the resultant spread of venereal disease'. R. Droescher, quoted in Mark Derby, ed., *Kiwi Compañeros: New Zealand and the Spanish Civil War* (Christchurch: Canterbury University Press, with the Labour History Project NZ, 2009), p. 99.

67   Borkenau, pp. 19, 22. Borkenau discusses Bakunin's influence on Spanish anarchism and his views on the possibility of anarchist revolution in Spain where working people, like the Russians, 'held freedom higher than wealth, where they were not yet imbued with the capitalist spirit' (p. 19). See also pp. 14–17 and 19–20.

68   Texidor to Mangan, 23 June [1938?]. Houghton, MS Am 1816, Folder 94 (1).

69   Borkenau, pp. 299–300.

70   Derby, pp. 96–97, 105.

71   Umberto Marzocchi, *Remembering Spain: Italian Anarchist Volunteers in the Spanish Civil War*, expanded second edition (London: Kate Sharpley Library, 2005), p. 10.

72   Borkenau, p. 169.

73   George Orwell, *Homage to Catalonia* (London: Penguin, 1989), p. 196.

74   Randolph Churchill, quoted in Angela Jackson, *British Women and the Spanish Civil War*, Routledge/Canada Blanch Studies on Contemporary Spain (London, USA and Canada: Routledge, 2002), p. 5. Jackson argues that

Churchill in fact misrepresented public attitudes: opinion polls in 1938–39 revealed considerable support for the Republic, although some questions were admittedly leading.

75 'Jesús Jiménez' was probably written in 1941–42, but it remained unpublished until *In Fifteen Minutes You Can Say a Lot* appeared in 1987. Cantonigròs also informs the setting of another story, 'San Toni', which Greville wrote around 1944. It too remained unknown until published online in 2006 (*Brief*, 34, pp. 85–119).

76 Antony Beevor, *The Battle for Spain* (London: Weidenfeld and Nicolson, 2006), p. 332. See also Jackson, p. 162.

77 *The Selected Poems of Federico García Lorca*, ed. by Francisco García Lorca and Donald M. Allen (New York: New Directions), p. 181.

78 Marjorie was soon to leave for the Continent to paint and would not return to England until after the Second World War: she was 'planning to go to Paris and is now studying Trotsky in bed – I do not know if there is any connection', reported Greville to Mangan in January 1939. Houghton, MS Am 1816, Folder 94 (1).

79 Texidor to Mangan, 23 June [1938?]. Houghton, Ms Am 1816, Folder 94 (1).

80 *Diary of a Militia Woman*, unpublished and undated. SLNSW, ML-MSS 5235, Box 1, Folder 5.

81 Holroyd, *Augustus John*, pp. 38, 588.

82 Albert Meltzer, *I Couldn't Paint Golden Angels: Sixty Years of Commonplace Life and Anarchist Agitation* (Edinburgh: A.K. Press, 1996), Chapter 3. Downloaded from https://www.katesharpleylibrary.net/jwsvjx. According to Holroyd, Augustus John tried and failed to complete the Queen's portrait for decades; it was finally presented to her in 1961, by which time she was the Queen Mother. Holroyd describes it as still 'disarmingly unfinished, and no masterpiece' (*Augustus John*, p. 473).

83 Texidor to Mangan, undated [1939?]. The following paragraph quotes from this letter and two others dated 23 June and 26 November, both to Mangan and probably from 1938. Houghton, MS Am1816, Folder 94 (1).

84 Alien internment record card for Werner Droescher, 16 November 1939, National Archives UK (HO 396170 Dem-Ehf)

85 Alien internment record card for Margaret Droescher, 5 December 1939, National Archives UK (HO 396170 Dem-Ehf)

86 *The Internment of Aliens in Twentieth Century Britain*, ed. by David Cesarani and Tony Kushner (London: Routledge, 1993), pp. 150–51.

87 Miriam Kochan, *Britain's Internees in the Second World War* (London: Macmillan, 1983), p. 34.

88 Reportedly at Churchill's request, Diana and her husband Oswald Mosley (leader of the British Union of Fascists) were later allowed to live together in a cottage in the prison grounds until their release in 1943 for health reasons.

89 The manuscript is held in the State Library of New South Wales, ML-MSS 5235, Box 2, Folder 15.

2. Not so much as a moo

1   My discussion of New Zealand's wartime demographics draws on Taylor, *The New Zealand People at War*; here, pp. 853–54.

2   Introduction to *New Zealand Short Stories*, ed. by O.N. Gillespie (London: Dent, 1930), p. v.

3   Charles Ferrall and Rebecca Ellis, *The Trials of Eric Mareo* (Wellington: Victoria University Press, 2002), p. 107.

4   Anyone born in New Zealand was automatically a British subject, not a New Zealand citizen, until the 1948 British Nationality and New Zealand Citizenship Act. Aliens who met certain requirements, including length of residence, could become British subjects / New Zealand citizens by applying for naturalisation – except during wartime. Taylor, p. 851.

5   Quoted in Taylor, p. 862.

6   According to Vincent O'Sullivan, this was E.H. McCormick's response to an incident involving Sargeson and the builder George Haydn. See O'Sullivan, 'Funnier, Meaner Sargeson Beyond This Good Life: Review of *Frank Sargeson: A Life* by Michael King', *New Zealand Books*, 1995, 1–4, p.4, and also *An Affair of the Heart: A Celebration of Frank Sargeson's Centenary*, ed. by Graeme Lay and Stephen Stratford (Auckland: Cape Catley, 2003), p. 45.

7   All quotes in this paragraph are from Taylor, pp. 860, 859, 875.

8   Unless stated otherwise, all comments and views attributed to Werner in this chapter are from his memoir *Towards an Alternative Society* (1978). UAkld, MSS & Archives 90/6.

9   Texidor to Mangan. 4 August 1941. Houghton, MS Am 1816, Folder 94 (1).

10 Quoted in Lyman Tower Sargent, 'Utopianism and the Creation of New Zealand National Identity', *Utopian Studies*, 2001, 12.1, pp. 1–18 (p. 5).

11 See Waitangi Tribunal, *The Kaipara Report* (Wellington: Waitangi Tribunal, 2006), chapter 2, https://forms.justice.govt.nz/search/Documents/WT/wt_DOC_68333936/Wai674final.pdf (accessed 10 November 2017).

12 Sir Henry Brett and Henry Hook, *The Albertlanders: Brave Pioneers of the 'Sixties* (Auckland: The Brett Printing Company Ltd, 1927), pp. 233–34.

13 This and other recollections from 'Oral reminiscences of Gladys Salter', compiled by Rosamunda Droescher in January 1979 and held with the Texidor papers at the University of Auckland Library. MSS & Archives A-198.

14 This paragraph draws on Roy Shuker, *Educating the Workers? A History of the Workers' Education Association of New Zealand* (Palmerston North: The Dunmore Press, 1984); the comment about 'gossip' was made by long-serving WEA tutor-organiser Arnold Hely (p. 122). Shuker comments that during and after the Depression, the WEA was increasingly divided over whether it should also act as a force for social and political change. Its leaders in the Auckland region, which covered Paparoa, firmly believed it should; they reasserted the branch's trade union links and commitment to the working class, to the dismay of some members (pp. 42, 104).

15 His lecture was probably based on the recent 'Approach to Poetry' course he had taught for the WEA in Auckland, covering linguistic and poetic theory, along with the plays of Shakespeare and Webster. ATL, Auckland WEA programmes, MS-Papers-7709-03.

16 Both quotes are from Sargeson, *Never Enough: Places and People Mainly* (Wellington: Reed, 1977), pp. 60–61.

17 The family occupied two cottages in their time in Paparoa. The first was high on a ridge-top and the second was down in a valley surrounded by eroded hills. It was at the second cottage that Greville painted the floors blue and set up her writing tent.

18 Quoted in 'Introduction to "San Toni"', ed. by Evelyn M. Hulse, *Brief*, 2006, 34, pp. 85–119 (p. 97).

19 Kurzke to Sargeson, undated. ATL MS-Papers-1760-09.

20 Texidor to Mangan, 4 August 1941. Houghton, MS Am 1816, Folder 94 (1).

21 The teacher is quoted in Hulse, p. 98.

22 Texidor to Sargeson, 8 July [1949?]. ATL, MS-Papers-0432-182.

23 Both the statements and the Authority's decisions are held at Archives New Zealand. AAAC489, Box 215, Record AL19479 (Greville) & AAAC489, Box 38, Record AL3546 (Werner).

24 More than nine-tenths of New Zealand's wartime refugees were put in this class. Taylor, p. 868.

25 Berkeley Dallard to Major Folkes, 20 May 1942; Folkes to Dallard, 31 October 1942. Archives NZ, AAAR 493, Box 31, Record 1941 50 73.

26 *Never Enough*, p. 64. Recalling this episode more than seventy years later, Cristina remembered that Greville would strip to the waist and deliberately shake her breasts up and down for the benefit of the hidden watchers.

27 *Never Enough*, p. 68.

28 Unpublished workbook, undated (Australia). UAkld, MSS & Archives A-198, Box 1, Folder 6.

29 Texidor to Duggan, undated [1945?]. ATL, MS-Papers-1760-09.

30 'Katherine Mansfield is dead. Before her there was no one comparable with her. Since her I am aware of no one unless we have now met him . . . It is Sargeson or nobody, and I now say Sargeson,' wrote *Listener* editor Oliver Duff that year. 'Look We For Another?', *New Zealand Listener*, 25 October 1940, p. 19.

31 Sargeson, *Never Enough*, p. 63.

32 Unpublished workbook, undated (New Zealand?). UAkld, MSS & Archives A-198, Box 1, Folder 7.

33 Sargeson to E.P. Dawson, 23 February 1942. ATL, Michael King, Research papers, 97-042-20/02.

34 Unpublished workbook, undated (Australia?). UAkld, MSS & Archives A-198, Box 1, Folder 6.

35 Evans, *Penguin History of New Zealand Literature*, p. 143.

36 Otti Binswanger, *'And How Do You Like This Country?' Stories of New Zealand* (Christchurch: Brookes, 1945), pp. 76–85.

37   Allen Curnow, 'House and Land', in *A Book of New Zealand Verse, 1923–45*, ed. by Allen Curnow (Christchurch: Caxton Press, 1945), p. 159.

38   It needs to be said that as an emerging writer working in a second language, Binswanger for the most part lacks the narrative technique to realise her ambitions. A more successful representation of the themes that interest her is to be found in Christchurch artist Douglas MacDiarmid's unsettling painting of Binswanger, *The Immigrant* (1945). Here, he portrays his friend as an out-of-scale and uncompromising figure standing in a spatially-distorted modernist setting – forever fixed, says Leonard Bell, as 'an outsider presented uncomfortably inside', an unsettled envoy from elsewhere (*In Transit*, p. 21; see also Bell's more recent *Strangers Arrive*, p. 204). For more on Binswanger, see Livia Käthe Wittmann, 'Living Without Regrets', in *'And How Do You Like This Country?' Stories of New Zealand*, by Otti Binswanger, Germanica Pacifica, v. 5 (Frankfurt am Main: Lang, 2010), pp. 77–118.

39   This quote and next: Texidor to Mangan, 4 August 1941. Houghton, MS Am1816, Folder 94 (1).

40   Memorandum, Douglas Ross to T.P. Pain (both members of the Aliens Authority, Whangarei), 16 March 1943. Archives NZ, AAAR 493, Box 31, Record 1941 50 73.

3. In the leper colony

1   Greville set out her impressions of Auckland in a letter to Mangan, 4 August 1941. Houghton, MS Am 1816, Folder 94 (1).

2   Quoted in Lay and Stratford, eds, *An Affair of the Heart*, p. 341.

3   Texidor to Duggan, undated [1947?]. ATL, MS-Papers-1760-09.

4   Unless stated otherwise, all comments and views attributed to Werner in this chapter are from his memoir *Towards an Alternative Society* (1978). UA, MSS & Archives 90/6.

5   Sturm, *Anna Kavan's New Zealand*, p. 52.

6   By this time, Kavan had already returned to England and was working with Cyril Connolly on the journal *Horizon*. After Hamilton's release from prison in 1946, he returned to Separation Point.

7   Farrell Cleary, 'Introduction', in *Free Society: A German Exile in Revolutionary Spain* by Werner Droescher (London: Kate Sharpley Library, 2012), p. 4.

8   10 February 1943, in *Letters of Frank Sargeson*, ed. by Sarah Shieff (Auckland: Vintage, 2012), p. 58. Werner's publications in other genres were wide-ranging and include 'Fairburn's Bogey', a defence of jazz co-written with Duggan (*Music-ho: Owen Jensen's music news-letter*, 4.3, Jan-Feb 1946); numerous scholarly articles on philology, the German language and pedagogy; and his memoirs (see p. ii for details).

9   Wolfskehl to Kurt Heinrich Wolff, 8 October 1945; *Poetry and Exile: Letters from New Zealand 1938–1948*, trans. by Nelson Wattie (Lyttleton: Cold Hub Press, 2017), p. 193.

10   Texidor to Duggan, undated [1944?]. ATL, MS-Papers-1760-09. For
     Duggan's views on Lemora, see Richards, *To Bed at Noon*, p. 79. Copious
     amounts of this ferocious citrus wine, brewed by the Migounoff family in
     Matakana, lubricated many North Shore social gatherings.

11   Except where stated otherwise, the comments about Greville in this
     paragraph draw heavily on Richards, pp. 86, 62–63.

12   Duggan to Texidor, Thursday [1944?]. ATL, MS-Papers-1760-10.

13   Michael King, *Frank Sargeson. A Life* (Auckland: Viking, 1995), p. 279.

14   Texidor to Duggan, undated. ATL, MS-Papers-1760-09.

15   Maurice Duggan, 'Beginnings', *Landfall*, 1966, 20.4, pp. 331–39 (p. 334).

16   Sargeson to E.H. McCormick, 20 December 1945, in Shieff, ed., *Letters*,
     p. 90.

17   Quotations in this paragraph are from Sargeson, *More than Enough: A
     Memoir* (Wellington: Reed, 1975), pp. 93, 51.

18   Evans, p. 185.

19   Quoted in King, *Frank Sargeson*, p. 203.

20   Mason, 'A Local Habitation and a Name', in Dudding, ed., *In Celebration,
     for Frank Sargeson at 75*, p. 243.

21   Copland, 'First Reading: Only Meeting', in Dudding, ed., pp. 264–65.

22   Dennis McEldowney, quoted in H. Winston Rhodes, *Frank Sargeson*,
     Twayne's World Authors Series, New Zealand, (New York: Twayne
     Publishers, 1969), p. 168.

23   Vincent O'Sullivan, 'Funnier, Meaner Sargeson Beyond This Good Life:
     Review of *Frank Sargeson: A Life* by Michael King', *New Zealand Books*,
     1995, 1–4 (p. 4).

24   Michael King may have been the first to use the term 'Sons of Sargeson' in
     print (in his 1995 biography of Sargeson), but its pedigree is considerably
     longer. It plays with the label given to the contemporary followers of
     Elizabethan poet and dramatist Ben Jonson, who were known variously
     as the 'tribe' or 'sons of Ben'. The term can also be traced to W.H. New's
     study of the short story in Canada and New Zealand, *Dreams of Speech and
     Violence* (Toronto: University of Toronto Press, 1987), one section of which
     is subtitled 'Frank Sargeson & Sons, 1900–1970'.

25   Sargeson to Alec Pickard, 29 May 1945. Shieff, ed., *Letters*, p. 79.

26   Sargeson to Duggan, 9 June 1944. Shieff, ed., *Letters*, p. 75.

27   Sargeson's influence on the development of New Zealand fiction has
     attracted much critical attention. While some writers described his
     influence as 'liberating' and positive (David Ballantyne and others, 'A Letter
     to Frank Sargeson', *Landfall*, 7, 1953, p.5), he was also accused of shaping
     mid-century fiction in his own image and fostering 'a literature of deficiency'
     (K.O. Arvidson, 'Review of *The Cunninghams* by David Ballantyne',
     Landfall, 1965, 19, pp. 69–73). Even decades later, he was accused of
     investing New Zealand fiction with 'the same beige moral tone . . . the same
     dreary humanism . . . the same truncated, banal dialogue occupying itself

with similar issues, confrontations and characters' (*The New Fiction*, ed. by Michael Morrissey, Auckland: Lindon Publishing, 1985, p. 16). Sargeson himself later commented that while trying to enable talent, he had ended up unwittingly encouraging imitation; instead of 'opening up something for New Zealand', he had shut down its literary possibilities, he said. See Michael Beveridge, 'Conversation with Frank Sargeson', in *Conversation in a Train and Other Critical Writing*, ed. by Kevin Cunningham (Auckland: Auckland University Press / Oxford University Press, 1983), pp. 153–54.

28   Sargeson to E.P. Dawson, 17 February 1944. Shieff, ed., *Letters*, pp. 67–68.

29   'September 1, 1939'. First published 1940. W.H. Auden, *Selected Poems* (London: Faber and Faber, 1979), pp. 86–89.

30   Frank Sargeson, 'Henry Lawson', in Cunningham, ed., *Conversation in a Train*, p. 125.

31   Sargeson regularly reported on his changing practices and ambitions to friends; this quote and others in the paragraph are from his letters to E.P. Dawson on 16 February 1944, 27 October and 5 November 1943. Hocken, MS-2404/002.

32   E.H. McCormick, *Letters and Art in New Zealand* (Wellington: Dept. of Internal Affairs, 1940), p. 182.

33   These remarks on Sargeson's personal life draw on two important sources: John Newton, 'Surviving the War', *Journal of New Zealand Literature*, 2013, pp. 84–106; and Kai Jensen, *Whole Men: The Masculine Tradition in New Zealand Literature* (Auckland: Auckland University Press), pp. 118–126.

34   Sargeson's comments in this paragraph are from letters to Glover, 9 August 1937; to Gaskell, 14 January 1944; and again to Glover on 10 February 1943. Shieff, ed., *Letters*, pp. 14, 66, 57–58.

35   Newton, pp. 87–88.

36   Denys Trussell, *Fairburn* (Auckland: Auckland University Press / Oxford University Press, 1984), pp. 249–50.

37   Here I quote the shifting opinions about Wolfskehl that Sargeson expresses in *More Than Enough*, pp. 105, 111; in a letter to Glover, 10 February 1943, in Shieff, ed., *Letters*, p. 58; and finally in a rueful letter to Phoebe Meikle, 23 July 1977, ATL, Dr Michael King Papers, 97-042-20/02.

38   Sargeson visited Europe in 1927, absorbing as much of England's cultural life as he could and embarking on a walking tour of the Continent. His accounts of this journey (he wrote a memoir, 'A New Tramp Abroad', soon after returning to New Zealand and revisited it in his autobiography more than forty years later) reveal his ambivalent and changing view of the experience, as do the recollections of his friends. In 1973, Sargeson said he had felt crushed by the Old World's 'intolerable weight of civilization' and inescapable odour of staleness and decay (*Once is Enough*, p. 115). But Janet Frame remembered him showing her postcards of his European travels with 'such a look of wild longing, almost of agony at what was gone, that I felt near to tears' (*An Autobiography*, p. 249). Sargeson confessed to Duggan in

February 1945 that despite being 'so very much a N.Z.er', he still 'suffer[ed] badly from a European hangover' (ATL, MS-Papers-1760-08).

39   Frame, *An Autobiography*, p. 270.

40   Sargeson, *Never Enough*, p. 61.

41   This term was coined by the English critic James Wood in his essay 'On Not Going Home', *London Review of Books*, 36.4 (2014), 3–8 (p. 6).

42   Sargeson, *Never Enough*, p. 62.

43   This quotation and next: Texidor to Duggan, 21 September 1951. ATL, MS-Papers-1760-09, and to Sargeson, 14 July [1950?]. ATL, MS-Papers-0432-182.

44   Sargeson to E.P. Dawson, 25 April 1944, in Shieff, ed., *Letters*, p. 70.

45   This paragraph draws on Sargeson's obituary, 'Greville Texidor 1902–1964', p. 136.

46   'An Annual Affair' appeared in Dan Davin's *New Zealand Short Stories* (1953), the first New Zealand volume in the Oxford University Press series 'The World's Classics' (republished in 1976). In more recent anthologies, 'Home Front' was included in Vincent O'Sullivan's *Oxford Book of New Zealand Short Stories* (1992) and 'Anyone Home?' in the *Penguin Book of New Zealand War Writing* (2015), edited by Gavin McLean and Harry Ricketts. An extract from *Goodbye Forever* appeared in *The Auckland University Press Anthology of New Zealand Literature* (2012), edited by Jane Stafford and Mark Williams.

47   Mangan to Texidor, 10 April 1956. UA, MSS & Archives A-198, Box 1, Folder 2.

48   This quote and the next from Sargeson, *Never Enough*, p. 63.

49   Some years later, when Sargeson advised Cristina that 'An Annual Affair' had been chosen for the Oxford University Press 'World's Classics' series (1953), he described it as 'really your story' (29 March 1953. Private collection of Cristina Patterson Texidor).

50   Sargeson, *More Than Enough*, pp. 113–14; Texidor to 'June', undated. ATL, MS-Papers-1760-09.

51   Unnamed correspondent to Michael King, undated. ATL, MS-Group-0667, 97-042-20/12.

52   Sargeson, *More Than Enough*, p. 111.

53   Frame, *An Autobiography*, p. 249.

54   Jasmin Brandt, 'Garvin Robert Gilbert: An Account of His Life and Work' (MA thesis, University of Canterbury, 2002), p. 6. All ellipses in original, apart from the second.

55   Early in their friendship, Frame showed Sargeson a draft of her story 'An Electric Blanket' but was so disappointed by his unsympathetic response, 'I resolved not to show him more stories, and I kept my resolve, later showing him only the beginning of my novel' (*An Autobiography*, p. 249).

56   Sargeson to Pickard, 17 February 1942. In Shieff, ed., *Letters*, p. 49.

57   Texidor to Duggan, undated [1945?]. ATL, MS-Papers-1760-09.

58 New, *Dreams of Speech and Violence*, p. 160.

59 She expressed her views on *When the Wind Blows* in an undated letter [1945?], ATL, MS-Papers-1760-09; her comments on *I Saw in My Dream* are from a letter to Sargeson from Australia [1950?], ATL, MS-Papers-0432-182.

60 This section, 'Someone who knows exactly what one is trying to do', quotes extensively from the many letters Texidor and Duggan exchanged in 1944 and 1945. As they are mostly undated, I have not given individual references. The sources for all such quotes are ATL, MS-Papers-1760-10 and 1760-09.

61 Sargeson to E.P. Dawson, 17 February 1944, in Shieff, ed., *Letters*, p. 67.

62 Richards, p. 62.

63 John Reece Cole, 'Jabberwocky and Back to the Fern Roots', *PEN Gazette*, 94 (1975), p. 3.

64 While Greville told Duggan the translations were 'very good', Cristina recalls her mother lamenting that Spender was a poet whose Spanish was poor, while Gili had excellent Spanish but was no poet.

65 The italics are mine. Duggan to Texidor, 16 May [1945?]. ATL, MS-Papers-1760-10.

66 There are strong echoes of Rhys's *Good Morning, Midnight* (1939) – the tone of sardonic bitterness, an unanchored and forsaken protagonist, a vividly-rendered Left Bank setting. Certain details in 'Aller Retour' also recall *Quartet* (1928), Rhys's reworking of her complicated relationship with Ford Madox Ford and his wife while her own husband was in prison. The wallpaper in the rackety hotel room of Texidor's protagonist, for example, depicts 'gilded birds nesting in a profusion of purple flowers that distill the passagery scent of lovers . . . The birds have withdrawn into the bowers on the dark walls'; in the room of Rhys's Marya, 'An atmosphere of departed and ephemeral loves hung about the bedroom like stale scent . . . The wallpaper was vaguely erotic – huge and fantastically shaped mauve, green and yellow flowers sprawling on a black ground'. *Quartet* (London: Penguin, 2000) p. 87. Despite the striking affinities between the women and their work, I have been unable to find any direct evidence that Texidor knew Rhys's fiction well. After the Second World War, it was largely forgotten until the publication of *Wide Sargasso Sea* in 1966. See Carole Angier, *Jean Rhys* (Harmondsworth: Penguin, 1985), p. 67.

67 Sargeson to Duggan, 19 May 1945. ATL, MS Papers-1760-08

68 He described his methods in these terms somewhat later, in a letter to John Reece Cole, 1 April 1955. Shieff, ed., *Letters*, p. 199.

69 Sargeson, 'Texidor', p. 137.

70 Unpublished workbook, undated (Australia). UA, MSS & Archives A-198, Box 1, Folder 6.

71 Duggan's biographer Ian Richards comments that 'bloody good' (and variants thereof) was at this time the young writer's highest form of critical praise. *To Bed at Noon*, p. 79.

72 Sargeson to Dawson, 16 February 1944. Hocken, MS-2404/002.

73 *Never Enough*, p. 64.

74 Calas, also known as Nikos Kalamaris, was a Greek poet and champion of European surrealism and the avant-garde who sought exile in America in 1940.

75 His comments to both Dawson and Gaskell are reported in King, pp. 261–62.

76 Sargeson to McCormick, 20 December 1945, in Shieff, ed., *Letters*, p. 89.

77 Sargeson to Dawson, 19 October 1945 in *Speaking Frankly: The Frank Sargeson Memorial Lectures, 2003–2010*, ed. by Sarah Shieff (Auckland: Cape Catley, 2011), p. 85.

78 Richards, p. 84.

79 Sargeson, *Never Enough*, p. 63.

80 At least in theory, gender relations among Barcelona's anarchists were egalitarian and sexually-progressive, unfettered by traditional roles and constructs such as monogamy.

81 Interview with Cristina Patterson Texidor, 22 April 2015.

82 Richards, p. 88.

83 Texidor to Duggan, undated. ATL, MS-Papers-1760-09.

84 Texidor's comments in this paragraph are from undated letters to Cole (ATL, MS-Papers-4648-17) and Duggan (ATL, MS-Papers-1760-09). To Duggan, she added: 'I am now beginning to suspect that I am a sinister old Auntie myself & this is why they are rather horrible.'

85 King, pp. 268, 276–78.

86 Sargeson's comments in this paragraph are from letters to Dawson (14 September 1944. Hocken, MS-2404/002) and Heenan (29 December 1948, in Shieff, ed., *Letters*, pp. 113–14).

87 All remaining quotes in this section, unless stated otherwise, are from four undated letters Texidor sent Duggan, probably in 1946–47. ATL, MS-Papers-1760-09.

88 As well as the version published in *In Fifteen Minutes You Can Say a Lot*, the manuscript of a longer version is among Greville's papers held at the State Library of New South Wales. It differs most obviously in its fuller treatment of Lili's European past.

89 Sargeson describes the 'handsome Jewess' in a letter to William Plomer, 1 December 1946. ATL, MS-Papers-0432-186.

90 'New Zealand: An Answer to an Inquiry' in Sturm, pp. 161–62.

91 Texidor to Duggan, undated [June 1947?]. ATL, MS-Papers-1760-09.

92 The responses to Greville's pregnancy quoted in this paragraph are from Cole to Sargeson, 2 March 1947 (ATL, MS-Papers-0432-025), Sargeson to Dawson, 23 March 1947 (Hocken, MS-2404/003) and Sargeson to Cole, 5 June 1947 (in Shieff, ed., *Letters*, p. 99).

93 A.R.D. Fairburn, 'New Zealanders You Should Know: Dr G.M. Smith', *Action – The Thinker's Digest*, 1944, 26–27 (p. 26).

94 In the early 1920s, it had emerged that Smith was not married to his purported wife, Lucy; she was, in fact, a former patient with whom he had

eloped to New Zealand, leaving the erstwhile Mrs Smith in Scotland with their four children. When these details were disclosed, Dr Smith was briefly dismissed by the Rawene Hospital Board. But he was soon reinstated and, after his divorce was finalised, he and Lucy were officially wed. As his anaesthetist – she had no medical qualifications, but G.M. trained her – Lucy was both instrumental to his work and a mollifying restraint on his more abrasive behaviour. A memorial sundial in the grounds of the Rawene Hospital reads: 'In memory of Mrs L.M. Smith. The calm foundation of her husband's turbulent world and his anaesthetist. She followed him.' See F. Rogers, 'Smith, George Marshall McCall', *Dictionary of New Zealand Biography. Te Ara – the Encyclopedia of New Zealand*. https://teara.govt.nz/en/biographies/4s32/smith-george-marshall-mccall. Accessed 1 July 2017. One of Smith's grandsons is the Scottish novelist Alexander McCall Smith.

95 The 'Northern News', 1928. Quoted in Graham Kemble Welch, *Doctor Smith: Hokianga's 'King of the North'* (Auckland; Hamilton: Blackwood and Janet Paul, 1965), p. 75.

96 Phil Amos, quoted in James McNeish's radio production 'Smith's Cure: Portrait of a Scots Maverick' (Wellington: NZBC Concert Programme, 1976). Unless stated otherwise, all quotes in the next paragraph are from the script or McNeish's research notes. ATL, James McNeish Papers, MS-Papers-7811-186, 'Smith's Cure'.

97 Kemble Welch, pp. 123–29.

98 G.M. Smith, *Notes from a Backblocks Hospital* (Christchurch: The Caxton Press, 1938), pp. 109–17.

99 Sargeson's account of this first meeting is in *Never Enough*, pp. 41–42.

100 King, p. 199. The remaining quotations in this paragraph are from the same source (p. 210).

101 Kemble Welch, p. 135.

102 Drs Bernhardt Kronig and Karl Gauss, quoted in Mark Sloan, M.D., *Birth Day: A Pediatrician Explores the Science, the History and the Wonder of Childbirth* (New York: Ballantine Books, 2009).

103 Dr Bertha Van Hoosen, quoted in Judith Walzer Leavitt, 'Birthing and Anesthesia: The Debate over Twilight Sleep', *Signs: Journal of Women in Culture and Society*, 6.1 (1980), 147–64 (p. 149).

104 Sally Pairman, 'From Autonomy and Back Again: Educating Midwives across a Century, Part 1', *New Zealand College of Midwives Journal*, 33 (2005), 4–9 (pp. 5–6). American paediatrician Dr Mark Sloan argues that twilight sleep never truly disappeared anywhere, but simply morphed into the standard childbirth practices found in most developed counties until at least the 1970s. He goes on to describe an 'assembly line . . . of heavy sedation and amnesia' in which women typically gave birth 'in a haze of anesthetic medications and tranquilizers' (*Birth Day*).

105 Smith, *More Notes*, p. 70.

106 Texidor to Sargeson, 15 November [1949?]. ATL, MS-Papers-0432-182.

107 Smith, *More Notes*, pp. 73–74, 89–90, 106–7. Unless stated otherwise, all quotes in this paragraph are from this source.

108 Smith, quoted in Kemble Welch, p. 135.

109 McNeish.

110 Kurzke to Sargeson, 8 August 1976. ATL, MS-Papers-4261-097. According to Kate, Greville practised yoga in Australia and, when in London, had once accompanied Kate to a Hampstead yoga centre: '[But] she was bitterly disappointed as the monk was pale white and she had expected some handsome Indian who would only wear a loincloth and who would tie himself in knots or at least get into the lotus position.'

111 Later, in Spain, Rosamund was formally christened Rosamunda; as an adult, she has generally been known by this name or Rosa.

112 Texidor to Duggan, undated [1947?]. ATL, MS-Papers-1760-09.

113 Sargeson to E.P. Dawson, 17 January 1948, in Shieff, ed., *Letters*, pp. 101–102.

114 Texidor to Duggan, undated [1947?]. ATL, MS-Papers-1760-09.

115 Richards, pp. 103–4.

116 Texidor to Duggan, two undated letters [1947 and 48?]. ATL, MS-Papers-1760-09.

117 Sargeson to Dawson, 13 June 1948. Hocken, MS-2404/003.

118 Sargeson to J. Heenan, 3 September 1948. Archives NZ, IA1W2578 237, Record 158 206 87.

119 Quoted in Jones, *Picking Up the Traces*, p. 256.

4. Australia and after

1 A.R.D. Fairburn, 'Fog over the Tasman', *Mail* (Adelaide, 7 June 1947), p. 7. Max Harris's response 'Australia's Bad Neighbor Policy', also quoted here, appeared in the *Mail* on 5 July 1947, p. 4.

2 Unless stated otherwise, all comments and views attributed to Werner in this chapter are from his memoir *Towards an Alternative Society* (1978). UAkld, MSS & Archives 90/6.

3 This quote and the next are from Texidor to Duggan, 29 December [1948?]. ATL, MS-Papers-1760-09.

4 Texidor to Cole, undated [1947?]. ATL, MS Papers 4648-17.

5 This quotation and next are from Texidor to Sargeson, undated [1948?]. ATL, MS-Papers-0432-182.

6 Werner's remarks to Sargeson this paragraph and next are from his letters of 7 February 1949 and 16 November 1948. ATL, MS-Papers-0432-182.

7 This paragraph draws on Jayne Persian, *Beautiful Balts: From Displaced Persons to New Australians* (Sydney: NewSouth Publishing, University of New South Wales, 2017), especially pp. 1–15 and 76–81.

8 Quotes in this paragraph are from Texidor's letters to Sargeson, 12 June and 8 July 1949 (ATL, MS-Papers-0432-182) and to E.P. Dawson, [1949?] (UAkld, MSS & Archives A-198, Box 1, Folder 3).

9   Texidor to Cole, 25 October [1949?]. ATL, MS Papers 4648-17.

10   Texidor's observations in this paragraph are from her letters to Sargeson, 1
     November [1950?] (ATL, MS-Papers-0432-102) and Duggan, October 1950
     (ATL, MS-Papers-1760-09).

11   Persian, *Beautiful Balts*, p. 156.

12   Texidor to Sargeson, 8 July [1949?]. ATL, MS-Papers-0432-182.

13   Texidor to Duggan, undated [1950?]. ATL, MS-Papers-1760-09.

14   Texidor to Cole, 25 October [1949?]. ATL, MS Papers 4648-17.

15   Texidor's comments to Sargeson in this paragraph are from letters of 12
     September [1949?] and 16 June [1951?]. ATL, MS-Papers-0432-102.

16   *Here & Now*, March 1951, pp. 21–24.

17   Sargeson to E.P. Dawson, 19 July 1949. Hocken, MS-2404/003.

18   Texidor to Duggan, October 1950. ATL, MS-Papers-1760-09

19   Texidor to Sargeson, 12 September [1949?]. ATL, MS-Papers-0432-182.

20   Sargeson, *Never Enough*, p. 66. Phillip Wilson called it 'the product of a sick
     mind' in his review 'Despair in the Sun', *New Zealand Listener*, 30 September
     1949, p. 16, while Sargeson judged it a 'masterpiece' (*Never Enough*, p. 64).

21   W. Droescher to Sargeson, undated [1949?]. MS-Papers-0432-182.

22   Laurence Pollinger (Pearn, Pollinger & Higham Ltd) to Sargeson, 10 January
     1945. ATL, MS-Papers-0432-102.

23   This comment and the next are quoted by Allentuck in 'Greville Texidor's
     These Dark Glasses: Bloomsbury in New Zealand', *World Literature Written
     in English*, 1980, 19.2, pp. 227–32 (p. 229).

24   The Fund agreed to contribute a £50 loan, to be repaid from book sales,
     and a £50 grant. W. Droescher to Sargeson, 7 February 1949. ATL, MS-
     Papers-0432-182.

25   Sargeson to Texidor, 27 April 1949. UAkld, MSS & Archives A-198, Box 1,
     Folder 2.

26   Texidor to Sargeson, 8 July [1949?]. ATL, MS-Papers-0432-182.

27   Most reviews of the novel described Victor as Ruth's lover. However, Greville
     was adamant that her character 'though at present rather dishevelled [was]
     not the sort of girl to have "lovers"'. Indeed, she told Cole, not many of the
     English who fought in Spain ever 'succumbed physically'. She was exasperated
     by the reviewers' apparent belief that Ruth would have done so: apart from
     being historically inaccurate, 'this . . . makes her behaviour unintelligible to
     me'. Texidor to Cole, 25 October [1949?]. ATL, MS-Papers-4648-17.

28   To scholar Dale Benson – whose doctoral thesis 'A World Like This: Exis-
     tentialism in New Zealand Literature' (University of Otago, 2000) examined
     the influence of European existentialism on various New Zealand writers –
     In Fifteen Minutes You Can Say a Lot expresses 'the development of a kind of
     existentialist sensibility' unprecedented in New Zealand fiction (p. 182).

29   At various times, *Penguin New Writing* published Sartre's Spanish Civil
     War story 'The Wall', which challenges conventional rhetoric about wartime
     heroism (no. 4, March 1941); Yuri Olyesha's 'Love' (no. 9, September 1941);

William Chappell's 'The Sky Makes Me Hate It' (no. 13, April–June 1942); and Lehmann's own essay 'The Search for the Myth' (no. 30, 1947), among others.

30 Connolly's Trou-sur-Mer is said to be based on the town of Cagnes-sur-Mer, north of Cassis between Cannes and Nice.

31 Duggan to Texidor, 21 September [1950?]. ATL, MS Papers-1760-10.

32 Cyril Connolly, *The Rock Pool* (London: Hamish Hamilton, 1947), p. xii.

33 Sargeson, *Never Enough*, p. 65; his other comments this paragraph are from the obituary he wrote for *Landfall*, 'Greville Texidor 1902–1964', p. 135.

34 Patrick Macaskill, 'Comments on the Year's Fiction', *Arts Year Book*, 1950, 6, pp. 145–48 (p. 148).

35 Wilson, p. 16.

36 J.C. Reid, *Creative Writing in New Zealand: A Brief Critical History* (Auckland: Whitcombe and Tombs, 1946), p. 61.

37 Sargeson to McCormick. In Shieff, ed., *Letters*, p. 129.

38 J.C. Reid, 'Review of *These Dark Glasses* by Greville Texidor', *Landfall*, 1949, 3.4, pp. 376–78 (p. 377). All Reid quotations are from this source.

39 Texidor, 'Letter to the Editor', *Landfall*, 1950, 4.2, p. 177. All quotes in this paragraph are from this source.

40 This quotation and next: Sargeson to Texidor, 18 July 1950. UAkld, MSS & Archives A-198, Box 1, Folder 2.

41 Allentuck, p. 230. Other comments in this paragraph are from: Kurzke to Sargeson, undated, ATL, MS-Papers-4261-097 (unless stated otherwise, all quotations from Kate in this chapter are from these letters); R. Droescher to F. Barrowman, 7 July 1987, SLNSW, ML-MSS 5235, Box 5, Folder 12; Duggan to Sargeson, 19 October 1950, ATL, MS-Papers-4261-044.

42 Texidor to Sargeson, July [1950?]. ATL, MS-Papers-0432-182.

43 This quotation and next: Texidor to E.P. Dawson, undated [1949?]. UAkld, MSS & Archives A-198, Box 1, Folder 3.

44 Sargeson to Duggan, 19 May 1945. ATL, MS Papers-1760-08.

45 Texidor to Sargeson, 1 November [1949?]. ATL, MS-Papers-0432-182.

46 Texidor to Duggan, 12 September 1950. ATL, MS-Papers-1760-09. Eighteenth-century Kenwood House, on the edge of London's Hampstead Heath, was one of the few London landmarks Greville recalled with fondness.

47 Duggan to Texidor, 23 November 1950. ATL, MS Papers-1760-10. Other letters quoted in this paragraph are from Texidor to Duggan, 2 November 1950, ATL, MS-Papers-1760-09, and Texidor to Sargeson, 15 November [1950?], ATL, MS-Papers-0432-182.

48 Duggan to Sargeson, 28 December [1950?]. ATL, MS-Papers-4261-044.

49 Jane Grant, *Kylie Tennant: A Life* (Canberra: National Library of Australia, 2006), p. 54. Grant suggests Tennant considered the comparison – first made after the publication of her novel *The Battlers* (1941) and frequently repeated – a slur on her originality.

50 Texidor to Sargeson, 15 November [1950?]. ATL, MS-Papers-0432-182.

51   The central character in Greville's unfinished story 'Tui' is based on Miriam.

52   Except where stated otherwise, all quotations in this paragraph are from Anne Coombs, *Sex and Anarchy: The Life and Death of the Sydney Push* (Victoria: Penguin, 1996), pp. vii, ix, 17 and 57.

53   Neil Hope, quoted in Bill Harcourt, 'The Push', *The National Times*, 3 February 1975, pp. 28–31 (p. 31).

54   Bill Harcourt gives an account of the Push's heroes and heroines in his article, p. 28.

55   Elizabeth Farrelly, 'When the Push Came to Shove', *Sydney Morning Herald*, 4 April 2009, https://www.smh.com.au/national/when-the-push-came-to-shove-20141112-9qi9.html.

56   Coombs, p. 57; James Franklin, 'The Push and Critical Drinkers', in *Corrupting the Youth: A History of Australian Philosophy* (Sydney: Macleay Press, 2003) Online edition available at https://web.maths.unsw.edu.au/~jim/contents.html.

57   Max Harris, John Reed, Sunday Reed, Barrett Reid and others founded this literary magazine (1951–55) after the collapse of *Angry Penguins* (1940–46). Its title exploited the earlier Ern Malley hoax – see chapter 3.

58   David Mustard, originally known as Gopal Deobhankar, became an eminent mathematician and taught at the University of New South Wales for more than thirty-five years. He played a key part in the publication of Greville's work in 1987; after his mother's death, he found the 'blue suitcase' containing much of Greville's unpublished work and returned it to her family. See John Slee, 'David Mustard. Mathematician, Mountaineer, Aesthete 1930–2001', *Sydney Morning Herald*, 3 August 2001, section Obituaries. Available at https://web.maths.unsw.edu.au/~jim/mustard.htm.

59   R. Droescher to F. Barrowman, 7 July 1987, SLNSW, ML-MSS 5235, Box 5, Folder 12.

60   Texidor to Hamilton, May [1952?]. ATL, MS-Papers-5597-03.

61   W. Droescher to Duggan, 5 May 1953, ATL, MS-Papers-1760-09.

62   'Radio Plays This Week', *South Coast Times and Wollongong Argus* (NSW, 24 August 1953), p. 2.

63   Texidor discussed 'The Laughing Spirit' in several letters to Duggan during July 1953, which I quote from here. ATL, MS-Papers-1760-09.

64   John Quinn, 'Plays with a Message to Make You Think', *Mail* (Adelaide, 29 August 1953), p. 41.

65   Texidor to Duggan, May 1953. ATL, MS-Papers-1760-09.

66   Greville's comments in this paragraph are from letters written to Duggan between January and May 1953 (ATL, MS-Papers-1760-09) and to Sargeson in July (ATL, MS-Papers-0432-182).

67   Barrett Reid told radio producer Ron Blair this in 1987. ABC, 'Radio Drama and Features Preview', July 1988. SLNSW, ML-MSS 5235, Box 5, Folder 12.

68   R. Droescher to F. Barrowman, 7 July 1987. SLNSW, ML-MSS 5235, Box 5, Folder 12.

69   Correspondence of Joy Hester and Sunday Reed, quoted in Janine Burke, *The Heart Garden: Sunday Reed and Heide* (Sydney: Vintage, 2004), p. 327.

70   Preston to Texidor, 25 July 1960. UAkld, MSS & Archives A-198, Box 1, Folder 2.

71   Unpublished typescript, SLNSW, ML-MSS 5235, Box 2, Folder 17.

72   Texidor to Sargeson, 16 June [1953?]; her comments about 'An Annual Affair' are from her letter of 1 January 1954. ATL, MS-Papers-0432-182.

73   The child who features in 'Jesús Jiménez', for example, appears in another guise in *Diary*, where the central character's packed suitcases signal her decision to abandon – and perhaps betray – the cause she has fought for, just as they do for the narrator of 'Time of Departure'. And, echoing 'Santa Cristina', a minor character in *Diary* dreams of a shellfish 'with an eye like a sea snail', an image later subsumed into a dream of death, where 'fear lay cold, looking up with a cold black eye, the eye of the shellfish'. Texidor's refusal to date her drafts makes it impossible to determine which iteration came first.

74   Judy Simons, *Rosamond Lehmann* (Basingstoke: Macmillan, 1992), p. 9.

75   In the following discussion, all quotes are sourced from multiple drafts in Box 1 of Texidor's papers at the State Library of New South Wales (ML-MSS 5235).

76   In some drafts, Magda is called Marga or Margaret; elsewhere Texidor experiments with Clare, Eve, Em and Kay (her ultimate preference for 'Magda' is consistent with the increasing overlay of biblical imagery that becomes more apparent in successive drafts). Martin is sometimes called Jan. The Cruz brothers, with whom Magda becomes romantically entwined, have numerous alternative names – Liberto, Progreso, Pedro, Juan, Garcia and more. For clarity, I have used the characters' names as they appear in what I consider Texidor's most finished drafts, although an absence of dates makes sequencing them an inexact science.

77   According to Rosamunda Droescher, the Conejero brothers, of mixed Andalusian and Catalan origins, were printers whom Greville met when working as a translator in Barcelona in the early days of the Civil War. It was through the Conejeros' influence and intervention that she was able to join the anarchist militia, even though women were by that point in the war technically banned from enlisting (see chapter 1).

78   Katherine Bail Hoskins, *Today the Struggle: Literature and Politics in England during the Spanish Civil War* (Austin & London: University of Texas Press, 1969), p. 244. The quotations from Auden's 'Spain', 1937, and Cornford's 'Full Moon at Tierz', 1936, are from *Poems for Spain*, ed. by Stephen Spender and John Lehmann (London: The Hogarth Press, 1939), pp. 55–58 and 26–29.

79   For an account of Styron's abandoned novel, *The Way of the Warrior*, see James L.W. West, *William Styron, A life* (New York: Random House, 1998), pp. 398–399, 432–433 and elsewhere.

80   Texidor to Sargeson, 26 December [1954?]. ATL, MS-Papers-0432-182.

81   Sargeson to Texidor, 27 April 1949. UAkld, MSS & Archives A-198, Box 1, Folder 2.

82   Lyndsey Stonebridge, 'Theories of Trauma', in *The Cambridge Companion to the Literature of World War II*, ed. by Marina Mackay, Literature Online, Cambridge Companions to Literature (New York: Cambridge University Press, 2009), pp. 194–206 (p. 200).

83   Suzette A. Henke, 'Modernism and Trauma', in *The Cambridge Companion to Modernist Women Writers*, ed. by Maren Tova Linett, Literature Online (Cambridge; New York: Cambridge University Press, 2010), pp. 160–71 (p. 164). H.D. was the writing name of Hilda Doolittle. Her multiple personal tragedies during and immediately after the First World War provoked severe post-traumatic stress symptoms for which Sigmund Freud prescribed scriptotherapy, or 'writing as healing'. According to Henke, H.D. found relief from 'the most deleterious effects' of her wartime traumas through writing the autobiographical novels *Bid Me to Live* (1960, written 1939) and *Asphodel* (1992, written 1921–22).

84   Stonebridge, p. 196.

85   Unpublished workbook, undated. UAkld, MSS & Archives A-198, Box 1, Folder 7. Other quotes in this paragraph are from her letter to Duggan, 21 Sep 1951. ATL, MS-Papers-1760-09.

86   Quoted in Burke, p. 308.

87   Rachel Barrowman, *A Popular Vision: The Arts and the Left in New Zealand, 1930–1950* (Wellington: Victoria University Press, 1991), p. 49.

88   R. McC., 'Bad Verse and Good Criticism', *Sydney Morning Herald*, 29 December 1945.

89   Quoted in Harcourt, p. 30.

90   Texidor to Duggan, 3 July [1953?]. ATL, MS-Papers-1760-09.

91   B. Reid to R. Droescher, 27 January 1988. SLNSW, ML-MSS 5235, Box 5, Folder 12.

92   See Gordon J. Turnbull, 'Classification', in *Psychological Trauma: A Developmental Approach*, ed. by Dora Black and others (London: Gaskell, 1997), pp. 19–30 (p. 22). My very general discussion of a very complex condition draws on Turnbull's account of key international developments in the classification and categorisation of PTSD.

93   Quotes from letters to Duggan, 21 Sep 1951 and 1947 (ATL, MS-Papers-1760-09); she told Sargeson that a return to Europe seemed 'too late' in an undated letter from 1953 or 1954 (ATL, MS-Papers-0432-182).

94   Gill Leahy, quoted in Coombs, p. 277.

95   Texidor to Duggan, 18 July [1953 or 54?]. ATL, MS-Papers-1760-09.

96   See for example Jenna L. McCauley and others, 'Posttraumatic Stress Disorder and Co-Occurring Substance Use Disorders: Advances in Assessment and Treatment', *Clinical Psychology*, 19.3 (2012), https://doi.org/10.1111/cpsp.12006.

97   Mark Brown, 'Son of WWII Photographer Lee Miller Welcomes Kate

Winslet Biopic Role', *The Guardian (Online Edition)*, 4 October 2015, https://www.theguardian.com/culture/2015/oct/14/son-lee-miller-second-world-war-photographer-welcomes-kate-winslet-biopic-role.

98   Texidor's comments about her mother are from her letters to Mangan, January 1944 (Houghton, MS Am 1816, Folder 94 (2)), and Sargeson, undated [1953?] (ATL, MS-Papers-0432-182).

99   Undated typescript, 'Death of Editha'. SLNSW, ML-MSS5235, Box 2, Folder 13.

100 Reported in Texidor to Cole, 25 October [1949?]. ATL, MS-Papers-4648-17.

101 She expressed these feelings in letters to friends – for example, to Sargeson on 12 September [1950?] (ATL, MS-Papers-0432-182) and in her workbook, where she wrote that 'in the colonies . . . [n]othing has ever happened.' (UAkld, MSS & Archives A-198, Box 1, Folder 6).

102 Texidor to Duggan, 3 March 1953. ATL, MS-Papers-1760-09.

103 Quotes in this paragraph come from letters to Duggan, 6 December 1954 and 14 December [1953?]. ATL, MS-Papers-1760-09.

104 Julian Coman, 'Eighty Years on, Spain May at Last Be Able to Confront the Ghosts of Civil War', *Observer* (London, 29 May 2016), International edition, http://www.theguardian.com/world/2016/may/29/national-museum-spanish-civil-war-barcelona.

105 Kurtzke to Hamilton, undated. ATL, MS-Papers-5597-03.

106 This paragraph quotes from the Texidor–Mangan correspondence of 1955–56 in Houghton, MS Am 1816, Folder 94 (2) and Folder 520 (1); also Mangan's letter to Manolo Texidor of 17 November 1955 (Folder 794).

107 Wald, 'The Pilgrimage of Sherry Mangan', pp. 94–98.

108 All quotes here are from the Texidor–Mangan correspondence of 1955–56, Houghton, MS Am 1816, Folders 94 (3) and 520 (1).

109 Texidor to Sargeson, undated [1957?]. ATL, MS-Papers-0432-182. Other quotes this paragraph are from Texidor's letters to Mangan, April–July 1956. Houghton, MS Am 1816, Folder 94 (3).

110 This paragraph quotes from Texidor's letter to Sargeson, undated [1957?] (ATL, MS-Papers-0432-182) and to Mangan, undated [1956?] (UAkld, MSS & Archives A-198, Box 1, Folder 3).

111 Mangan to Manolo Texidor, 27 May 1960. Houghton, MS Am 1816, Folder 794.

112 This paragraph quotes from two letters by Texidor to Sargeson [1957?], ATL, MS-Papers-0432-182.

113 See Sargeson's letters of mid-1956 to numerous friends, and Frame herself, in Shieff, ed., *Letters*, pp. 238–50.

114 Frame, p. 325; Michael King, *Wrestling with the Angel* (Auckland: Penguin, 2000), p. 168.

115 Greville's comments in this paragraph are from two undated letters to Sargeson, ATL, MS-Papers-0432-182. Presumably Frame's manuscript was her novel *Uncle Pylades*, which she worked on during her stay on Ibiza. Frame, p. 335.

116 Mangan to Texidor, 3 May 1960. UAkld, MSS & Archives A-198, Box 1,
     Folder 2.
117 Mangan to Texidor, 19 December 1960. Houghton, MS Am 1816, Folder
     520 (3).
118 Kurzke to Sargeson, undated, ATL, MS-Papers-4261-097
119 According to Greville, in an undated letter to Werner [1961?]. UAkld, MSS
     & Archives A-198, Box 1, Folder 3.
120 Texidor to Mangan, undated [1960?]. MS Am 1816, Folder 94 (3). The
     remaining quotations in this paragraph are from letters exchanged between
     Mangan, Greville and Werner in 1961. UAkld, MSS & Archives A-198, Box
     1, Folders 2 and 3.
121 Quotes from Mangan in this paragraph are from his letters to Greville on 19
     March 1957, 2 March 1960 and 19 December 1960. UAkld, MSS & Archives
     A-198, Box 1, Folder 2.
122 Mangan died in Rome on 24 June 1961. Earlier that month, he sent Greville
     a letter joking that as his freelance work was drying up, he expected to 'starve
     to death about the third week in June' (2 June 1961, UAkld, MSS & Archives
     A-198, Box 1, Folder 2).
123 Both quotes from undated letters to Werner, 1961. UAkld, MSS & Archives
     A-198, Box 1, Folder 3.
124 Texidor to R. Droescher, 5 December 1961. UAkld, MSS & Archives A-198,
     Box 1, Folder 3.
125 Sargeson, Never Enough, p. 68.
126 Unpublished workbook, undated (Australia). UAkld, MSS & Archives
     A-198, Box 1, Folder 6.

5. The secret of her unsuccess?

1   Unpublished workbook, undated (Spain). UAkl, MSS & Archives A-198,
    Box 2, Folder 2. This is also where she refers to 'the secret of my unsuccess'.
2   Jones, Picking Up the Traces, p. 341; Patrick Macaskill, 'Comments on the
    Year's Fiction', Arts Year Book, 1950, 6, pp. 145–48 (p. 148).
3   Sargeson, 'Greville Texidor 1902–1964', p. 135.
4   Texidor, unpublished workbook, undated (Australia?). UAkld, MSS &
    Archives A-198, Box 1, Folder 6.
5   British Fiction After Modernism: The Novel at Mid-Century, ed. by Marina
    Mackay and Lyndsey Stonebridge (New York: Palgrave Macmillan, 2007),
    p. 1. Other critical texts that helpfully expand traditional understandings
    of what literary modernism was (or is) include Kristin Bluemel's
    influential Intermodernism: Literary culture in mid-twentieth-century
    Britain (Edinburgh: Edinburgh University Press, 2011) – which defines
    intermodernism as both 'a complex theoretical enterprise' and a body
    of overlooked writing with common temporal, stylistic and ideological
    characteristics – and Morag Shiach's 'Periodizing Modernism' in The Oxford

Handbook of Modernisms, ed. by P. Brooker et al. (Oxford; New York: Oxford University Press, 2010), pp. 17–30.

6   Texidor to Mangan, 7 March 1956. Houghton, MS Am 1816, Folder 94 (3).

7   Kurzke to Sargeson, undated. ATL, MS-Papers-4261-097.

Index

Page numbers in **bold** refer to images

Lorca, Francisco García 211
Lowry, Bob 14, **15**, 17, 26, 123

'Maaree' (short story) 48, 50, 115, 213, 214
Macalister, Molly 26, 120
Macaskill, Patrick 196
MacDiarmid, Douglas 269n.38
Mangan, Sherry 34, **55**, 56, 73, 84, 86, 108, 111, 117, 134–35, 150, 229, 230, 231, 233, 235–37, 246
    'For Keeps' 230
Mann, Thomas 131
Manners, Lady Diana (later Cooper) 45, 47
Mannin, Ethel 61, 64
Mansfield, Katherine 40
Mansill, Bill and Val 205
Māori 18, 104
    Hokianga 165, 167, 168, 171
    Kaipara 102
    The Laughing Spirit (radio play) 210
Maragall, Joan 264n.53
Mareo, Eric 97–98, 104
Mason, Bruce 126
Mason, R.A.K. 16, 26, 119
Masson, André 57
McAuley, James 222
McCahon, Colin 24
McCormick, Eric 26, 120, 267n.6
McNeill, Dorelia 41
McWilliams, Donald 14, 15, **15**
Meltzer, Albert 86
Miller, Lee 224
modernism 8, 11, 13, 21, 24, 154, 190, 192–94, 199, 212, 221, 244
    see also intermodernism
Moonbeam Magic (film, 1924) 47–48, **49**
Morland, Andrew 83
Morland, Dorothy 83, 93
Mosley, Diana 92, 266n.88
Mosley, Oswald 266n.88

Mount View, Hazelbrook 205, **206**, 208–10, 212, 213, 215, 220, 222, 223, 238, 239, 242
Mulgan, John, *Man Alone* 16
Munster, George 209
Mustard, David 209, 279n.58
Mustard, Lucy 209, 242

Nation 209
National Joint Committee for Spanish Relief 93
nationalism 18–19
    see also cultural nationalism
Nazism 18–19, 21, 57, 64–65, 91, 92, 98, 111, 183
Nettleship, Ida 42
New Directions (journal) 150
New Life Colony 121
New Poems (1934) 16
New, W.H. 138
New York 50
New Zealand Listener 152, 196
New Zealand Literary Fund 8, 188
New Zealand New Writing (Gordon, ed.) 115, **151**
New Zealand Short Stories (Davin, ed.) 8, 154, 212
North Shore Group 26, 119–22, 162–64, 190, 193, 233

Orman, Felix 47
Orwell, George, *Homage to Catalonia* 71, 77, 265n.65
O'Sullivan, Vincent 127

pacifism 102, 121, 137
Paparoa, Northland 99–105, **106**, **107**, 108–17, 210, 243, 268n.17
Paris 50, 52, 56
Park, Ruth 204
Patterson, Keith ('Spud') 225, **226**, 228, 233
Patterson Texidor, Cristina 205, 224, **226**, 272n.49